Gloster Met

Britain's Celebrated First-Ge

Phil Butler and Tony Buttler

An imprint of
Ian Allan Publishing

Gloster Meteor
© 2006 Tony Buttler and Phil Butler

ISBN (10) 1 85780 230 6
ISBN (13) 1 85780 230 6

Published by Midland Publishing
4 Watling Drive, Hinckley, LE10 3EY, England
Tel: 01455 254 490   Fax: 01455 254 495
E-mail: midlandbooks@compuserve.com

Midland Publishing and Aerofax are imprints of
Ian Allan Publishing Ltd

Worldwide distribution (except North America):
Midland Counties Publications
4 Watling Drive, Hinckley, LE10 3EY, England
Telephone: 01455 254 450   Fax: 01455 233 737
E-mail: midlandbooks@compuserve.com
www.midlandcountiessuperstore.com

North American trade distribution:
Specialty Press Publishers & Wholesalers Inc.
39966 Grand Avenue, North Branch, MN 55056
Tel: 651 277 1400   Fax: 651 277 1203
Toll free telephone: 800 895 4585
www.specialtypress.com

Design and concept
© 2006 Midland Publishing and
Stephen Thompson Associates
Layout by Sue Bushell

Printed in England by
Ian Allan Printing Ltd
Riverdene Business Park, Molesey Road,
Hersham, Surrey, KT12 4RG

Visit the Ian Allan Publishing website at:
www.ianallanpublishing.com

Contents

Title page: **A head-on shot of a Meteor F Mk.III, showing the wing shape used on the Mk.I, Mk.III, early production Mk.IV, and the later Mks 10, 11, 12, 13 and 14.** via Phil Butler

Below: **An early production Meteor F.4, still with the long-span wing.** via Tony Buttler

Introduction

The Gloster Meteor is one of the most well known, and one of the most successful, of British military aircraft. The story of its development from wartime testing and use to its service in a multitude of roles with a host of RAF squadrons, and its export to many foreign air arms, is a fascinating one.

Surprisingly perhaps, at the time of writing, it is believed that there is no major historical book on the Meteor currently in print and, with a number of new model kits of various marks of the type recently hitting the market, it seemed sensible to try to fill this gap. In the past, the type has been the subject of a good number of books and many magazine articles which have examined their subject to differing degrees of depth (and in some cases accuracy). One of the best narratives is *Meteor* by Brian Philpott (Patrick Stephens 1986), a book that drew on a large volume of primary source material but which is no longer in print. Another excellent book and also out of print is *Meteor – Gloster's First Jet Fighter* by Steven J Bond (Midland Counties Publications 1985), a different type of work that gave superb detail for the individual airframes.

Whilst this Aerofax will serve as a good introduction to new readers who are not familiar with the overall story of the Meteor, we have taken the opportunity to include as much previously unpublished information as possible while giving less coverage to the areas which have been 'done to death'. In particular documents at the National Archives (formerly the Public Record Office) and in the hands of the Jet Age Museum have allowed a detailed narrative to be put together for the early design and development period and for the initial flight test programmes. For example this embraces some good coverage of the Metropolitan-Vickers F.2-engined prototype DG204 which was lost early in its career.

Accurate construction and overseas sales data has also been included (some of that for the first time as well) which should make this work an important reference. Finally, over the years the authors have also acquired a good

An air-to-air photo of Meteor NF.11 WD597. Product development resulted in a very different appearance for the later Marks. Armstrong Whitworth Aircraft NF66, via Phil Butler

number of previously unpublished high quality photographs of Meteors, some in colour, and their inclusion will give the modelling world extra reference material to work with.

It has been a pleasure for the two of us to work together on such an interesting subject. However, a publication such as this still needs the assistance of many people. A big thank you must go to John Adams, Valerie Adams, Peter Berry, Chris Butler, Peter Green, Coen van den Heuvel (Flash Aviation), John Horningtoft, Tim Kershaw and the members of the Jet Age Museum, Gerry Manning, Eric Morgan, Wg Cdr Trevor Price, Ian White, Aart van Wijk and finally the staff of the National Archives.

Phil Butler and Tony Buttler,
January 2006

Glossary

A&AEE	Aeroplane & Armament Experimental Establishment	D	Drone (unmanned aircraft)	NF	Night Fighter
AAM	Air-to-Air Missile	DTD	Director of Technical Development	NGTE	National Gas Turbine Establishment
AFDS	Air Fighting Development Squadron	EAAS	Empire Air Armament School	OCU	Operational Conversion Unit
AFS	Advanced Flying School	ECFS	Empire Central Flying School	OFU	Overseas Ferry Unit
AMDP	Air Member for Development and Production	EFS	Empire Flying School	OTU	Operational Training Unit
ANS	Air Navigation School	ETPS	Empire Test Pilots School	PR	Photo Reconnaissance
APS	Armament Practice Station	F	Fighter	RAAF	Royal Australian Air Force
ASI	Air Speed Indicator	FAA	Fleet Air Arm	RAuxAF	Royal Auxiliary Air Force
AWA	Armstrong-Whitworth Aircraft	FCCS	Fighter Command Communications Squadron	RAE	Royal Aircraft Establishment
AWOCU	All Weather Operation Conversion Unit	FEAF	Far East Air Force	RATOG	Rocket Assisted Take-Off Gear
BLEU	Blind Landing Experimental Unit	FEAFES	Far East Air Force Examining Squadron	RIAT	Royal International Air Tattoo
C&TT Sqn	Communication and Target Towing Squadron	FR	Fighter Reconnaissance	RNethAF	Royal Netherlands Air Force
CAACU	Civilian Anti-Aircraft Co-operation Unit	FRS	Flying Refresher School	RNZAF	Royal New Zealand Air Force
CEV	Centre d'Essais en Vol	FRU	Fleet Requirements Unit	RRE	Royal Radar Establishment
CF	Communications Flight	FTS	Flying Training School	SAM	Surface-to-Air Missile
CFE	Central Fighter Establishment	F(TT)	Fighter (Target Tug)	SBAC	Society of British Aerospace Companies/Society of British Aircraft Constructors
CFS	Central Flying School	FWS	Fighter Weapons School	T	Trainer
CGS	Central Gunnery School	GWDS	Guided Weapons Development Squadron	TAF	Tactical Air Force
CRD	Controller of Research and Development	IAS	Indicated Air Speed	THUM Flt	Temperature and Humidity Flight
CSE	Central Signals Establishment	ITF	Instrument Training Flight	TRE	Telecommunications Research Establishment
CU	Conversion Unit	JCU	Jet Conversion Unit	TT	Target Tug
		JSTU	Joint Service Trials Unit	TTF	Target Towing Flight
		MAP	Ministry of Aircraft Production	TWU	Tactical Weapons Unit
		MEAF	Middle East Air Force	WRE	Weapons Research Establishment
		MU	Maintenance Unit		

An air-to-air of a formation of No 85 Squadron Meteor NF.14s (WS741, WS740, WS723) taken on 24th May 1954. Armstrong Whitworth NF348, via Ray Williams

Chapter One

Origins

The development of the jet engine or gas turbine, the brainchild of Frank Whittle, is one of the most celebrated of all aviation stories. The first fruits of a long research and development programme was the Gloster E.28/39 research aircraft which made its first very short flights, of several hundred yards length, during taxi tests at Brockworth airfield on 8th April 1941. Its official first flight, a seventeen minute trip, was made from Cranwell on 15th May 1941, and these events represent some of the most historic moments in aviation history. Any reader wishing to acquire a detailed account of the story of the two E.28/39 research aircraft is recommended to read *Jet Pioneers: Gloster and the Birth of the Jet Age* by Tim Kershaw (Sutton 2004). Suffice it to say these were extremely successful aeroplanes which, in part, had resulted from an excellent working relationship between Frank Whittle and his Power Jets organisation and the Gloster Aircraft design team under George Carter's leadership. The second machine, W4046/G, was lost in a crash but the first aircraft, W4041/G, was used for research throughout most of the war and in April 1946 it passed into the hands of the Science Museum to be preserved.

However, despite various suggestions for fitting guns to the little E.28/39, in truth it was never a suitable airframe to turn into a fighter aircraft – this machine was really only intended to test the Whittle engine and for use in general experimental work. Fighter capability would require a different aeroplane and the resulting project was to become the Gloster Meteor. This aircraft holds the distinction of being the first British jet fighter to fly, the first to enter RAF squadron service and to go into combat but, during the mid-war years when it was created, no-one could have predicted that it would serve so successfully for so long and in so many versions. In addition, for a pioneer aeroplane the Meteor was to prove highly profitable in the export market, something not every 'first of type' has managed to achieve.

First Signs

It was quickly realised that the development of a twin-engine single-seat fighter powered by jets would be the best route to take, but such a type would have to be started from scratch. Studies had shown that if long range was required a jet-propelled aircraft would have to be optimised for high altitude but, because of its high ground speed and high rate of climb, the type could also be adapted to form a fine interceptor, provided short range was accepted. In truth,m long range was impracticable because it would require a volume of fuel that would destroy the weight advantages

The original 'Pioneer' (more correctly the E.28/39) prototype, photographed at Farnborough. The shot shows the small additional fins on the tailplane, fitted in 1944 after the crash of the second prototype aircraft.
via Tony Buttler

offered by the new engine. A single-engined type offered advantages over any multi-engined arrangement but the new fighter would require a military load of at least 1,500 lb (680kg) and the thrust ratings expected in the short term from current and new Whittle jets would make a single-engined type unsuitable; rate-of-climb for example would be inadequate. Attention therefore moved to the twin-engine arrangement and Gloster Aircraft was the natural choice to produce the new type.

On 10th April 1940 the Ministry of Aircraft Production's Director of Technical Development (DTD), W S Farren, asked George Carter to investigate in more detail a proposal from the Royal Aircraft Establishment (RAE) at Farnborough for a fighter weighing 8,500 lb to 9,000 lb (3,856kg to 4,082kg) and carrying 1,500 lb (680kg) of warload. At the time Carter was looking at an 11,000 lb (4,990kg) aeroplane with a 3,000 lb (1,361kg) load but Farren felt that the former was a better application of two Whittle W.2 power units. He added that 'If you could

manage to include four 20mm (or even two 20mm) combined with a certain amount of 0.303in, it would give us a far higher speed and operational height than any other aircraft we have in view, with an armament which would be fully able to deal with anything for which such a performance would be essential – namely the high speed lightly armed or unarmed bomber'. He noted that Carter's proposal had merits of its own 'and we may well decide ultimately to build both', but his present view was that the lighter project should come first. A general arrangement drawing and brief performance data were requested as soon as possible.

Carter provided a full scheme very quickly. On 2nd May Farren saw him again and confirmed that they would proceed immediately with a design on these lines. He also instructed Carter to begin a mock-up straight away while RAE had the essential wind tunnel work already planned out and was to proceed with it in collaboration with Carter and Whittle. Figures calculated separately by Carter, the Ministry's staff and RAE were all in fairly close agreement and suggested that the fighter's weight would fall within the 8,700 lb and 9,000 lb (3,946kg and 4,082kg) range and it would actually carry 1,800 lb (816kg) of warload. The gun armament was to be four 20mm cannon, or two 20mm and six 0.303in (7.7mm) machine guns, top speed was between 400mph and 430mph (644km/h and 693km/h) at sea level and 450mph to 470mph (724km/h to 756km/h) at 30,000ft (9,144m), and range about 750 miles (1,207km).

Once the twin-engine fighter had become reality, the next step was to deal with the problems of its design. The close proximity of the two engine nacelles to the fuselage gave rise to a very poor wing junction, which was likely to result in a breakdown of the flow and an early

stall of the wing between the nacelles and fuselage. In addition the thick section would produce compressibility effects over this part of the wing. However, mounting two engines in the fuselage would restrict accessibility. The decision to use two engines, mounted along the wing away from the fuselage, proved a major benefit to the eventual Meteor because it gave the airframe the ability to accept a number of different types of engine. This was both as a testbed and service aircraft and did much to extend what was to become a long and very successful operational career. In comparison de Havilland's first jet fighter, the DH.100 Vampire, had a single power unit in a short pod fuselage and this prevented the type from being used as an engine test bed.

A report dated 26th October 1940 noted that the basic design of Gloster's jet fighter was simple and straightforward and the structure had been specially designed to incorporate all possible facilities for quantity production. To this end forgings and stampings had been eliminated wherever possible and special attention given to the bench assembly of the various units and components. There was the problem of a possible shortage of machine tool equipment and so, wherever possible, machining operations had been planned on the basis of a straight cut and simple turning. At this stage the design looked really quite similar to the aircraft as built, although it was actually a two-seater. The most important features that did not survive through to the prototypes were an elliptical-shaped wing and a different tailplane.

The Specification issued to cover the twin-engined jet fighter was called F.9/40 and this document was completed on 14th November 1940. Operational Requirement OR.86 was also raised for the project and stated that the 'salient advantage of this system of propulsion

is the possibility of speeds, particularly at high altitudes, which would not be possible by the orthodox arrangement of engine and airscrew. To make full use of the possibilities available a small aeroplane is essential. It is vital for the success of the project that every item of Service equipment which is not absolutely essential should be eliminated.' Two Whittle Type W.2B jet propulsion engines were the quoted powerplant and the fighter's top speed at 30,000ft (9,144m) was not to be less than 430mph (692km/h). There were few other performance requirements but, when taking off from a grass surface with full fuel and military load, the aircraft had to be capable of crossing a 50ft (15m) screen within a distance of 600 yards (549m) in still air. On landing the aircraft should come to rest in not more than 700 yards (640m), again with full fuel and weapons aboard. F.9/40 quoted either six 20mm cannon with 120 rounds each or four with 150 rounds per gun.

It appears that the Specification was drawn up without much RAF input. On 3rd October 1941 Air Marshal Sholto Douglas wrote to Air Vice Marshal R S Sorley at the Air Ministry to report that he felt that Fighter Command should have been consulted prior to the formation of the specification for the Whittle fighter (such a step had apparently been standard practice for previous specifications). He added that the aircraft's estimated performance seemed satisfactory but Douglas would have liked more endurance. For the time being the fighter was known as the 'Gloster F.9/40'.

At this time Gloster was also working on a twin-piston-engined night fighter to Specification F.18/40, a design that was actually a development of an earlier fighter built to F.9/37 (the first of two prototypes had flown in April 1939). By December 1940 however, it was becoming clear that Gloster's design capacity was insufficient to undertake both projects and one of them would have to be dropped. At a meeting held on 18th December the F.18/40, unofficially known as the Reaper, was placed on a lower priority. The Gloster F.18/40 was a competitor to the proposed night fighter versions of the Bristol Beaufighter and de Havilland Mosquito and it was actually May 1941 when a final decision was given not to proceed with the project further.

However, on 9th January 1941 Lord Beaverbrook, head of the Ministry of Aircraft Production (MAP), told Gloster 'I wish you to concentrate your design strength on the twin-engined Whittle fighter. This will be your main contribution to my development programme. It is of unique importance [and] to assist you on making this effort, work on the night fighter will

DIAGRAM OF CONSTUCTION.

GLOSTER INTERCEPTOR FIGHTER

WHITTLE GYRONE ENGINES

SKETCH No 2160

Drawing dated April 1940 which was prepared for a report on the proposed sub-contract manufacture of the F.9/40. It also happens to show the original wing and tail arrangement, which differed quite markedly from the aircraft as built. Note the spelling mistake!
National Archives AVIA 15-477

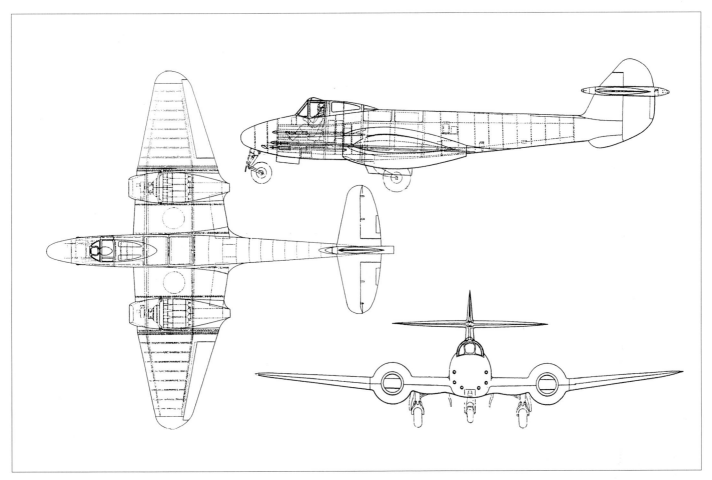

Official Gloster drawing dated June 1941 which shows the six-cannon armament grouped in the nose. Eric Morgan

stop. A pressure cabin must be provided as soon as possible. On this you should collaborate with Westland, who are to design a Merlin-engined fighter with a pressure cabin'. The project he referred to was the Westland Welkin high-altitude fighter with two Merlin piston engines which first flew in November 1942. George Carter duly liaised with Westland on the design and operation of pressure cabins and the information gained was to prove valuable for the F.9/40.

In addition, by the end of 1940 Gloster had received instructions to proceed at all speed with the completion of the twin-engine jet fighter and its design now had to take precedence over all other work. Sir Henry Tizard, at the time working for the Ministry of Aircraft Production, attached great importance to it despite the concept of a jet fighter being unproven – he felt that it should be possible for such an aeroplane to achieve practical success in time to influence the war. On 24th January 1941 Tizard told the Vice Chief of the Air Staff that the Ministry's Research Department was now satisfied that the Whittle engine had reached a sufficient stage of development to permit the placing of production orders.

Throughout the winter of 1940/41 the project took an important place in the discussions for the future development programme, which were held at the highest level between the Ministry of Aircraft Production and the Air Staff. MAP was created in May 1940 to relieve the Air Ministry of the responsibility for the procure-

ment and supply of aircraft and equipment – its functions were taken over by the Ministry of Supply in April 1946. The Air Staff was part of the Air Ministry, the civilian body which governed the RAF, and one of its major functions was to develop new aircraft and to decide which types should be put into production. During this period the Air Staff was strongly in favour of proceeding with Gloster's specialised F.18/40 piston night fighter (see above) and, with the prototype E.28/39 still yet to fly, was hesitant to decide on the F.9/40. It was MAP who sustained the Air Staff's interest in the jet fighter and, once the E.28/39 had successfully demonstrated jet-powered flight, the latter finally interred the piston-powered project.

Frustratingly, at this stage it was not possible to judge how much power would be generated by Whittle's engine. Tizard had made calculations for the jet fighter's performance against the Supermarine Spitfire III with varying levels of engine thrust. At a rating of 1,400 lb (6.2kN) the new aircraft's all-round performance as an interceptor would only just be as effective as the Spitfire because it had a poorer take-off and rate of climb and a service ceiling approximately the same; however, it would be a much faster aircraft than the Spitfire III at 35,000ft (10,668m) altitude with a maximum of 390mph (628km/h) against the Spitfire's 280mph (451km/h). At 30,000ft (9,144m) the speeds were closer, 345mph (555km/h) for the Spitfire and 397mph (639km/h) for the F.9/40, but 1,600 lb (7.1kN) of thrust offered a potential

436mph (702km/h) for the F.9/40 at this height and 1,800 lb (8kN) thrust 470mph (756km/h). In both cases the higher thrusts also offered a much higher ceiling with 1,800 lb (8kN) giving 46,500ft (14,173m) against the Spit's 38,000ft (11,582m). In Tizard's view the main effort had to be concentrated on producing an engine able to give not less than 1,600 lb (7.1kN) of static thrust at sea level.

An interim report from Gloster showed that a six 20mm Hispano cannon installation had been examined but a total of four was currently planned, the two extra weapons being regarding as overload above an aircraft weight of 10,000 lb (4,536kg). By mid-January 1941 the assembly of the cockpit, fuselage and full wing mock-up were all well under way. A brochure was completed in February for the new fighter which showed a span of 43ft 0in (13.11m), length 41ft 3in (12.57m), wing area 374ft^2 (34.78m^2) and an all-up-weight of 10,650 lb (4,831kg), or 11,020 lb (4,999kg) with six cannon. Fitted with 1,640 lb (7.3kN) W.2B engines it had an estimated top speed of 385mph (619km/h) at sea level and 440mph (708km/h) at 30,000ft (9,144m), a sea level rate of climb of 3,220ft/min (981m/min) and a ceiling of 46,000ft (14,021m); with 1,800 lb (8.0kN) engines the equivalent figures were 400mph (644km/h), 460mph (740km/h), 3,860ft/min

(1,177m/min) and 47,000ft (14,326m). Official documents make frequent references to Whittle's Gyrone, which was actually the codename for the Whittle engine. A final Mock-Up Conference was held on 11th February 1941 and it was estimated then that the first prototype would be flying by the end of the year.

Frank Whittle's career is well documented but, prior to the publication of Tim Kershaw's book, George Carter, the Meteor's designer, has received less publicity. Carter's achievement in bringing both the E.28/39 and Meteor to fruition with a brand new type of engine, and with relatively little trouble, has rarely been acknowledged as strongly as it should have been. Quite correctly Whittle has received a great deal of attention for developing the power unit but his excellent working relationship with Carter was vital. Carter had joined Sopwith Aviation in 1916 as the company's chief draughtsman and he later became chief designer for Hawker Engineering, the company that replaced Sopwith after the latter went into liquidation in 1920. His products included the Horsley bomber and Hornbill fighter but he was succeeded as chief designer in 1925 by Sydney Camm. Carter moved on to design the Crusader seaplane for Short Brothers at Rochester in readiness for the 1927 Schneider Trophy competition and then in 1937, after periods at de Havilland and Avro, he became Gloster's chief designer. Here his first project was the F.9/37 piston fighter, to be followed by the E.28/39 jet pioneer and then the Meteor.

Carter's efforts were recognised by the award of a CBE in 1947, and in 1948 he became Gloster's technical director. From 19th July 1943 Richard Walker assumed full responsibility for the F.9/40 (Meteor) programme so that Carter could move on to prepare more new designs. One was a stillborn jet fighter proposed in 1946 for the Chinese Nationalist Government, and there is strong evidence that Carter did much of the design work on the Gloster Javelin, the company's last jet fighter which flew in 1951. George Carter finally retired in 1958 and died in February 1969.

During his early career Richard Walker spent periods at RAE Farnborough, the Blackburn Aeroplane Company at Brough and Hawker Aircraft. In 1933 he began two years as a consultant to AB Svenska Järnvägsverkstädernas (later SAAB) and later was responsible for the design of the wing for the Hawker Hurricane fighter. Walker joined Gloster in 1937 as assistant chief designer and was much involved with the design of the E.28/39 and F.9/40 projects and in 1948 succeeded Carter as the company's chief designer. As such he saw the Javelin into service but the Gloster factory was eventually closed in 1963. Walker then spent time with the former Armstrong Whitworth and Avro design teams, who with Gloster had all become part of the Hawker Siddeley Group. Richard Walker died in April 1982.

Mention should also be made of Gloster's general manager, Frank McKenna. He had to plan the F.9/40 fighter's production and, with insufficient capacity available within his own company's facilities, this would have to include major sub-contracting arrangements. In fact with so many companies becoming involved this proved to be a substantial task. One problem for example, was to maintain a high standard of interchangeability between the various components involved, a problem that was solved by Gloster making it a condition that the tools and parts made by all sub-contractors should strictly adhere to the limits specified on the master drawings.

First Orders

It was clear by the end of December 1940 that if the jet fighter was required at all then it would be required in very large numbers and this was sufficient for Sir Henry Tizard to arrange for production plans to be drawn up with 'great enthusiasm and activity'. One of Air Vice Marshal Tedder's last acts before he left MAP (to move on to another post) was to call a meeting on 13th October 1940 to discuss the subject, and the figures laid down at this time as the basis for planning were eighty

airframes and at least one hundred and sixty jet engines per month.

On 14th February 1941 an order was placed for twelve prototype F.9/40s under contract number SB.21179/C.23(a) and these were given the serial numbers DG202 to DG213; the contract price was envisaged as being £200,000. By December 1942 the number of prototypes to be flown had been reduced to seven but the total was eventually increased to eight when it was decided to complete DG209 to allow a trial installation to be made of the Rolls-Royce W.2B/37 engine. The centre section of DG210 was also completed but further work on this aircraft was cancelled after a decision was made not to use it as the second aircraft fitted with the Metropolitan-Vickers F.2 engine. It appears that DG210 to DG213 were never formally cancelled, but the need for their completion was negated because of delays in the delivery of their engines.

Four of the first five airframes were hand-built in Gloster's experimental facility at Bentham, the exception being the third aeroplane which was built in Gloster's Cheltenham shop. During the war all prototypes and production aeroplanes had the suffix 'G' added to their serials, which signified 'Guard': a sign of just how secret and important these machines were that they were to have guards allocated to them at all times while on the ground. This suffix was authorised for use on all Meteor prototypes on 11th June 1942.

At the start of 1942 the maiden flight of the first prototype was now expected in May and, overall, work on the airframes proceeded with relatively few problems, apart from some of the sub-contractors who fell behind with their deliveries. On 8th August 1941 orders were confirmed for three hundred F.9/40s but the aircraft's Whittle engine was having problems. The original W.1, which powered the E.28/39, had performed satisfactorily but during tests at Power Jets the W.2, which offered more thrust and was the progenitor of the F.9/40's W.2B, was showing signs of blower surging well before full power was reached; it was also running hotter than expected.

In fact at this stage it proved impossible to achieve a thrust level that was acceptable for flight while keeping the jet pipe temperature within the required limits and this problem was to be the cause of several delays with more than one prototype. Later on, as part of the overall operation of jet engines, orders were also given forbidding the use of Whittle-type power units on dusty aerodromes. Eventually the Whittle engine was to be held up repeatedly by both technical and political problems, including working relationships with sub-contractors, and these troubles

were to push back the date of the F.9/40's first flight on several occasions.

The background to the engine's problems (and the jet story itself) has been heavily documented in many works (such as *Genesis of the Jet* by John Golley, Airlife 1996), so what needs to be noted here is a general summary of the situation. Whittle's own company was called Power Jets and was based at Lutterworth but it was not big enough to take on the full development and production job. It was a small firm which had negligible capital of its own, was backed heavily by Government money and, according to the Ministry's Controller of Research and Development, was completely without production knowledge or facilities. Previously Power Jets had worked in co-operation with British Thomson Houston (BTH), who had wide experience in turbines but none in aviation. This company had been brought in after the established aero-engine companies had decided that they would have nothing to do with jet propulsion for the time being.

By the time the F.9/40 programme was under way the Whittle engine work was being shared with the Rover Car Company at Coventry, but the working relationship between subcontractor and Power Jets was, to say the least, never as comfortable as that between Whittle's organisation and Gloster. The overall poor performance by Rover, which was not an established aero-engine company, was to bring some of the biggest delays and in 1943 its role was passed into the hands of Rolls-Royce. In its struggles to produce the W.2B Rover had tried hard to build up a research organisation and had met with a certain amount of success, but the company's basic experience in the field was non-existent and its limited knowledge had frequently led Rover to erroneous conclusions. Rover had designed a 'straight-through' version of Whittle's engine in an attempt to ease the production difficulties on the original Whittle unit and this brought a lack of trust with Power Jets. Although Rolls-Royce had no jet engine design experience, it did have a great deal of research, development and production experience. Rolls put Stanley Hooker in control and he and Whittle were to work together extremely well. Consequently the Whittle engine programme began to move forward with much greater pace and energy.

However, long before the arrival of Rolls-Royce, two other jet propulsion engines had appeared from sources outside Power Jets. The first was called the H.1 and was designed by Frank Halford and built by de Havilland, the other came from Metropolitan-Vickers and was built to the general designs of the Royal Aircraft Establishment. This second engine, called the F.2, was expected to have a static thrust of 2,300 lb (10.2kN) and featured an axial-flow compressor when both Whittle's and Halford's

units employed a centrifugal compressor; the latter was a much more straightforward and simple arrangement but was less efficient in operation. The F.2 consisted of a nine-stage axial compressor delivering air to an annular-style combustion chamber. The hot gases leaving this chamber drove a two-stage turbine and then passed into an exhaust system which was similar to that of other jet propulsion engines. Halford's engine was roughly similar to Whittle's except that it used a single-sided impeller in the compressor rather than the double entry type employed by Power Jets. Very quickly a decision was made that some of the F.9/40 prototype airframes should be used to air-test these alternative engines.

Like BTH, Metropolitan-Vickers also had no experience with aero-engines but the company was brought into the picture for the same reasons; here however, the aero-engine company Armstrong-Siddeley was associated with them to help evolve the F.2 into a form fit for use in aircraft. In addition Metropolitan-Vickers did have a production background that in due course could allow them to produce the F.2. Armstrong Siddeley currently had no piston engine under design and when its most recent projects, the Wolfhound and Deerhound, were stopped in 1941, Lord Brabazon had promised the company that it should come in with the jet 'on the ground floor'. Its designers were now in slow time doing research work on a co-axial engine that might employ a two-stage blower and a two-stage turbine. Overall there was by now a wide scope of design teams working on jet developments, although the actual numbers of staff employed as direct labour were still relatively small. The science of jet propulsion was, as yet, in its infancy and none of the engines which it was hoped would be put into production had actually emerged from the research stage.

Installing the MetroVick F.2 in the F.9/40 airframe was difficult. Carter had three options – slinging the engine under the present spars so

keeping them straight, kinking up the front spar and retaining the present type of banjo back spar or making a larger banjo with a removable top for the front spar (the banjo was a 'spar frame' that was wrapped around the engine's body). The first was the simplest solution because it meant that practically no spar redesign was necessary and Carter was proposing to take this route, along with the Dowty undercarriage. The second idea was structurally awkward and, in the Ministry's words, looked unpleasant, while the third would be less difficult but would lead to a weight increase of 400 lb (181kg). The underslung engines would introduce problems with pitching moment, and an increase in drag, and Carter was asked to get together with RAE to satisfy himself on the aerodynamics of the scheme. If it was found to be safe and the effects on the performance were not 'disastrous', it was agreed that everyone would settle on the underslung format since it was undoubtedly the quickest solution and would rapidly get the engine into the air.

This indeed was the method eventually turned into hardware with the nacelle placed beneath the wing rather than in it, in an arrangement which looked more attractive to the eye but brought other changes such as having to lengthen the landing gear. In fact the new landing gear would create problems of its own (see Chapter Two) but the different nacelle also brought an 80 lb (36kg) increase in overall weight. The first Gloster drawing of this version is dated 30th May 1942 and numbered P.118. (Note: Gloster's apparent 'P' project number series noted in many books actually relates to a series of drawing numbers for planned or unbuilt aircraft designs. Some show a three-view but others, with a different P-number, might show for example the same design's internal detail. Consequently not every P-number represented a new aircraft layout.)

The F.2 version's different nacelle arrangement also pushed the centre of gravity (CofG)

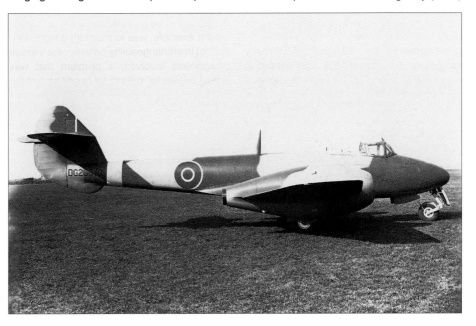

F.9/40 prototype DG206 with de Havilland H.1 engines. Note the fatter nacelles.

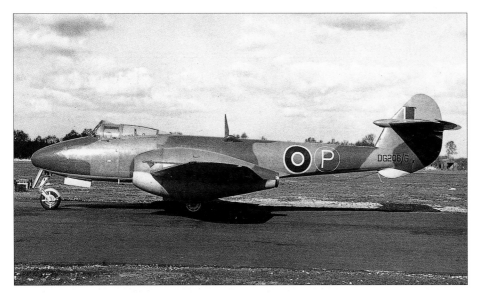

The Goblin-powered F.9/40 prototype DG206 at RAE Farnborough during March 1944.
DERA Neg No 51674, via Tony Buttler

540mph (869km/h) if allowance was made for compressibility. The estimated sea level rate of climb was 9,100ft/min (2,774m/min) falling to 4,800ft/min (1,463m/min) at 30,000ft (9,144m), and the aircraft would take 4.4 minutes to reach 30,000ft. De Havilland, a company with wide engineering experience and a sound production background, had entered the jet field comparatively late in the day. However, by using its own, Halford's and other people's experience, it was able to evolve a practical running engine in the H.1 in a remarkably short time, and taking it through to production was not expected to be a problem.

Gloster's first full brochure for an H.1-powered F.9/40 (later known as the Meteor Mk.II) was written in November 1942. It had either four or six cannon, and the lengthened spar for the centre section with the redesigned nacelles; there were other relatively minor changes to compensate for the increased gross weight. Some difficulties did arise because of the rather unusual mass distribution caused by locating these rather heavy power units with their CofGs

Official Gloster drawing showing the MetroVick F.2-powered F.9/40M prototype with four cannon. The line above the cockpit shows the original outline before modifications were introduced. Eric Morgan

backwards. Consequently 170 lb (77kg) of forward ballast was needed to retain the balance because it was now expected that the fuel tankage, which was behind the CofG, was to be increased to 300 gallons (1,364 litres) – it was George Carter's intention to introduce this extra fuel capacity in the near future. The approximate all-up-weight for the type with 300 gallons (1,364 litres) of fuel was 12,000 lb (5,443kg) and the mock-up for the F.2-powered F.9/40 was officially examined on 29th September 1942 and again on 21st January 1943. DG204 was the prototype allocated as a test bed for the engine and was known as the F.9/40M (M for MetroVick). The F.2 later became the F.2/4

Beryl and, after the war, this and MetroVick's other engine projects were taken over by Armstrong-Siddeley Motors and formed the basis of the Sapphire, which was used by several of the next generation of jet fighters and bombers.

Installing the de Havilland H.1 was much simpler than the F.2 since the front wing spar could go right through but, because the engine itself was somewhat larger in diameter than the Power Jets W.2B, it needed a larger banjo for the front spar with a wider nacelle. Otherwise the installation job for the Halford engine was much along the lines of the W.2B. Early estimates made in November 1941 suggested a top speed of 565mph (909km/h) at sea level, or

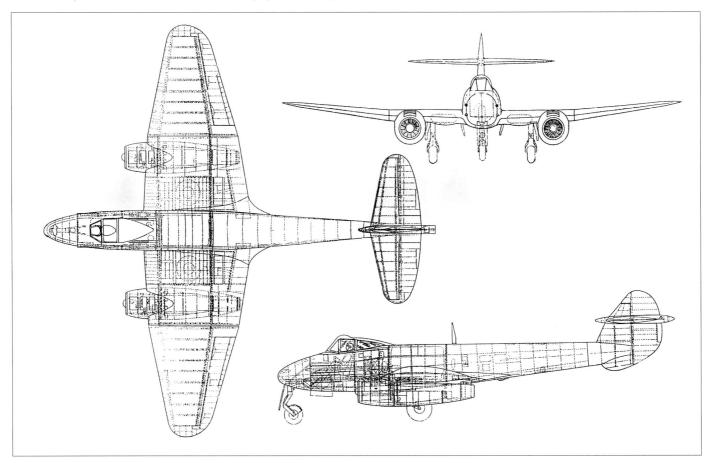

well behind the front spar. Span was 44ft 4in
(13.51m), length 41ft 4in (12.60m), gross wing
area 387ft^2 (36.0m^2) and all-up-weight with four
cannon 13,300lb (6,033kg). Each engine gave
2,500lb (11.1kN) of thrust and so the estimated
top speeds were higher than for the W.2B –
470mph (756km/h) at sea level and 490mph
(788km/h) at 30,000ft (9,144m) for what was in
all respects a fully operational aeroplane. Operational ceiling was 45,000ft (13,716m) and
absolute ceiling 48,000ft (14,630m).

Fully developed, the H.1 was expected to
give 3,000lb (13.3kN) of thrust which made
speeds in excess of 500mph (805km/h) at
40,000ft (12,192m) a possibility; exceptional
rates of climb to high altitudes were also predicted, 40,000ft being reached in about fifteen
minutes. The estimated speed range from sea
level to 50,000ft (15,240m) was described as
phenomenal and, with 330 gallons (1,500
litres) of fuel aboard, the endurance at
40,000ft (12,192m) was nearly one hour. The
operational ceiling was expected to be
52,000ft (15,850m). As a result Gloster
declared that this version may thus be considered as 'a formidable fighter proposition
and one that may well play a significant part in
future operations'.

**F.9/40 prototype DG204 with MetroVick F.2
engines in underwing nacelles.** Eric Morgan

With so much work on jet engine development, together with the ever increasing pressure of work on conventional engine and
propeller development, the Ministry needed to
expand its staff to cover and control the situation. On 15th December 1942 it was agreed that
the knowledge of gas turbines had reached a
stage which demanded much greater attention
and so it was decided to set up a separate
Deputy Directorate within the Engine Development Directorate. This would have the sole
responsibility for gas turbine engines and was
to be known as DD/RDE(T); Dr Roxbee-Cox

was selected for the post of Deputy Director.

The main security codename given to the
F.9/40 was 'Rampage' but by September 1941
it was unofficially being called 'Thunderbolt'
and, indeed, some Ministry files make reference to this name. On 19th February 1942 the
Ministry's H J Allwright confirmed that it had
been agreed that the type should still be
referred to as the 'Gloster F.9/40', instead of
using names that were unauthorised. These
now also included 'Meteor', and later on 'Millet'
was used to screen the F.9/40's first flights.
Gloster itself was loath to suggest a name since

the company felt that the secrecy of the project would be better safeguarded if the aircraft was referred to by its specification number. Allwright noted that a name was more likely to excite speculation than a specification number and, for anyone knowing the British system, the use of a name would inform them that a production order was in existence.

In fact, giving a new British military aeroplane a suitable name has often been a long and serious business, even during the war, and a large volume of correspondence on the subject of the F.9/40 was to pass between the manufacturers and MAP. Some of the names apparently suggested by the Ministry included Scourge, Terrifier, Thunderbolt (again), Tempest and Cyclone, but Thunderbolt was in fact used by the American Republic P-47 piston fighter, Tempest became the latest in the line of Hawker piston fighters and the Cyclone was an American piston engine produced by the Wright company. Other alternatives included Avenger (for which Gloster expressed a preference), Skyrocket, Dauntless and Tyrant. However, Avenger was given to the torpedo bomber produced by the American Grumman company and so in late February 1942, or soon afterwards, the F.9/40 jet fighter was officially named Meteor, although late in the piece Gloster had also suggested Annihilator, Ace and Reaper.

By September 1943 the Meteor's production plans were expected to embrace two types of engine – the Whittle as developed by Rolls-Royce and the H.1 as developed by de Havilland. The reasons behind this were complex, as noted by R S Sorley on 11th September. It was expected that the enemy was likely to introduce jet aircraft into operational use during 1944 which meant that the Meteor had to be in service with the RAF the same year. As early as possible, and not later than the end of 1944, the Meteor would also need to have engines of the highest thrust available from developments of both of these engine types. New advances from Rolls, such as the B.37 engine, were very promising but were likely to be inferior in thrust to later developments of the H.1 – the H.1's potential was considered to be far greater and its successful development would make the Meteor a much more formidable aircraft. In addition, it was expected that a replacement aircraft type would be necessary by 1945.

In the event only two of the prototypes, DG206 and DG207, were to fly with de Havilland's engine because it was found that its endurance was insufficient to allow a sufficiently long flight time at high altitude. As the Goblin, the H.1 was also used to power production examples of the de Havilland Vampire. However, delays with Rover-built W.2B units were to result in the near-cancellation of the whole Meteor project. In fact Rover's inability to produce airworthy engines forced MAP to halt work on this version of the fighter and it was at this point that the size of the prototype order was reduced. Then, when it had become clear

that the H.1's development programme was proceeding relatively smoothly, a decision was made on 26th September 1942 to give the de Havilland engine precedence over the Metro-Vick F.2 and the version was to be 'pushed forward on high priority'. This move eventually ensured that the first Meteor to fly would actually be prototype DG206 fitted with the H.1.

First Metal

On 16th June 1942 Ministry representatives visited Gloster Aircraft to take a close look at the state of progress with the prototypes. The first machine was very well advanced, it had both engines installed and was due to start ground running at Bentham just before the end of the month. Breaking down of the airframe was expected to start during the first week of July in readiness to move the aircraft to Newmarket, which at the time was the intended venue for its first flight. If things went smoothly it was hoped that taxying tests could begin during the second week of July. The second airframe was a long way behind the first (around ten to twelve weeks) and had fallen back considerably from the programme arranged the previous 8th April; it was hoped that this gap could be reduced. The third aircraft (being built at Cheltenham) was about one month behind the planned schedule and the fourth machine had barely been started. About one hundred and thirty men were now working in the Experimental Shop and another thirty were based at Cheltenham, but it was considered that an extra ten to fifteen men would do much to accelerate the programme as a whole.

On 28th March 1943 Stanley Hooker reported on the current position of the W.2B's development. The engine being built at Barnoldswick was basically the original W.2B design but was known as the W.2B/23 after the introduction of a modified fuel and combustion system. This particular type of engine had now been subjected to some 1,800 hours of test bench development running at Barnoldswick, and also at Waterloo Mill, Clitheroe, and a further 1,200 hours had been completed by Power Jets. In addition three W.2B/23 units had accumulated flight experience – one had completed a twenty-five hour test mounted in the tail of a modified Vickers Wellington bomber and this had been followed by a second which had so far done thirteen hours. The third W.2B/23 had completed ten hours flying in W4046/G, the second of the E.28/39 research aeroplanes.

The Wellington was simply acting as a flying testbed and, although offering good mechanical and operating experience, it was very unsuitable for estimating the engine's performance. In fact the difference in the Wellington's performance with the W.2B on or off was very small. It is worth noting that this aircraft was to be the first of several piston-powered bombers, mainly Avro Lancasters and Lincolns, to serve as testbeds for jet engines during the 1940s. The jet engine lent itself to test installations in various piston-powered aeroplanes which was

fortunate because there was a need to acquire as much airborne experience as possible as early as possible. Indeed in the early days of the jet programme in 1939, leading to the two E.28/39 prototypes, drawings were actually prepared for a jet-powered version of the Avro Anson reconnaissance and training aircraft. Hooker felt that it would be highly desirable to test the W.2B/23 in an F.9/40 airframe, the engine having passed all of the necessary tests for flight clearance at 1,400 lb (6.2kN) thrust; 1,600 lb (7.1kN) was the expected maximum thrust.

The Rover-designed 'straight-through' engine was called the B.26 and Rolls-Royce now had a redesigned version called the B.37 well under way. This was being designed to give 2,000 lb (8.9kN) of thrust and, since 90% of the unit was identical to the B.26, it was anticipated that the new engine would be ready for flight in six to nine months. Gloster Aircraft had already done a mock-up of a B.37 installation in the F.9/40 and found that it could go in with very little modification. The estimated top speed with these engines, even with the 1,400 lb (6.2kN) rating, was described by Hooker as 'exceptionally good' and, at sea level and high altitude, considerably exceeded the figures for the Supermarine Spitfire Mk.IX with the Merlin 66 and the North American Mustang with a similar piston engine, particularly at sea level and high altitudes. The rate of climb was not quite as good as the piston types but still appeared to be adequate, particularly when the 2,000 lb (8.9kN) rating was available. As noted previously, DG209 was the airframe chosen for the W.2B/37 trial.

Hooker now commented that, in the past, most emphasis had been laid on the jet aeroplane's altitude performance but his data showed that their sea level performance was equally outstanding (in contrast to some official documents, several of which have been referred to). For example, with 2,000 lb (8.9kN) thrust engines the F.9/40 would be around 100mph (161km/h) faster than the Spitfire or Mustang at sea level and the objection to this had always been the jet's high fuel consumption at sea level. On analysis however, Hooker's team had found that the endurance of the F.9/40 with 300 gallons (1,364 litres) of fuel was equal to that of the Spitfire IX, even at sea level for speeds above 300mph (483km/h). With piston engines it was necessary to enrich the mixture at high powers in order to suppress detonation, and in this case unburnt fuel had to be thrown away on the exhaust gases due to there being insufficient air in the cylinder to burn the available fuel. Such a condition was impossible on jet propulsion engines for the simple reason that these ran with an enormous surplus of air far exceeding the requirements of any fuel supplied.

The question of production capacity for the F.9/40 Meteor was also considered over a long period. Gloster was also experiencing increasing demands for production of the Hawker

Typhoon piston fighter-bomber. There was some consideration towards extending the facilities at Stoke Orchard aerodrome near Bishop's Cleeve, which was one of Gloster's dispersal units and, other than Staverton, the only one with flying facilities adjacent. However, a substantial development programme was planned for the F.9/40 Meteor prototypes and it was agreed that a runway 2,000 yards (1,829m) long would be needed for the flight tests, and for testing production aircraft, at least until such time as the flying techniques of the type were fully known and the reliability of the engines had been fully established. It was realised that uprooting the now firmly entrenched Typhoon production from Stoke Orchard sheds would be unwise while Gloster's Brockworth site was regarded as unsuitable.

Discussions between the Ministry and Glosters during June 1942 also made it clear that, due to the experimental nature of the job, development of the jet fighter would be very closely allied to production and should be done as near to Gloster's main drawing office and factory as possible. The matter had become one of urgency and a search was made for a suitable airfield, which included a visit to the satellite aerodrome at Moreton Valence, situated off the Bristol Road about twelve miles from the Gloster works. An inspection found this venue to be ideally situated and its runways, with small extensions, would be quite suitable. At the time there were no buildings on the aerodrome, other than huts, and the only aircraft based there were a few trainers dispersed from Staverton. In due course this was to become Gloster's main test airfield and operated right through the Meteor and succeeding Javelin jet fighter programmes. Sadly, today it has long been closed and much of the main runway sits underneath the M5 motorway.

Returning to the prototypes, Newmarket Heath was chosen as the test airfield for the initial Meteor flights but was soon dropped because it was too far away from the Gloster factory, and it lacked support facilities. RAF Cranwell, the venue for the E.28/39's first flight, was chosen instead and DG206 was transported there by road on 12th February 1943, the wings being removed for the purpose. Nevertheless, the size of the DG206's wing centre section, which overhung the sides of the Queen Mary trailer, meant that several telegraph poles had to be moved out of the way en route to allow the lorry to pass. After making the Meteor's first flight there, security problems at Cranwell meant that DG206 went to Newmarket Heath for its next sorties. In the event RAF Bar-

ford St John, near Banbury, was to be used for further flights with DG206, and also for the first flights of DG202 and DG205, and two blister hangers were temporarily erected at Barford for support purposes.

As noted earlier, by mid-June 1942 W.2B units built by Rover had been installed in DG202 and some ground running followed on the 29th, but these engines did not give enough power for the aircraft to be able to take off. By mid-September the second prototype had been completed as far as was possible without its engines. It was the delays with these power units that brought the H.1-powered DG206 to the head of the queue in readiness for flight. Gloster's chief test pilot, Gerry Sayer, had flown the maiden flight of the E.28/39 and also undertook the first F.9/40 Meteor taxi runs but tragi-

cally, on 21st October 1941, he was killed while flying a Hawker Typhoon. His successor as chief test pilot, Michael Daunt, became the pilot for the first Meteor flight. Daunt's number two at Gloster was John Grierson and, to help with the Meteor test flying load that would follow, John Crosby-Warren also joined the test pilot team.

Many still regarded the new jet-powered aircraft with suspicion. Some staff at the Air Ministry felt the Meteor was a serious waste of effort and that a large number of highly-skilled specialist personnel could be more profitably employed on alternative types, like the de Havilland Mosquito powered by the Rolls-Royce Merlin 61 piston engine. On 26th October 1942 R S Sorley, Assistant Chief of the Air Staff (Technical Requirements), wrote a memo that outlined the Air Staff's general thinking. The

The Rolls-Royce W.2B/23 Welland engine which powered the first production Meteors.
Rolls-Royce Heritage Trust

The Rolls-Royce Derwent V engine powered the Meteor Mk.IV and later Marks.
Rolls-Royce Heritage Trust

first Meteor with the Whittle W.2B was indeed down on thrust, the second H.1 variant would be quite good and the third, with fully developed Whittle engines, a superior type. But Sorley declared that, on service entry, the Meteor would then be surpassed at high altitude by the Westland Welkin. He concluded that the Meteor 'will do no more than serve as a useful high speed type for a very short while, but it will provide us with a jet-propelled aircraft on which to gain experience of the new technique'. He felt that if they dropped the 'Whittle' fighter they would 'gain little in alternative productive effort over the next twelve to eighteen months and it would prejudice the advancement of jet technique, certainly from a Service point of view'.

Indeed at this stage the fighter's future was uncertain because, with the W.2B powerplant, it was expected to be outclassed by orthodox fighters, except possibly in speed. During November 1942 the whole question of its future was under active consideration at the Ministry of Aircraft Production and MAP's Controller of Research and Development (CRD) had recommended that the present order should be reduced to around fifty aeroplanes. That number would still allow the essential engine development effort to proceed and provide sufficient aircraft for the very necessary service training needed for this new type of aircraft and propulsion. Even with so much development work ahead it was agreed that fifty was a reasonable compromise at this stage.

However, the jet fighter was sufficiently flexible from the point of view of its ability to operate at varying heights. At this stage jet fighters were seen essentially as 'interceptors'. The peculiarities of their climbing performance, coupled with a high forward speed, was such that it would usually be possible for this type of fighter to engage an enemy flying at great height sooner than could a normal fighter. One attractive feature about this class of aircraft was that it would always be able to out-dive the normal piston type. The thrust increased with speed and there was no danger of straining the engine since the power unit would actually tend to slow down as the dive speed increased.

As an aside, by January 1943 Gloster had begun work on another new fighter which was designed to Specification E.5/42 and powered by a single H.1 engine; in some respects the design itself was based on the original E.28/39 research aircraft. Delays in getting the Meteor airborne plus the availability of de Havilland's more powerful engine had helped the push for an alternative jet fighter. Three E.5/42 prototypes were planned as a second-string project but, despite being seen in many respects as a more desirable aircraft, the project eventually faded away and was replaced by a larger single jet fighter, the Gloster E.1/44 Ace. This flew in prototype form, but not until 1948, and was not a success. However, it was eventually to be a major influence on the Meteor programme because the second E.1/44 featured a new high set tailplane which did prove successful, and this was adopted for the F Mk.8 version of the Meteor (see Chapter Three).

It goes without saying that jet engines and jet aircraft were 'Top Secret', and on 13th August 1943 attention was drawn by the Minister of Aircraft Production to the strict necessity for avoiding any reference to jet-powered aircraft in the press. In fact it was vital that no reference of any sort should be made to the development, production or flight of jet aircraft, although there was no objection to any articles that examined the theory of jet propulsion in general. This subject had come to the fore because a reference had appeared in the April 1943 issue of the American publication *Esquire*. Information on the development of jet engines and aircraft in Britain was finally released to the national press on 6th January 1944.

This chapter has outlined much of the complexities and complication associated with the design and development of, not just a new combat aircraft but a new engine to power it as well. In May 1943 the overall planning included, as one of the sub-contractors, the Standard Motor Company, and this organisation was expected to build twenty-five Meteor I centre sections per month. This particular firm is noted here because a Ministry report has been found which states that Standard's Meteor I shop would function as a separate factory and, as such, would require the following – two private cars, two utility vans, two 2-ton or 3-ton lorries and two 40ft (12.20m) Queen Mary trailers. The value of this equipment was £3,500. This item illustrates so clearly that, despite the very advanced nature of the new jet engines and aircraft, which were designed using the most advanced technology of the time, putting them into production still required some very basic ingredients. A high proportion of the manufacture of the F.9/40 prototypes and early production Meteors was undertaken by sub-contractors. For example, besides Standard's wing centre sections (which were additional to the company's other contracts for Airspeed Oxfords and de Havilland Mosquitoes) Bristol Tramways built front fuselage sections.

EE401 is a standard Meteor III in the camouflage scheme that appeared on most production F.I and F.III aircraft. The code 'MK' is a personal code of the Wing Commander Flying at RAF Middle Wallop. *The Aeroplane,* via Tony Buttler

Chapter Two

Prototypes

DG202/G, the first F.9/40 prototype, fitted with the original W.2B/23 engines and very narrow jet pipes. It made its first flight on 24th July 1943. IWM MH.4852

The previous chapter highlighted the problems experienced in getting the various types of jet engine ready for flight and gave the reasons why the de Havilland H.1 prototype, DG206, became the first airframe to fly. This event took place on 5th March 1943 at RAF Cranwell in Lincolnshire, the aircraft being piloted by Michael Daunt, but the flight was terminated after just three and a half minutes. On reaching 200mph (322km/h) air speed indicated (ASI) he found that it proved impossible to stop the aircraft yawing from side-to-side in violent fashion. Consequently, Daunt reduced speed to 150mph (241km/h) ASI, where it did become possible to control the machine, and landed immediately. The problem was traced to an unbalanced rudder and the first attempt to cure the fault was to fit trimmer cords, which worked well. Later the rudder's trailing edge was thickened and, in due course, DG208 introduced an enlarged fin/rudder arrangement with flat sides and a torpedo fairing at the fin/tail intersection. Not a good start, but the problem had not resulted from the new powerplant.

With so many different prototypes and engines involved, it seems wise to break down this part of the story with an examination of the career of each F.9/40 prototype in turn. This

also gives the opportunity to write about DG204 in some detail, the Metropolitan-Vickers F.2-powered machine which had a short life and, consequently, has been mentioned only relatively briefly in previous accounts. However, before detailing their flight test programmes, it is worthwhile including some notes from two official reports. Both were written by H J Allwright at the Ministry of Aircraft Production and, as summaries of the overall programme on the dates they were compiled, they give a fine illustration of the state of progress of each prototype and the delays suffered by the late delivery of power units. In fact they illustrate the various aspects of a prototype test programme for a new type of aeroplane very well.

The first is dated 1st April 1943 and records that DG202 was being prepared for the installation of two Whittle W.2/500 engines. The airframe was having to be re-conditioned following storage at Newmarket in 'bad conditions', but it was expected to be ready well before the engines were available; their arrival was unlikely for some two months (in fact the W.2/500s were never fitted). DG203 was fully-equipped and had been ready for flight since September 1942, since when it had been used for miscellaneous trial installations and, more

recently, for pressure cabin development work. The two MetroVick F.2 engines for DG204 had now been delivered and the aircraft was within three weeks of completion, apart from the undercarriage units which it had been known for some time would determine the final completion date. The best promise from Dowty was the third week in April and, on this basis, it was thought that DG204 would probably fly in May. The heavier nosewheel loads of this aircraft were expected to accentuate the undercarriage troubles now being experienced (which are described later).

DG205 was the 'skeleton aircraft' for Rover W.2B engine testing and was within two weeks of completion. Rover W.2Bs of 1,250 lb (5.6kN) thrust had been delivered on 24th February but, by general agreement, this aircraft would not fly until flight experience had been accumulated on the H.1 testbed (DG206); thus it was unlikely that DG205 would fly, at the very least, for two weeks. DG206 of course, had

already flown but was now being taken to Newmarket from Cranwell for taxying tests with a modified nosewheel unit, which it was hoped would give 10ft/sec (3.05m/sec) vertical velocity characteristics with freedom from 'bottoming'. Allowing for re-erection of the airframe, alterations to the front fuselage and drop testing of the new undercarriage, taxying could begin in about a week's time. However, the problems of rudder over-balance had still to be overcome and the first step to deal with it had been the thickening of the rudder trailing edge.

DG207 was to be the full Mk.II prototype with the H.1 engine and the assembly of the centre section of this aircraft was just beginning. On the other hand DG208 was to have W.2 units (plus air brakes) and the centre section for this aircraft was expected to be cleared on about 9th April. In general there had been a number of criticisms of the rate of progress at Glosters but Allwright noted that, from the above, the construction of the airframes would not delay the flight trials of any of the prototypes except DG204, and here it was the undercarriage from Dowty that was causing the delay. In fact he considered that Glosters' performance in building five prototypes in a little over two years (and the first in eighteen months) was extremely meritorious, particularly considering that the company had lacked detailed information on the engines until just a few months ago.

Allwright's second report is dated 10th September 1943. DG202 had flown on 24th July and completed two and a half hours flying up to the 30th. Since then no engines had been available for it and so no further flying had been accomplished. The machine was now undergoing preparation for handing over to Rolls-Royce for engine test flying; engines had now been received and it was hoped that DG202 would be handed over in about ten days. The pressure cabin development on DG203 had proceeded up to 'a satisfactory standard' and it had now been decided that this aircraft would be used for W.2/500 flight testing. One engine had been received and the second was due at the end of the week so, allowing for re-assembly, flight testing was expected in about ten days. The Whittle W.2/500 was acknowledged by RAE as a promising design which offered a take-off thrust of 1,800 lb (8.0kN) and steady thrust of 1,600 lb (7.1kN), an improvement over the W.2B.

Testbed prototype DG204 had carried out taxying tests on 3rd August during which it was found that the idling thrust of the MetroVick F.2 power units was excessive. The engines had been returned to the manufacturers to be modified to improve this condition and were due back at Glosters the following week-end, so a first flight was possible during the week beginning 13th September. DG205 had now completed twenty hours of flying and the aerodynamic development process had been proceeding, but bad weather had delayed the flying programme considerably. Further modifications to improve the F.9/40's aileron control

had recently been made although, as yet, no results were available. A torpedo fairing for the tailplane fin junction had also been fitted and an improvement had definitely been effected.

A third period of engine test flying had been completed on DG206 during August and this had brought the flight time up to seven hours and the total engine running time to fifteen hours. The engines themselves had since been taken away for examination but currently were back in the aircraft and flying was due to recommence at any moment. Construction was proceeding with low priority on Meteor II DG207, but it was expected to be ready for flight in early December. It was anticipated that DG208 would be ready for its first flight in three to four weeks and it was during the period between these two reports that the decision was made to build an eighth prototype (DG209) to carry out the trial installation of the Rolls-Royce W.2B/37. This aircraft was to be completed by the end of the year.

These reports show very clearly the hive of activity that was now surrounding the development of the jet fighter in Britain. It should still be remembered that the full designation for these aircraft during the war years was DG202/G, DG203/G, etc, to signify their Top Secret nature and to ensure that they were 'guarded' at all times. The individual careers of the F.9/40 Meteor prototypes was as follows.

DG202

This aircraft began its initial engine runs at Bentham on 29th June 1942 with Rover-built W.2B/23 units in place and three days later it was moved by road to Newmarket. Taxying began on 10th July but was suspended because of problems with the undercarriage, and in fact these did not restart until 18th December after some Hawker Typhoon wheels and tyres had been fitted. In 1943 plans were made to fit W.2/500s but were cancelled before DG202 went by road to Barford St John on 22nd May of that year. Michael Daunt took it on its first flight on 24th July and in early November it was flown to Rolls-Royce's Balderton site for engine development flying, principally as the W.2B/23c Welland testbed aircraft.

After being damaged by an engine failure on 13th December 1944, and having logged a total of 367 flight hours, DG202 was taken to Gloster's Moreton Valence site for repairs and reconditioning. On 11th August 1945 the by now veteran prototype was flown to Abbotsinch in readiness to carry out some engine running, taxying and deck handling on board the aircraft carrier *Pretoria Castle*, a trials carrier converted from a passenger liner and moored in the Firth of Clyde. To do this DG202 had to be dismantled and taken aboard on a lighter. These operations were successful and lasted until 26th August (much later proper 'airborne' landings were carried out on the fleet carriers *Illustrious* and *Impacable* using 'hooked' Meteor Mk.III EE337). After retirement, DG202 served as a 'gate guardian' at RAF Yatesbury and in 1958

the importance of this rare airframe was recognised which, fortunately, ensured that it was saved. Today DG202 is preserved at the Aerospace Museum at RAF Cosford.

DG203

DG203 was flown, primarily as an engine testbed, with two different Power Jets engines, the W.2/500 and W.2/700, both of them more powerful developments of the W.2B. It was Frank Whittle's hope that these units might have been put into production but this never happened. W.2/500s were in place for the machine's maiden flight from Moreton Valence on 9th November 1943 and W.2/700s were installed in early 1944. Surging had been experienced on the W.2B-powered aircraft but the W.2/500 was found to be surge free and ideal for solving the Meteor's control problems. However, when DG203 was preparing for its second flight the port impeller disintegrated and wrecked the engine. Michael Daunt described the W.2/500 as an extremely good engine. The W.2/700s were actually substitutes and offered 1,700 lb (7.5kN) of thrust, which allowed DG203 to reach 464mph (747km/h) at 20,000ft (6,096m). After spending several months under repair following a single-engine wheels-up landing on 22nd April 1944, DG203 was used by Gloster Aircraft for pressure cabin development. In April 1946 it became ground instructional airframe 5928M.

DG204

This aircraft reached Barford St John in June 1943 for its intended first flights with the Metropolitan-Vickers F.2, but, because of the powerplant's high idling thrust, the test programme progressed no further than taxying trials held during July. Excessive idling thrust was one of many new problems and characteristics associated with the introduction of jet propulsion and meant that extra effort had to be made to keep the aircraft under control on the ground or when in cruise flight. DG204's MetroVick F.2/1 engines had an idling thrust of 365 lb (1.62kN) per unit, which for all practical purposes was too high, and so they had to be removed and modified, the alterations reducing the figure to 230 lb (1.02kN) per engine.

Nos 1 and 2 engines were re-installed but, after the first handling flight, an accident occurred to No 2 during a ground run when a piece of an inspector's coat was drawn into the air intake. This necessitated a change to the spare No 6 power unit which, with No 1, was installed for subsequent tests. Although later expected to give rather more power, the take-off thrust of DG204's engines was nominally 1,800 lb (8.0kN) at 7,300rpm. Excluding the radio and its mounting, DG204's all-up-weight with 300 gallons (1,364 litres) of fuel aboard was 12,190 lb (5,529kg).

DG204 was eventually dismantled and moved by road to RAE Farnborough. Wg Cdr H J Wilson flew the aircraft on its eleven-minute first flight on 13th November 1943 and further

engine runs were attempted during the following week, after which the power units were changed. The second flight (with replacement engines) was made on the 19th December, another followed on the 22nd, four on the 25th (yes Christmas Day!) and further flights were planned for 4th January 1944; they were shared by Wilson and Sqn Ldr W D B S Davie. During the two flights completed in the week before Christmas DG204 achieved a speed of approximately 375mph (603km/h) but one flight made on the 25th gave a disappointing top speed of 350mph (563km/h) at 7,350rpm and 2,700ft (823m) altitude. Preliminary analysis showed that one of the engines was giving a thrust approximately 5% below the static bench figures.

Tragically, during the second flight of 4th January (intended to be a climb to 20,000ft [6,096m] and then to continue to 25,000ft [7,620m] for stall investigations) the compressor in DG204's port engine broke up and burst out of the nacelle, causing the aircraft to crash near Farnborough. The machine was destroyed after just twelve minutes flying and Sqn Ldr Davie was killed when he was hit by the aircraft after baling out (ejection seats were not yet available).

It is believed that the compressor failed through over-speeding and the pilot may have lost control while he was trying to return to base – the end of the tail structure also failed and broke off in the air. There was a clear blue sky and many of the Establishment's staff, enjoying their lunch break, were able to observe DG204's jet plumes as it flew overhead. Suddenly it began to execute some large gyrations in its flight and to

break up, and the detached tail section actually landed on the roof of the RAE Foundry, not far from the engine testbeds. Altogether, wreckage was spread over a distance of 13 miles (21km) south of Farnborough and required a long search to collect it all. Examination showed that the compressor drum had suffered a crystalline fracture and, when it failed, it then sliced through the airframe. It was also apparent that the fuselage structure had failed in an unusual way which afterwards prompted some special strength tests to be made on the fuselage and tail of another Meteor.

After the loss, RAE's C W R Smith, C Kell and T G Woodford compiled a report covering the results of testing undertaken on DG204 thus far. The objective of this aircraft's test programme had been to obtain engine performance data, but it was also hoped to include some aerodynamic tests as well. Due to the crash of course, the tests were terminated at an early stage and it appears that only nine flights that contributed to the test programme were completed. During the early stages trouble was experienced with the nosewheel tyre skidding during landing runs, and so a few extra handling flights had been necessary whilst this was being corrected. The parts of the programme that were completed were position error tests and calibration of the air temperature thermometer, level speeds at 3,000ft (914m), 15,000ft (4,572m) and 20,000ft (6,096m), covering a range of engine speeds, and just one reliable climb to 15,000ft (4,572m). The time taken to reach 15,085ft (4,598m) was eight minutes and fourteen seconds, the mean rate of climb being 1,830ft/min (558km/min).

DG204/G, the MetroVick F.2-powered F.9/40, at the Gloster experimental department, Bentham, being prepared for engine runs before its first flight. This shows the underslung axial-flow engines, the first British axial-flow jets to fly. Arguably this was the most elegant of the F.9/40 prototypes. ATP 12306F, via Tony Buttler

Engine starting was accomplished using an external mechanical flexible drive which RAE declared was dangerous, unwieldy and caused delays, but future units were expected to have a self-contained electric starter. Previously, during July 1943, an F.2 engine had been air-tested in an Avro Lancaster bomber and the report noted that the actual engine starts on DG204 were good, with little flame, and a vast improvement over that achieved with the Lancaster installation. A limitation was imposed on accelerating the engine from idling speed (3,300rpm) up to 5,000rpm to avoid the danger of compressor stalling, but this was a cause of anxiety to the pilot as the manually-controlled rate of acceleration depended entirely on his judgement. This was particularly disadvantageous in the case of the aircraft undershooting or otherwise requiring more power during the landing approach, and would remain until the danger of compressor stalling during rapid acceleration had been eliminated. The pilots also felt that the 230 lb (1.02kN) idling thrust was still too high and resulted in a difficult landing approach and excessive braking. In fact, in view of the braking troubles with the aircraft, it was preferred to land with 'dead' engines if the approach was unimpeded.

Although compressor stalling was experienced on the ground, on no occasion was a stall observed during flight, even at 20,000ft (6,096m) where the actual speed of 7,340rpm corresponded to a corrected ground level speed of 7,700rpm. The precaution of reducing the speed of one engine to cruising rpm, whilst maintaining the other at climbing speed, was taken during the climb from 15,000ft to 20,000ft (4,572m to 6,096m) to avoid the danger of both engines stalling simultaneously.

A number of points and criticisms were raised by the two pilots. The machine was considered to be rather 'rough' to fly, and the controls were found to be heavy. At 20,000ft (6,096m) the pilot reported that DG204 'wallowed' during level flight, this term being described as a combination of rolling and low frequency 'snaking'. Comment was also made regarding the small cockpit, especially when the pilot was clad in high-altitude clothing. The pilot also had to release the control column in order to operate the two-lever jettisonable hood arrangement, which was not thought to be a good situation.

In addition the difficulty of 'baling out' from this type of machine was raised because of the relative position of the cockpit to the main wing and the high tailplane. This seems particularly unfortunate after the pilot of DG204 was killed when the aircraft was lost. An ejection seat would probably have increased his chances of survival substantially, which is backed up by the report when it states 'this point needs consideration and recommendations. Possibly the safest method to get out of the cockpit would be by some forced ejection means which should be considered particularly on this aircraft.' Although DG204 is the subject here, this point applied to all of the F.9/40 prototypes and to early production Meteors (in fact an ejection seat was not introduced into the Meteor until the arrival of the Mk.8 described in Chapter Three).

In conclusion RAE confirmed that the accident to DG204 had limited the information obtained, but from the available results the performance fell below the anticipated values. In addition the acceleration, stalling and idling thrust caused anxiety to the pilots and, together with the starting technique, needed to be improved at the earliest moment. Otherwise the F.2 power unit was satisfactory. Finally, RAE stated that it was interesting to record that the noise of this machine in the air was less than other jet propulsion aeroplanes. The attached graphs showed that DG204, with a mean speed of 7,200rpm for each engine, achieved a maximum of 373mph (600km/h) at 15,000ft (4,572m), while 7,350rpm gave 385mph (619km/h) at that height and 361mph (581km/h) at sea level; a brief record for 7,460rpm shows a maximum 384mph (618km/h) at 5,570ft (1,698m). The flights indicated that the top speeds recorded were about 25mph (40km/h) down on estimates at the high end of the speed range while rate of climb was 15% less, but the profile drag from the underslung nacelles was also found to be more than had been predicted.

DG205

This was the Rover W.2B test aircraft and reached Barford St John by road on 23rd May 1943. Daunt took it on its first flight (of twelve minutes duration) on 12th June and reported that these engines gave an unimpressive performance in take-off and climb. In addition the elevator tab was too sensitive and the hydraulic pump 'sounded like the hammers of hell!' However, he also observed that 'there are distinct possibilities for the F.9/40 as an operation low-level [ground-attack] fighter'.

DG205 was used for extensive flight control development and for measuring take-off and landing performance. In August 1943 an 'acorn' or bullet-shaped fairing was fitted to DG205 over the intersection of fin and tailplane and in October the aircraft was flown to Moreton Valence because the Barford site was due to close. By 12th December DG205 had completed 106 flights shared between Gloster

pilots Michael Daunt, John Grierson and John Crosby-Warren, RAE's H J Wilson and also two Americans, Col E K Warburton of the US Army Air Force and Frank Kelley from Bell Aircraft. Kelley was in England to make the first UK flight of RJ362, the Bell YP-59A Airacomet jet fighter that was to be tested by RAE Farnborough to compare it with current British types. On 27th April 1944 DG205 crashed at Moreton Valence having recorded just over eighty hours flying time.

The Aircraft and Armament Experimental Establishment (A&AEE) at Boscombe Down was the organisation that tested new aircraft and equipment intended for use by the UK's air forces. Between 24th and 29th February 1944 four A&AEE pilots visited the Gloster works and flew DG205 and DG208 in order to gain preliminary experience and impressions of this aircraft, with its new 'revolutionary' mode of propulsion, and to assess its handling qualities. Most of the flying was done with DG205 at 11,300 lb (5,126kg) weight and a total of five short flights were made. On the whole the cockpit layout was described as fairly reasonable but some improvements to the instruments and throttle position were needed and, for comfort, the seat could also be tilted back a few degrees. Starting the engines was simple and, in general use, the handling was very straightforward, but a restriction of ten seconds minimum opening time from idling to full power was seen to be a handicap.

Taxying was normal, though the response to the throttles was much slower than with a conventional piston aircraft, and the take-off was straightforward and easy without any tendency to swing (swing to the side while on the runway was a feature of piston-powered aeroplanes due to the torque created by the rotating propeller). The take-off run was fairly short but the initial climb was poor. Engine surge was experienced on one climb at 13,000ft (3,962m) but was not very noticeable and easily avoided by an increase in speed or decrease in height or power.

In general flying it was found that the controls were very badly harmonised and had to be improved. The rudder was immovable at ordinary level speeds and diving speeds after the first few degrees of movement, the elevator was too heavy whilst the ailerons were too light at low to moderate speeds. The elevator was the least satisfactory of the three, but could profitably be lightened, and the rudder was very heavy indeed from moderate speeds upwards; within the initial range of rudder movement, however, the response of the aircraft was good. The ailerons were very light and effective but completely lacked feel and self-centring qualities up to about 250mph (402km/h) ASI. Above that speed they became heavier being satisfactory at about 300mph to 350mph (483km/h to 563km/h), but a little heavy at 400mph

(644km/h). In bumpy conditions a directional oscillation of the aircraft was present which could also be induced in calm air by applying a little rudder and then centralising the control. The oscillations were fairly quick (of frequency about one to one and a half seconds) and, although the amplitude was small, the movement was quite pronounced whilst the decay was very gradual. This feature was serious since it impaired the aiming accuracy and so had to be eliminated.

The elevator trimmer was found to be too sensitive and had an excessive amount of backlash, but the rudder trimmer was acceptable. There was hardly any change in longitudinal trim with the engine and the change with flaps and undercarriage was very small. Owing to a lack of aileron trimmer a left-wing-low tendency at low speeds, which changed to right-wing-low at high speeds, could not be trimmed out. The aircraft appeared to be statically stable with stick fixed and also gave the impression of being dynamically stable. The A&AEE pilots concluded that the Meteor 'was an easy aircraft to fly and the comparative quiet and freedom from vibration are pleasing qualities, but the control harmonisation must be improved'.

Clearly plenty of development flying needed to be done. However, the pilots' notes from this visit were described as tentative and some of the conclusions 'might be modified as experience was gained'. In addition, on 4th September 1943 Wg Cdr Wilson had reported that he 'was very pleased with the general handling of the aircraft apart from the ailerons. I think it is an

excellent aircraft and all it wants now is more thrust to make it a very excellent fighter'. He also noted that very slight swing occurred when one engine was out at 300mph (483km/h) ASI. The ailerons were to prove quite difficult to get right and several modifications were made to try and find a solution. Spring tabs were fitted, and also mass-balanced weights, short extensions on the trailing edges were tried and the metal shrouds around the leading edges were cleaned up, but all to no avail. Improvements in one area usually created problems in another and, for some time, it proved practically impossible to furnish the F.9/40 with light aileron feel through the aircraft's full flight envelope at height.

Having made reference to two official flight test reports, it is worth remembering that in those far off World War Two days there was no computer-aided design and monitoring equipment – the test pilot and his engineering colleagues had to plan each flight very carefully and explore a new aircraft's flight envelope in small relatively easy stages. The pilot was able to make some notes on a knee pad, or had to rely on his memory, but there was hardly any special data-recording equipment.

DG206

The delays with the Whittle power units meant that it was well into 1943 before flight-standard W.2B engines would become available, so the first flight-ready prototype was DG206, the de Havilland H.1 testbed (this aircraft and DG207 were also designated F.9/40H). By 12th January two engines had been delivered, but were

DG206/G, the Halford H.1-powered Gloster F.9/40, was the first Meteor to fly. The engine cowling looks similar to that for the W.2B, the most obvious difference being the small air intake (just visible in this photograph below the yellow 'P' prototype marking on the fuselage). The purpose of the bulge next to the aerial on the fuselage is not known. DERA Neg. 51673, taken at RAE Farnborough, 3rd March 1944

de-rated to 2,000 lb (8.9kN) for early tests, and Michael Daunt began some preliminary taxi runs on 3rd March. Having also done some of the taxying in the Whittle-powered DG202 he found that the H.1 'provided a rather different set of answers' – for example, because the de Havilland unit gave more thrust, and DG206 was heavier at 11,500 lb (5,216kg), the nosewheel shock absorber showed signs of using more travel.

In fact, quite a lot of development work was to be needed on the F.9/40 Meteor's undercarriage, particularly with the nosewheel strut and different main wheels to improve brake cooling. The wheel/brake assembly was the key and the undercarriage problem was exacerbated on the longer-legged version used by DG204. In fact, after DG205's first flight the port wheel inner tube actually burst as a result of the heat generated by the brakes during taxying and landing. The taxi tests included leaving the ground for a moment at 110mph (177km/h) but the engines performed perfectly, though they were described as noisy.

As recorded already the first flight was made at RAF Cranwell on 5th March but it was far from

DG208/G, the seventh F.9/40, powered by Rolls-Royce Wellands, and seen here with a revised fin shape. Photographed at Moreton Valence, where it was used for air-brake development by Glosters. IWM ATP.12627F.

easy to keep the existence of jet aircraft secret – apart from service personnel seeing aeroplanes with no propellers there was always that distinct noise for the public to hear. During the early history of jet aircraft development and test flying the aircraft themselves were only allowed to fly from specially cleared airfields, which in practice had amounted to concentrating them eventually at Barford St John and Farnborough. This suited Gloster well but naturally did not satisfy the engine suppliers, Rolls-Royce or de Havilland, who were most anxious to operate them from airfields closer to their own factories.

In due course the various contractors were allowed to use their own airfields and, as R S Sorley wrote on 6th August 1943, once jet aircraft were in the air 'it is impossible to conceal the fact that such aircraft are flying and it really does not matter where they are seen, whether in Gloucestershire or Hertfordshire'. In addition, once the de Havilland Vampire, Britain's second jet fighter, was ready to fly, it became even more difficult to conceal that all of these aircraft were in existence, so the airfield restriction was lifted. It must be noted that the security arrangements included strict operation when using land-line telephones or RT and, for example, Barford St John was never referred to by name – it was always 'Position X'.

Back at Cranwell, however, there was a different security problem. Some students from Turkey, a neutral country, were about to arrive for a course at the RAF College, so DG206 was moved by road to Newmarket for its next flight, which took place on 17th April. However there were problems here too, not least that the testing of this vital secret project had to be stopped for the fortnightly race meeting. There were also problems still to solve with the undercar-

riage which prevented any more flying until May, when seven sorties were completed, the last (and longest at twenty-nine minutes) being a cross-country trip to Barford St John on the 28th. Newmarket was far from ideal, for one reason because the runway surface condition was poor which meant that the fuel load had to be kept to a minimum. Consequently Daunt had to keep a close eye on the fuel gauges and this was the reason why the longest flight prior to the journey to Barford was a mere eighteen minutes (on 7th May). It was found however, that DG206 did handle well on one engine.

A total of nineteen flights were completed at Barford up to 24th September giving DG206 a total flight time of ten and a half hours. DG206's next move, without engines, was another road trip, this time to RAE Farnborough on 19th December. After receiving new power units it was flown on 2nd March 1944 by Wg Cdr Wilson and completed another five sorties during March and May. After that DG206 appears to have been little used.

The greater power of the derated H.1 engine over the W.2B/23 was offset by the higher drag of the fat nacelles and to see which version was faster, test pilots Daunt (in DG205) and John Grierson (in DG206) flew together between Barford St John and Brockworth at 7,500ft (2,286m) with full power applied for five minutes. In fact the aircraft held station neck-and-neck throughout to give identical speeds, and previous measurements which had found that the W.2B/23 was 10mph to 15mph (16km/h to 24km/h) faster were nullified by DG205's now rather poor surface condition. Early measurements had shown that DG206's H.1 engine would give 1,850 lb (8.2kN) of thrust at 8,950rpm, DG205's W.2B 1,745 lb (7.8kN) on

the bench at 17,150rpm. In fact the H.1 was designed to rotate at a much lower speed which was helpful in reducing demands on the bearings.

A report from Gloster's own pilots on their tests with DG205 and DG206, dated 14th September 1943, showed that left rudder had to be applied continually to maintain directional trim. Shallow dives were made at 320mph to 330mph (515km/h to 531km/h) at 22,000ft to 23,000ft (6,706m to 7,010m) and showed that the existing rudder and fin were liable to directional instability. It was also found that directional instability was worse at altitude than at lower heights. During the early stages of test flying, sorties could only be made up to about 33,000ft (10,058m), this being the limit on account of the surging characteristics of the engine.

DG207

This airframe was earmarked as the Meteor Mk.II prototype with the H.1b (Goblin) but production of the Mk.II was postponed indefinitely in August 1944 and eventually cancelled because Goblin production for the de Havilland Vampire was given greater priority. Consequently progress with the construction of this airframe was slow and it did not fly until 24th July 1945; John Grierson was the pilot and the venue was Moreton Valence. After the production programme had been cancelled there were plans to install two Nene units in DG207,

a new 5,000 lb (22.2kN) thrust engine from Rolls-Royce which was first bench-tested in October 1944. This particular aircraft's centre section could accommodate the larger engine, but a decision was made instead to use DG207 to help with further development of the Goblin. The aircraft went to Hatfield on 6th September but, in the event, was little used because its endurance was insufficient to allow time at the high altitudes which were needed for the then-current development work. On 5th November 1948, after a long period of disuse, DG207 went by road to RAF Locking to begin a period of service at No 5 School of Technical Training as ground instructional airframe 6591M. On 5th April 1955 it was moved to No 1 School of Technical Training at RAF Halton.

DG208

The next prototype in the series was fitted with the Rolls-Royce W.2B/23 and made its maiden flight from Moreton Valence on 20th January 1944. By 27th April it had completed forty-eight flights and the machine was used extensively on air-brake development and later for a trial installation of some strengthened undercarriage components used by later marks of Meteor. It was also used on some tests to try and solve the problems of directional instability, which included the introduction of a larger fin above the tailplane with a leading edge aligned with the section beneath the tail, plus the acorn fairing at the junction of fin and tail. In November 1946 it became ground instruction airframe 5862M. After Rolls-Royce had taken over the role formerly undertaken by Rover (before the first F.9/40 prototype flight) the W.2B/23 became the B.23, and in October 1943 it was named the Welland I. For its first F.9/40 flight the engine was cleared for 1,400 lb (6.2kN) thrust but this figure was soon increased to 1,600 lb (7.1kN). A hundred were eventually produced to power Meteor F Mk.1 production aircraft. (Note: Rolls-Royce has usually named its gas turbine engines after rivers, signifying the concept of constant flow.)

DG209

This was the Rolls-Royce W.2B/37 testbed and first flew from Moreton Valence on 18th April 1944 (this engine later became the Rolls-Royce Derwent). When it made its maiden flight it became the first Meteor to fly with more than 2,000 lb (8.9kN) of thrust per power unit, which gave a higher speed than any other installation so far. On 10th June DG209 was delivered to Rolls-Royce's Church Broughton facility to begin the engine's development flying programme and by 26th January 1946 this aircraft had completed 336 flight hours. That day it was flown from Church Broughton to RAE Farnborough for use in 'full-scale fire-prevention tests'. Later it was moved to Shoeburyness.

Side-on view of DG208/G, taken on the same day.
IWM ATP.12627D

DG210

As already noted this aircraft was never completed. However, it was intended to receive MetroVick F.2/4 engines (also known as the 'F.2 Mk.II') and work was still in progress on this aircraft well after the crash of DG204. In early July 1944 there were plans to build seventy F.2 engines by January 1946 and, for the F.2/4, 3,000 lb (13.3kN) of thrust was expected to be available by April or May 1945 with an increase to 3,500 lb (15.6kN) following around six months later.

General Knowledge

Along with the development flying of the various engines, all of the F.9/40 Meteor prototype airframes were used, to a greater or lesser extent, in the development of flying controls, air brakes, the fin/tailplane configuration or ancillary equipment such as instrumentation, fuel systems and pressure cabins. All of the early prototypes (except DG204) were built by Glosters at Bentham and then DG209 (plus the unfinished DG210) preceded the first Mk.I production Meteors on the new production line at Moreton Valence.

Teething troubles included engine surge and aileron instability at high altitude, the latter a new phenomenon never before experienced on other aircraft. Previous aeroplanes had suffered from light ailerons at high speed and low level but, as already noted, on the F.9/40 the ailerons became progressively heavy with speed at low level. More important it was eventually discovered that above 15,000ft (4,572m) they actually became light at all speeds and showed dangerous tendencies above Mach 0.65. Overbalance caused the joystick to try and slip out of the pilot's hands, a particularly unpleasant experience, but attempts to modify the ailerons brought difficulties elsewhere. Not until flat-sided ailerons were fitted well into 1944 was the instability cured, while a further problem of aileron flutter was removed by replacing the external mass balance with three smaller balances inside the wing.

Also noted earlier was the point that it was forbidden to fully open the throttles on early Meteors in under ten seconds but by May 1944 work was under way to clear the engines for instantaneous operation. That month speed limits were set for the aircraft at 400 knots (461mph/741km/h) below 15,000ft (4,572m) and Mach 0.70 above, and the aircraft needed extra outer wing riveting and new ailerons to help clear it for higher speed dives. The view out for the approach and landing and all flight conditions was excellent, but with the early style of canopy the rearward view was poor. Manufacturer's tests found the stall to be gentle but without warning and there were some compressibility problems (which are discussed in Chapter Three). Test flying eventually showed that the maximum level speed performance of a jet aircraft was extremely sensitive to changes in air temperature – a 10°F rise might cut the speed by 20mph (32km/h), for example from 405mph (652km/h) to 385mph (620km/h).

The introduction of jet propulsion was to radically change the design of aircraft compared to earlier generations of piston-powered machines. The Gloster Meteor itself was essentially a World War Two piston-type airframe fitted with jets, which in fact was the ideal direction in which to proceed with such a revolutionary development. It allowed a thorough assessment of the jet engine to be made before more advanced airframes became available and ensured enough experience was accumulated to allow the introduction later on of more advanced aerodynamic shapes like the swept wing. On 12th December 1947 the Gloster Aircraft Company produced a report that appraised some of the difficulties and changes that had been brought about by the application of the jet engine. It was called *Problems Met in Jet Aircraft Design, Particularly Gloster E.28/39 and Meteor*. Some of the difficulties highlighted were to have important effects on future design trends but others actually proved to be illusory.

Meteor F Mk.I EE214/G in flight. The Mk.I differed little from the prototype F.9/40s. IWM CL2955

Firstly, the absence of long airscrews had allowed the use of shorter undercarriages. Second, the change of slipstream from a large-area moderate-speed flow to a small jet of high velocity had led to a repositioning of the tail. The tail had to be placed away from the jet to avoid excessive inflow effects but it then suffered from a lack of slipstream velocity. When a tricycle undercarriage was fitted a large enough tail also had to be provided to lift the nose during take-off. In addition, it might be thought that, since the tail was outside the slipstream, the loss of stability normally experienced on the climb with propeller aircraft would be absent. In fact the tail was usually placed above the jet and the loss of stability on the climb due to jet inflow was actually quite marked. Even the Meteor, despite its high tail, suffered in this respect and would suffer even more with developments giving increased engine thrust. It had been found that this destabilising effect was absent if the tail was ahead of the jet nozzle, as per the E.28/39.

The absence of airscrews made a jet aircraft relatively clean with power off, which was an advantage in one-engine cruise but a disadvantage when speed had to be lost or when a descent from altitude had to be made quickly without exceeding the limiting speed. Also, to keep alight the engine burners it was necessary to maintain a certain minimum fuel consumption. The fuel consumption gave rise to an 'idling' thrust which at altitudes of the order of 40,000ft (12,192m) could be 'a serious embarrassment'. For this reason, and also because jet aircraft were inherently clean, effective air brakes were an essential feature of their

design. This same difficulty also occurred when coming into land, when speed had to be lost.

The next point was that jet engines did not open up as quickly as conventional piston engines and this disability was felt the most in a baulked landing (or in deck landing on carriers). Schemes had been developed whereby the engine was left running at a fairly high rpm while the thrust was spoiled by an obstruction placed in the jet aft of the nozzle – when this obstruction was removed high thrust was available immediately. Also, during cruise flight jets used a relatively large amount of fuel and making the space available to provide a sufficiently large capacity was a problem. In addition jet aircraft were also fast and, therefore, employed a relatively thin wing section, which meant that large amounts of fuel had to be carried in the fuselage.

Finally, it was noted that the absence of propeller and slipstream on jet aircraft lent

them for use in technical and scientific research. Flight tests made using the Meteor had established the fact that the aircraft's aerodynamic centre had moved forward and then back with increasing Mach number. This had provided flight confirmation of wind tunnel test results while the absence of the type of vibration associated with reciprocating engines had also enabled test instruments in the cockpit and auto-observer to be read accurately. In fact, during Meteor flight testing, instances had occurred where a vibrator had to be provided in the auto-observer box to prevent the delicate instruments sticking.

Meteor F.4 EE519, still in Second World War-style camouflage and carrying 500-lb bombs. This was a Gloster 'trial installations' aircraft, flown on bomb-dropping trials amongst other duties. Russell Adams P19/50C, via Phil Butler

Chapter Three

Day Fighters and Trainers

Gloster Meteor F Mk.I

This designation was allocated to the first production version of Gloster's jet fighter. All early production Meteors had provision to take either the Whittle W.2B or W.2/500 engine and at a meeting held on 8th June 1942 it was decided that the F.9/40 Meteor fitted with W.2B units should go ahead as an operational type, while the de Havilland H.1 and Metropolitan Vickers F.2 versions should continue on their present basis as flying testbeds. However, during this meeting it was also recognised that one or both of the latter might also become operational and, in due course, the H.1 was selected for a

planned production programme as the Meteor Mk.II (below).

By 6th April 1943 the F Mk.1 production order had been temporarily cut from three hundred machines to just twenty, a situation that was brought about by various delays and also doubts regarding whether the programme would go the distance. In the end only these twenty Mk.Is were to be built, with serials EE210 to EE229, because the follow-on orders

were switched to later marks. The first production aircraft, EE210, was flown by Michael Daunt on 12th January 1944 and, apart from having two 1,700 lb (7.6kN) W.2B/23 Welland I engines, it was in all respects a duplicate of prototype DG202. In fact the development process associated with this new form of propulsion was so extensive that numerous Mk.Is were to join the prototypes in the test programme, with several going to RAE Farnborough or A&AEE

An official photograph of the second production Meteor F.I, EE211/G, taken at RAE Farnborough in March 1945, after it had been fitted with extended engine nacelles to cure vibration and speed limitations arising from the original nacelle profile fitted to the Welland-powered F.9/40 prototypes and production F.Is.
ATP 13539B, via Tony Buttler

EE210/G, the first production Meteor F Mk.I, was dispatched to the USA after making its first flight on 12th January 1944, being flown again at Muroc Flight Test Base in California on 15th April. It was returned to England after being slightly damaged, and was later used for trials at RAE Farnborough. via Phil Butler

Boscombe Down. However, from 12th July onwards many Mk.Is were to make their way to No 616 Squadron. Mk.I EE215 became the first Meteor to be fitted with guns.

However, before EE210, the first production aircraft, became involved with any trials programmes it was to travel across the Atlantic. Brief mention was made in Chapter Two concerning the arrival of a Bell YP-59A Airacomet jet fighter at RAE Farnborough to allow a comparison to be made with current British jet-powered types. In reply EE210 was dispatched to the USA under 'Reverse Lend-Lease' for trials at Muroc Flight Test Base in California ('Lend-Lease' was the term that covered the supply of large amounts of military equipment to Britain from America during the war). The first flight at Muroc was made on 15th April 1944, the pilot being Gloster's John Grierson, but by December of that year EE210 was back at Glosters for repairs to be made to some damage sustained on the wing spar. On 17th May 1945 it flew from Moreton Valence to RAE Farnborough to begin its part in an investigation into 'snaking', a form of directional instability then thought to be characteristic of jet aircraft. EE210 made numerous flights at RAE over a period of several months before going to RAF Melksham on 4th March 1946 as ground instruction airframe 5837M.

The second Mk.I, EE211, made its first flight on 16th April 1944 and from mid-July was used by RAE for investigations into compressibility, a term which describes the problems created by the airflow over an aircraft's flying surfaces when it begins to approach the speed of sound. This is discussed in more depth towards the end of the chapter. EE211 was fitted with W.2B/23c engines and modified engine nacelles (below) and, finally, in April 1945 it was given W.2/700 power units. When EE211 returned to Moreton Valence on 24th April 1945 for tail load tests, it had received what were to be the definitive engines nacelles used by the Meteor F Mk.IV. After further service as ground

instruction airframe 5927M, EE211 was struck off charge on 8th April 1952.

Because of compressibility, early Meteors were Mach number limited to about 0.75 due to the onset of severe shock stalling over the engine nacelle, which created intense buffet. RAE tunnel tests revealed how airflow breakaway could be postponed by increasing the length of both the nose and rear of each nacelle, and this would also allow the machine to reach higher Mach numbers. Gloster fitted such extensions to EE211's nacelles before the aircraft returned to RAE on the 30th November 1944. Up to March 1945 flight testing revealed that EE211 now suffered no buffet up to Mach 0.81 and up to 4G and, over this range, the flow around the nacelles was perfectly satisfactory. By 27th April it had been possible to increase these limits to Mach 0.84 and 38,000ft (11,582m), the aircraft now being powered by W2/700 engines of 2,000 lb (8.9kN) thrust.

In fact at sea level the new nacelles improved top speed by about 60mph (97km/h) and, compared to the standard Mk.I Meteor, EE211's nacelle extensions delayed any unpleasant effects by about 0.1 Mach. The RAE concluded that the aircraft was now 'quite satisfactory and one of the best aircraft we have as far as high Mach Number characteristics are concerned'. However, the thrust from the W2/700 was still not enough to generate sufficiently high Mach numbers on the level, so to carry out any high-speed research the pilot would still have to take the machine into a dive which was a far from acceptable situation.

From September 1944 EE212, the third production Meteor, took part in handling and stability tests at A&AEE Boscombe Down (described shortly) and then on 26th January 1945 it flew to Moreton Valence to receive a new tailplane and end fins. In February it went to RAE to take part in the investigations into 'snaking' before, after being replaced by EE210 in this role, it returned to Boscombe. After having served as a ground airframe at

Henlow it was struck off charge on 21st September 1950.

As part of the on-going effort to improve the Meteor's directional oscillation and stability problems mentioned in Chapter Two, three A&AEE pilots visited Moreton Valence on 6th June 1944 to undertake flights in prototypes DG208 and DG209 and F Mk.Is EE211 and EE212; a total of six sorties were completed. Glosters had introduced different modifications to these aircraft – all had 5° of extra dihedral over approximately the outer 16in (40.6cm) of the span but with variations of trim tabs plus fabric or metal covering to the rudder, elevator and ailerons. It was found that the extra 5° of wingtip dihedral made no apparent difference to the directional oscillations and only EE212, with fabric on the upper portion of the rudder and metal covering below, and fabric elevator and ailerons, showed any improvement to the directional oscillation. This is just an example of the testing that was needed to prove this new type of aircraft and its powerplant. As an aside, it was noted that the increased power available to DG209 from its W.2B/37s had improved the performance appreciably, especially on take-off (the aircraft was actually called EE209 in the report). The other machines had W.2B/23 engines except for DG208 which had the W.2B/23c.

EE212 was based at Boscombe Down from September to December 1944 for handling trials. By now this aircraft had received two W.2B/23c units and also had 'heavy' ailerons and a modified fin and rudder – as such it was not entirely representative of either a Meteor Mk.I or the later Mk.III. The maximum weight at which the aircraft was handled was 11,670 lb (5,294kg) and a range of centres of gravity was covered. It was reported that, in general, the aircraft was pleasant and easy to fly and had good stability characteristics about all axes. However, the stick forces in untrimmed dives, and the stick forces required to pull out from trimmed dives, were considered too high for a fighter aircraft. At low speeds the elevator was light and effective but, overall, the ailerons were (deliberately) heavy and the rudder was heavy and rather ineffective. EE212's behaviour under asymmetric power conditions and during low-speed flight was good but the worst feature was again the directional oscillation, which was still under investigation. This particular aircraft displayed a critical Mach Number of 0.74 (the nacelle extensions introduced by EE211 were not fitted) and A&AEE considered that figure to be rather low for this type of aircraft.

EE213 took part in some armament and navigation tests at A&AEE and EE214 went to A&AEE in February 1945 to undertake a series

EE212/G, the second production Meteor F.I, which was used for flight trials at A&AEE Boscombe Down. This shot shows the early 'pop-bottle' nacelle design to advantage. IWM MH.4856

of trials with a large 100-gallon (455-litre) ventral tank in place. When compared to the other Mk.Is this produced no adverse effects to the type's general handling and, in fact, the presence of the tank was only made noticeable by the increase in the aircraft's take-off run. EE214 was also used to test sets of IFF (Identification Friend or Foe) and radio equipment. The next F Mk.I, EE215, went to Farnborough on 3rd September 1944 to carry out flight trials and experiments with early 'Mark I' reheat (afterburning). It then went to Power Jets Ltd at Bitteswell on 20th February 1945 for further reheat trials and became an instructional airframe at the National Gas Turbine Establishment (NGTE) in July 1949. The NGTE had been formed out of the former Power Jets company after the latter had ceased engine design and development in 1946. EE215 was also to become the first two-seat Meteor when its armament and ammunition were removed to allow an observer's seat to be added. The programme of research into a full-scale jet exhaust reheat system is described in some depth in Chapter Seven.

Other Mk.Is used for tests included EE219, which from 8th February 1945 took part in the 'snaking' investigation at RAE for which it received end-fins on the tailplane (these were removed in November). Reheat trials were also carried out using a Whittle W2/700 engine in Meteor I EE221, the aircraft joining Power Jets from 616 Squadron in February 1945; later on it operated with the National Gas Turbine Establishment (NGTE). EE223 served as the Rolls-Royce W.2B/37 (Derwent) intensive flying trials aircraft, arriving at Rolls-Royce on 7th March 1945 to begin this programme.

On 6th January 1945 EE227 left No 616 Squadron at Manston and flew to Moreton Valence to have its rudder cut down in size in readiness for yet another trials programme. Once these modifications were finished the aircraft flew to RAE on 4th February – in this form it had become the only T-tail Meteor and the first British T-tailed turbojet aircraft. The experiments at RAE were intended to try and help with the Meteor's directional stability but this modification offered virtually nothing in the way of improvements. Afterwards, on 7th March EE227 went to Rolls-Royce at Hucknall to have two RB.50 Trent propeller turbines installed. As such it became the first aircraft in the world to fly with a propeller driven by a gas turbine, a type of powerplant which today is called a turboprop (EE227 with this power unit in place is also described in the chapter on engine testbeds). In April 1948, EE227 went to A&AEE Boscombe Down for deck-landing trials and returned to Hucknall in October. It was struck off charge at RAE in 1949 and used for fire tests.

There were plans to fit EE229 with a Griffith wing section for another RAE research programme, but this was cancelled and the machine went direct to the RAF (Mk.III Meteor EE445 was the aircraft eventually fitted with the Griffith wing, as outlined in Chapter Seven). The remaining Mk.Is served entirely with the RAE's research and development Flight at Farnborough (T-Flight) and/or with No 616 Squadron. T-Flight was a joint RAF/RAE unit that carried out intensive flying trials with the Meteor F Mk.I.

The first proposal to form a special jet aircraft test flight at Farnborough specifically to help prepare jet aircraft for service with RAF was made in February 1943. On 12th February Dr Roxbee Cox, Deputy Director Research and Development Engines, reported that 'in view of the considerable number of aeroplanes [required] for experimental work … early steps should be taken to form a small flight whose sole duties are jet propulsion research and development'. He also suggested that the establishment should have three officers, that the nucleus of the maintenance staff should be drawn from NCOs and men who had gained experience at Power Jets and the Rover works at Barnoldswick, and that the flight should be stationed at Moreton Valence (which at the time was being prepared for jet aircraft operations). Finally he considered that the senior RAF officer of the Flight should be a pilot of the highest quality, with long experience of flying new types and working with research and development engineers.

However, on 15th March the Controller of Research and Development ruled that 'such flying of jet engines and jet-propelled aircraft as cannot be carried out by the firms under normal arrangements shall be centred in the RAE. For this purpose a separate flight of the Engine Flight shall be formed and shall be devoted exclusively to this work. This arrangement deals with the earliest phase of the development of jet-propelled aircraft. As soon as any type comes up for consideration for introduction into the Service, it is to go through the usual test procedures of the A&AEE in just the same way as other aircraft'.

On 18th March the new unit was designated the Tactical Flight or T-Flight (and not 'Turbine Flight' as noted in some publications) and the RAE's Director was asked to put in hand the necessary arrangements so that the flight could begin operating as soon as possible. By mid-April the arrangements for starting the Flight were well under way. While the F.9/40 prototypes and first production Meteors would in the first instance be flown by Gloster's test pilots, once they were passed out from the manufacturers a great deal of research, development and experimental flying needed to be done, with special pilots allotted for these tasks. This new Flight would concentrate the necessary flying in one place and its terms of reference included close collaboration with the Turbine Section of RAE, technical liaison with the manufacturing firms concerned and the training of RAF personnel.

The man put in charge of the unit was indeed very experienced. He was Gp Capt Hugh Joseph 'Willie' Wilson who was born in May 1908 and had joined the RAF in 1929. During the Battle of Britain Wilson was charged with undertaking research into the performance of the Spitfire, which included for a period an operational attachment to No 74 Squadron. He also became the first RAF pilot to handle jet aircraft and later on took No 616 Squadron with its Meteors into action against the V.1 flying bombs. In due course Wilson took part in the Meteor's attempts on the World Speed Record and also became the commanding officer of the Empire Test Pilots' School.

The Tactical Flight was formed at Farnborough in May 1944 but the first Meteors did not arrive until June. One of Wilson's tasks was to undertake a tactical appreciation of the Meteor, both from the point of view of air tactics and tactical application. It was known that the Meteor's engines suffered from certain limitations, such as range and rate of climb, and it would be important to know the powerplant's shortcomings in full so that this knowledge could then be passed to Rolls-Royce to guide them in the direction in which future developments of the jet engine should proceed.

Mk.III EE420, by now in a silver colour scheme and with the four-letter code markings that came into use in the 1947-1949 period. The code indicates aircraft 'B' of squadron 'RAA', which was No 500 Squadron, Royal Auxiliary Air Force (the 'R' in the code indicates 'Reserve Command', and 'AA' the lowest squadron number in that Command). via Phil Butler

The Meteor F Mk.1 was cleared for Service use on 17th July 1944 at a maximum permissible all-up-weight of 11,925 lb (5,409kg) and a maximum speed in calm air of 400mph (644km/h) up to 15,000ft (4,572m) and 450mph (724m/h) up to 8,000ft (2,438m). From the handling aspect the Mk.1 was mediocre but the top speed, although offering no improvement over current piston fighters, was available at sea level when a piston type's maximum was normally at high altitude. However, a speed of over 500mph (805km/h) was possible in a steep dive and, thanks to cockpit pressurisation, regular operations at heights above 40,000ft (12,192m) were also available. On 23rd July 1944 all of T-Flight's fighters and pilots flew to Manston to form the equipment and flying staff of No 616 Squadron.

Meteor F Mk.II

This was intended to be the version powered by the de Havilland H.1 Goblin engine and has already been referred to in Chapter Two. The production life of the Meteor was expected to be short and it was planned to utilise both W.2B/23 and H.1 powerplants, but thrust increases were urgently needed to counter an expected introduction of jet aircraft by Germany. Although in the short term it appeared to be the inferior engine, the H.1 was expected to give the better long-term thrust improvements. However, the H.1-engined production order was eventually cancelled although the intended airframes would appear as Mk.IIIs. DG207 remained the sole F Mk.II to be flown but in due course it did introduce an all-new canopy windscreen and hood. This was created after a close study had been made of a captured German Focke-Wulf Fw 190 piston fighter and was to become the standard for the Meteor F Mk.III.

As noted in Chapter Two, the reason behind the Mk.II cancellation was solely that the production of the H.1 engine had been allocated instead to the DH.100 Vampire fighter, and it was felt that an increase in the volume of manufacture would put too much strain on the resources at de Havilland. Apart from the slightly larger wing centre-section to accommodate the bigger turbines, which increased the span by 14in (35.6cm), externally the Mk.II Meteor would have been identical to the Mk.I.

It appears that in 1944 there was still some doubt in regard to just what effect the Meteor would have on its entry into service. The Vice Chief of the Air Staff (VCAS) wrote that 'it is difficult to foresee the extent to which the Meteor will take over from conventional single-engined fighters with reciprocating engines'. Comparisons of data had been made between the Meteor Mk.II and Mk.III and current piston types – the latest Spitfire and the new Supermarine Spiteful (both with Rolls-Royce Griffon 65), the Hawker Tempest II and F.2/43 (Fury) with Bristol Centaurus radial engines, and the de Havilland F.12/43 (Hornet) with two Rolls-Royce Merlins.

VCAS declared that the Meteor 'will be superior in performance to any other fighter which we shall have in operation in 1945 and 1946' and his figures showed that these improved versions of the jet always had the higher top speed. He added that this inferiority in speed of the reciprocating-engined fighters will increase above and below the altitudes of their maximum speeds because the variation in speed with altitude was very much less with jet-propelled types than with piston types. However, the Meteor itself possessed the aerodynamic characteristics of twin-engined aircraft, which meant that it might not be suitable as a replacement for more than a small proportion of the RAF's fighter force. The single-engined de Havilland jet fighter, the E.6/41 (Vampire), was expected to be entering production towards the end of 1945 and so would also influence the situation, because it would follow the characteristics of the highly manoeuvrable interceptor fighter more closely than the Meteor.

Meteor F Mk.III

This was the first version of the Meteor to be built in numbers and it also introduced the Rolls-Royce W.2B/37 Derwent I powerplant first tested in prototype DG209. Unfortunately, the pace of engine development was unable to keep pace with the manufacture of Meteor airframes and so, in the interim, the first fifteen F Mk.IIIs received W.2B/23c Wellands. The first of these, EE230, first flew in early September 1944 and the 2,000 lb (8.9kN) thrust Derwent Is were fitted to serial EE245 onwards. All of these production aeroplanes had short nacelles except for the final fifteen which introduced the longer version described above; however, some earlier machines were retrofitted with the long nacelle. Most of the first examples of the F Mk.III joined No 616 Squadron and the new mark brought with it, at last, a performance which was superior to piston-engined fighters. Certain examples were eventually to have the even more powerful 2,400 lb (10.7kN) Derwent IV installed.

On 2nd April 1946 the Air Fighting Development Squadron at West Raynham, part of CFE (the Central Fighter Establishment) and a unit that specialised in thorough evaluations of future RAF fighter types, issued a report on the Meteor III (EE248, EE281 and EE446 had joined the AFDS for a period to undertake tactical trials). The report also made a comparison between the Meteor and the Hawker Tempest V piston fighter which had served extensively in Europe during the final year of the War. The flight restrictions for the Meteor during these trials were 500mph (805km/h) IAS (because of structural limitations), a Critical Mach Number of 0.74, the undercarriage or flaps were not to be lowered above 155mph (249km/h) IAS and, if the undercarriage was down, the aircraft was not to be flown above 225mph (362km/h) IAS. Finally, intentional spinning was prohibited, aerobatics were not allowed above an all-up-weight of 12,300 lb (5,579kg) and the Meteor was not to be landed at weights above 12,000 lb (5,443kg).

Accurate speed and climb figures for the jet above 20,000ft (6,096m) were unobtainable during the trials owing to engine surging (a term given to a rumbling and bumping irregularity of airflow through the engine with a loss of rpm and thrust). This could also occur at ground level if the throttle was opened too quickly, which made the turbines accelerate less quickly and give irregular thrust while it was happening. The result of this could be a swing on the Meteor when one engine surged and so the situation was to be avoided by opening the throttles gradually.

Taking the Meteor III's flying characteristics first, the rudder was heavy but effective – however, owing to the fact that use of the rudder

Two views of one of the two 'Navalised Meteors', EE387, from a set of official photographs taken at A&AEE Boscombe Down. The arrester hook is evident. The two aircraft, EE337 and EE387, were both conversions from standard Meteor IIIs.
ATP 15556, via Tony Buttler

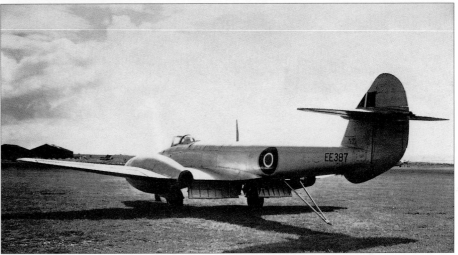

tended to increase snaking (instability in yaw) at medium and high speeds, this effectiveness was not seen as an advantage. The response to aileron movement was good but the stick force necessary to produce any particular movement was much heavier than on any modern fighter. The elevators were light and effective. Elevator and rudder trimmers were fitted and these were effective, especially above approximately 300mph (483km/h), and provided adequate trim throughout the speed range. There was no change of trim on 'unstick' or when the undercarriage was retracted, and the slight tendency to sink when the flaps were raised could easily be corrected by the elevators. On the whole the aircraft was pleasant to fly in calm weather.

At the lower end of the speed range the slightly greater care which had to be paid to control movements suggested that the measure of longitudinal stability decreased with speed. Above 250mph (402km/h) however, the balance between stability and elevator stick force for manoeuvring was pleasant and at no time did the aircraft tighten in turns. Due to the characteristics of the jet engine, the initial acceleration during take-off was moderate, and the climb when airborne was poor until the climbing speed was reached, after which the best rate of climb was obtained at a comparatively high air speed and small angle of climb. The slow acceleration occurred at low speeds in all circumstances.

The great disadvantage of the Meteor III from a tactical and general flying viewpoint was the heaviness of the ailerons throughout the speed range. At medium and high speeds evasive action and even moderate turns were found to be very tiring. It was also considered that the upright seating position and the low rudder pedals were a distinct disadvantage in combating the effects of 'G'. However, the almost complete absence of change of trim on a typical fighter sortie relieved the pilot a great deal. Under 'bumpy' weather conditions the aircraft became directionally unstable, the instability manifesting itself as moderate to bad 'snaking'. The only cure for this was to throttle back and reduce speed – the use of rudder only aggravated the situation.

The view from the cockpit both forwards and to the sides was described as 'excellent', but immediately behind the pilot's head the metal armour plating greatly restricted the view. In addition considerable distortion was noted when objects were viewed through the rear canopy. The Meteor III was a pleasant aircraft for low flying, having an excellent all-round view except that the view forward and down was partly blocked by the gyro gunsight. The four

20mm cannon armament was described as 'ideal', but at operational speeds the snaking made it unsuitable as a gun platform.

The Meteor III was faster than the Tempest V at all heights – the figures quoted were 465mph (748km/h) TAS at 1,000ft (305m) against 381mph (613km/h), 471mph (758km/h) against 416mph (669km/h) at 15,000ft (4,572m) and 465mph (748km/h) against 390mph (628km/h) at 30,000ft (9,144m). Comparative acceleration tests showed similar results, irrespective of height, and at 250/260mph (402/418km/h) Indicated Air Speed (IAS) in the Meteor and 8,000ft (2,438m) altitude their acceleration was identical. If the Meteor was flying at an indicated 190mph (306km/h) at this height, the Tempest V had a slight initial advantage but, after about thirty seconds and as the accelerating speed approached 300mph (483km/h) Meteor IAS, the jet drew away rapidly and was out of range, that is, 600 yards (549m), in about 1.5 minutes.

In deceleration/retardation trials performed at the Tempest V's maximum speed, it was found that when the Meteor did not use its dive brakes, and if the throttles of both types were closed, the Tempest would be behind the Meteor in a position to shoot it down almost immediately at all heights. However, when the dive brakes were used the position was

reversed but, after using them, it was necessary for the Meteor to retract the brakes to avoid dropping out of range. Under all conditions the Meteor III, with its lower wing loading, could turn inside the Tempest and could get onto its tail in about four turns. However, the piston aircraft could out-roll the jet very easily at all speeds, and the latter was therefore at a disadvantage in the initial manoeuvres of a combat.

Climb performance tests showed that the Meteor could do 3,850ft/min (1,173m/min) at sea level, against the Tempest's 4,000ft/min (1,219m/min), and at 20,000ft (6,096m) the figures were 2,450ft/min (747m/min) and 2,100ft/min (640m/min) respectively. In a pull-out and zoom climb at 40° with full throttle, from 500mph (805km/h) IAS, during the pull-out the two fighters were identical. However, immediately the nose of the Meteor came up to the horizon it started to pull away quite rapidly and, by the time it had reached 225mph (362km/h) (its best climbing speed) it was approximately 750ft (229m) above and 600 yards (549m) ahead of the Tempest. By steepening the angle of zoom the Meteor could convert this lead into a further height advantage and these facts applied at whatever height the zoom commenced. Finally, if both aircraft were dived from any set level conditions up to the Meteor's limiting speed, and the throttles were not opened

A view of the 'Navalised' Meteor EE337 about to 'take the wire' during deck-landing trials, probably on board HMS *Implacable.* Admiralty, via Tony Buttler

during the dive, there was nothing to choose between the two. If, however, the throttles were fully opened in a dive from 12,000ft (3,658m), the Meteor was 500 yards (457m) ahead of the Tempest by the time its limiting speed (500mph/805km/h IAS) was reached.

In conclusion the Meteor III was superior to the Tempest V in almost all departments. If it were not for the heaviness of its ailerons and its consequent poor manoeuvrability in the rolling plane, and the adverse effect of snaking on the aeroplane as a gun platform, it was stated that the Meteor would be a comparable all-round fighter with a greatly increased performance. From the maintenance point of view the Meteor was generally much easier than the Tempest, taking 48 man/hours to change an engine from the crate when the Tempest needed 105 man/hours (or 75 when certain components were already fitted). However, Tempest needed 0.15 man/hours to refuel and 0.10 man/hours to re-arm, using two auxiliaries, when Meteor took 0.20 and 0.15 man/hours respectively with four auxiliaries. The Tempest was powered by a Napier Sabre piston engine and had an all-up-weight of 11,500 lb (5,216kg); the Meteor III had two Derwents and an all-up-weight of 13,000 lb (5,897kg).

The difference in the maximum speed and height combinations between jet and piston fighters has been referred to already, but the AFDS report clarified the point. The effect of speed on the power and thrust of a turbine jet was different from that on a propeller and this affected the performance of the aeroplane and could be used to get and keep the tactical advantage. This difference could be stated in two ways, either that the thrust of the jet remained nearly constant throughout the speed range while the thrust of an engine driven by a propeller decreased as the speed increased, or, that the thrust horsepower of the jet increased as the speed increased while the thrust horsepower of the propeller remained nearly constant. Therefore, in a comparison between a jet-driven and propeller-driven fighter, the advantage at low speeds would lie rather with the propeller fighter for acceleration and climb, but at high speeds the jet would tend to have the advantage where it was enjoying an increase in available horsepower. There would be a definite speed at each height at which they were equal (unless a future jet was being considered which had greater power at all speeds) so the propeller fighter would try to fight at lower speeds while the jet would try to fight at higher speeds.

Returning to the Mk.III programme overall, following the successful deck handling trials made with prototype DG202 aboard HMS *Pretoria Castle,* during April 1948 two short-nacelled Mk.IIIs (EE337 and EE387) were modified to give further experience of deck landing jet aircraft in a second series of experiments. The changes were the fitting of Derwent 5 engines, a de Havilland Sea Hornet 'A' frame arrester hook and a strengthened undercarriage designed for a descent rate of 11.5ft/sec (3.5m/sec). Also the aircraft were lightened by the removal of non-essential equipment and the main undercarriage doors were removed to prevent them fouling the arrester wires. As such they were termed 'Navalised Meteors'.

After some landing assessment flights had been completed using a dummy deck on land, a trials programme comprising thirty-two flights onto HMS *Implacable* was begun by two A&AEE pilots. When EE337 made the first landing on 8th June 1948, it was the first time that a British twin-jet aeroplane had been received by a carrier – the pilot for this occasion being the legendary Capt Eric Brown. Landings were initially made after the aircraft had taken-off with 220 gallons (1,000 litres) of fuel aboard; that is, at a take-off weight of 12,150 lb (5,511kg) but this was later increased to 260 gallons (1,182 litres) and 12,500 lb (5,670kg).

Deck landings were most easily made by a technique involving a more gently sinking approach than in the 'British' sinking approach

method. The latter was a power-on approach at a steady rate of descent which was used in the tests but gave a very tail-down attitude at touch-down with a consequent violent pitch on to the nosewheel. For the new technique, based on that previously used with a de Havilland Vampire 1, the Meteor was brought in in a relatively shallow approach with the aircraft about 7ft to 8ft (2.1m to 2.4m) above the round-down. The stick was then eased forward until the aircraft was approximately in the 3-point attitude on first contact with the deck. Less pilot judgement was needed with this new method.

The pilots were both of the opinion that the Meteor as modified for these trials made an excellent deck landing aircraft, and had without doubt better deck landing qualities and characteristics than any jet aircraft tested by A&AEE to date. The lightness and effectiveness of the elevator at slow speeds, excellent throttle response on the approach, good view out and the tricycle undercarriage were all major factors behind this opinion. The hook position relative to the undercarriage was considered excellent and the only adverse comment was that all circuits and landings had to be made with the cockpit hood closed, due to the noise and discomfort experienced with the hood open. This was contrary to normal Naval practice. In the condition tested the Meteor's take-off performance from the carrier was described as 'good for a jet aircraft'. These trials proved so successful that a Mk.IV, EE531, was duly sent to Heston Aircraft to be fitted with folding wings.

Elsewhere, over a period of thirteen weeks EE336 completed a 300-hour programme of intensive flying at Khartoum to clear the type for operations in tropical conditions. The numerous tests that this required included cruising and all-out level flight over a height range from ground level up to 30,000ft (9,144m), climbs to 30,000ft using maximum climbing power and ground running under simulated sandstorm conditions. Oil temperatures and pressures, and jet pipe temperatures, remained within the limitations throughout all of the trials and it was concluded that the Mk.III Meteor was entirely suitable for operation under tropical conditions similar to those obtained in Khartoum.

Meteor F Mk.IV

As part of the overall jet engine development programme a new engine had been designed and built by Rolls-Royce which was called the Nene. This was too big to fit into the Meteor's engine nacelles but an 85.5% scaled-down version called the Derwent V, which offered 3,500 lb (15.6kN) of thrust, was also developed. Derwent V made its first run on the test bench on 7th June 1945 and a Meteor Mk.III, EE360, was then fitted with the new powerplant to become the F Mk.IV prototype (later, with the

official switch from Roman to Arabic numerals in June 1948, this variant became the F Mk.4). As such EE360 was flown by Eric Greenwood from Moreton Valence on 15th August 1945 and, thanks to the big increase in thrust, he was soon clocking 570mph (917km/h) at 10,000ft (3,048m). In addition, when compared to the earlier marks, the aircraft's acceleration was terrific which, in the eyes of the pilots, had turned the Mk.IV into a real hot rod. Consequently examples were modified for some attempts to be made on the World Air Speed Record, as described in a later chapter.

A large ventral tank was also fitted to the Mk.IV, to be followed later by wing tanks, and full harmonisation of the controls had now been accomplished which allowed the mark to give good handling through most of the flight envelope. The extra power took the machine pretty quickly towards its top speed and a slight nose pitch-up would warn the pilot of the onset of compressibility; design dive speed was now 600mph (965km/h). However, the extra speed available to the F Mk.4 presented some new problems.

The strength factor of the Meteor wing centre section was unlikely to take the increased performance, several aircraft having already been lost from wing break-up during high-speed dives. Rate of roll was also insufficient and, after some production aircraft had been built with the normal wing, a new cropped version that was 5ft 10in (1.8m) shorter was substituted on EE525. This improved the rate of roll by 80°/sec and provided enough strength to allow the carriage of two 1,000 lb (454kg) bombs under the wings. In spite of the higher take-off and landing speeds that resulted from this wing it was to become the new standard and the 'Clipped Wing F Mk.4' had specification F.11/46 written around it in November 1946. The mark was to serve extensively with the RAF as well as being the first Meteor to be exported in quantity. Other parts of the structure were also strengthened and a September 1946 report noted that the original Mk.IV was

cleared with long-span wings to a weight of 14,000 lb (6,350kg). The clipped Mk.IV had a normal weight of 14,700 lb (6,670kg), the higher figure being largely due to the addition of more nose ballast to maintain the longitudinal stability with the Derwent V and also the extended nacelles. Under maximum overload conditions the Mk.IV at take-off weighed 18,600 lb (8,437kg).

The Meteor proved to be a big success in the export market, much of which stemmed from some European demonstration tours by the manufacturer. In 1947 Gloster took a short-span F Mk.4 from the production line, removed the guns, painted it crimson red (carmine) and had it registered under the civilian registration G-AIDC as a private venture aircraft. A tour began in mid-April and proved a triumph, marred only by the crash landing of G-AIDC in Belgium after which it was brought home and rebuilt as the T Mk.7 G-AKPK.

Between November 1947 and May 1948 the Central Fighter Establishment checked out the Mk.IV for its ability to make day interceptions at 40,000ft (12,192m) without long-range tanks, in the process completing a large number of trial sorties. The work was confined to the aircraft's radius of turn at that height, the basic problems of interception under visual conditions at that altitude, various aspects of visual range and time to intercept plus the meteorological conditions experienced during flights at high altitude. It was found that a Meteor IV flying at 40,000ft (12,192m) and Mach 0.75 could fly through 360° in seventy seconds. This represented a 2.2G turn and a turning radius of 1.5 miles (2.4km), although actual interceptions were made at 2G and a practical radius of 1.75 miles (2.8km) because it appeared that the pilot was less able to concentrate on his instruments during an actual interception. At 35,000ft (10,668m) the minimum practical radius was 1.25 miles (2.0km).

During the six month period, on the days interceptions were carried out, contrails were

EE360/G was effectively the prototype F.IV, being used by Gloster to fine-tune the nacelle shape until that used on the Mk.IV was established. *The Aeroplane*, via Phil Butler

One of the first Meteor 4s to fly with clipped wings, the wing shape used on the later Mk.4s and the Mk.7, 8 and 9 versions. Gloster Aircraft, via Phil Butler

Meteor F.4 EE592 photographed at Moreton Valence in November 1946. ATP 14782D, via Tony Buttler

bomber covered between identification and the fighter's take-off. There were plenty of problems, including those induced by compressibility effects, and the trials indicated that successful evasive action could be taken by the bomber after it had sighted the fighter, provided long-range visual contact was made.

Meteor PR Mk.5 and F Mk.6

The photo reconnaissance PR Mk.5 was designed to replace Supermarine Spitfires in this role and F Mk.4 VT347 was converted into a prototype, the work involving the installation of both vertical and oblique cameras in a new nose unit but with the full gun armament retained. The camera nose could be supplied as a complete unit for fitting to standard Mk.4 aircraft (as an FR Mk.4) but in the Mk.5 two more vertical cameras were placed in the middle of the fuselage just aft of the main fuel tank; the short-span wings were retained. VT347's maiden flight in this form was made on 15th July 1949 but the aircraft broke up and crashed, in the process killing test pilot Rodney Dryland. It was established that the side skins

observed on two days out of every three while, on about one day in three, the trails were dense and persistent and materially increased the visual range, which provided an aid for target evasion. At 35,000ft (10,668m) and below the number of abortive sorties was 6.5%, but at 40,000ft (12,192m) the figure was 30%, mainly because the aircraft was nearing its useful ceiling, it had a greater tendency to technical unserviceability at such height (usually in pressurisation, hydraulics and instruments), and there was less margin for error for the pilot and his ground controller. It was found that, assuming the Meteor had a 35 knot (40mph/64km/h) advantage over the bomber, a pursuit interception from the instant the Meteor's wheels were rolling on take-off to the instant it overtook the bomber should be possible on 90% of occasions in 185 miles (298km) of the bomber's track. This did not include the distance the

around the centre fuselage fuel tank bay had failed and the resultant modifications meant that the PR Mk.5 was substituted by the FR Mk.9 (below).

The F Mk.6 is believed to have been a proposal made in early 1946 for a Meteor powered by Derwent 7s mounted in long nacelles. It had F Mk.4 short-span wings and the tail from the Gloster E.1/44 single-jet fighter (see later), but further refinements led to the F Mk.8, the ultimate single-seat Meteor, which thus prevented the Mk.6 from ever being built.

Meteor T Mk.7

In the early days of jet flight there were no two-seat trainers available to help pilots convert to this new form of propulsion. The stimulus for a conversion aircraft came when Gloster received an order for F Mk.4 Meteors for Argentina. Pilot training was also requested and the company found that teaching students

Meteor F.4 VT104 seen in a nice air-to-air shot. via Tony Buttler

VW411, a Meteor T.7 fitted with an F Mk.8 tail unit. A number of T.7s were fitted with the later-style fin design, which offered slightly improved handling characteristics, but it was never a standard fitment. This example was used for trials at the Royal Aircraft Establishment at Bedford and Farnborough (and previously at the BLEU Martlesham Heath). The aircraft also had a camera nose fitted in connection with these trials. via Phil Butler.

with instructors sitting on the outside of the aircraft was, to say the least, far from ideal; clearly a two-seater would be invaluable for Meteor operators worldwide. A private venture prototype with civil register G-AKPK was put together using sub-assemblies from the old and damaged F Mk.IV demonstrator G-AIDC. After rebuilding as a two-seater the aircraft was first flown in this form from Moreton Valence on 19th March 1948, Bill Waterton was the pilot. Ministry interest followed and in mid-May 1948 G-AKPK undertook a successful sales tour as a

demonstrator aircraft, the trip this time taking in some Mediterranean countries.

The design and construction of a two-seater dual control version of the F Mk.IV single-seat fighter was covered by Operation Requirement OR.238 and Specification T.1/47, dated 5th May 1947. The new variant was intended to give pilots experience in jet flight before they commenced their solo flying and also instruction in aerobatics, ground attack and air tactics. The specification declared that the extra cockpit was to have the least possible effect on the

present performance of the Mk.IV and allow the accommodation of one instructor and one pupil pilot. The pilot would fly the aircraft from the front seat and full dual control was required in the rear cockpit. Blind flying facilities were also requested and there was to be no provision for guns, rocket projectiles or bombs. Two Derwent Mk.V engines were to form the powerplant and the resulting trainer had a longer forward fuselage to accommodate the tandem cockpits; its heavily framed canopy was quite distinctive.

The first production Meteor trainer made its maiden flight on 26th October 1948 and deliveries took place between December 1948 (when the RAF received its first example) and 1954. The type went on to serve with a large number of RAF squadrons, the Fleet Air Arm and many overseas air forces. Despite being based on the F Mk.IV, some T Mk.7s received a different tail based on the Gloster Ace/F Mk.8 arrangement described shortly, and consequently these were sometimes known as T Mk.7½s. It was found that the Mk.7's longer

nose improved the Meteor's directional stability and in due course more powerful 3,600 lb (16kN) Derwent 8 powerplants were introduced. A&AEE handling trials made on an early production T Mk.7 showed that the type exhibited characteristics which were generally similar to the Meteor Mk.4. However, in general these could not be regarded as satisfactory for a trainer aircraft, except for pilots moving on to fly Meteors in the Service. At Mach numbers above 0.7 there was a rapid deterioration of manoeuvre margin, making the aircraft very heavy to manoeuvre at high Mach numbers.

Meteor F Mk.8

By 1947 it had become clear that the original Meteor would need a thorough updating if it was to stay competitive with its rivals so Gloster's design team began work on a 'second generation' aircraft. Some production F Mk.IVs had received a longer nose but the more forward position of the guns and their ammunition, relative to the whole aircraft, ensured that more pronounced movements in

Meteor T.7 VW443, fitted with a non-standard nose for experimental work. It was used for 'guidance and control trials' at RAE Farnborough. via Tony Buttler

Meteor T.7 WL349 of No 229 OCU, photographed at Chivenor in a silver scheme with Day-Glo patches applied. via Tony Buttler

the centre of gravity were experienced as the ammunition and fuel were used up. In fact the original Meteor tail arrangement was not suited to cope with this pitch-up instability. Fortunately a different type of angular tail was now available which had been flight tested by a prototype of Gloster's single-engine 'Ace' jet fighter. The 'Ace' was designed to Specification E.1/44 and first flown in March 1948, but it was not a successful aircraft in its own right and did not proceed beyond the prototype stage.

One proposal to fit a version of the E.1/44 tail to the Meteor appears to have been made in about November 1947. However, in January 1948 Air Commodore T E Pike, the Director of Operational Requirements (Air), or DOR(A), wanted to reconsider the idea after the E.1/44 had flown. He told Gloster that 'if flight indicates an improvement for the Meteor we will ask you to proceed with a trial installation'. The tail gave good results on the E.1/44 and an example of the new flying surface was eventually fitted to F Mk.4 Meteor RA382; a 30in (76cm) insert was also introduced into the fuselage forward of the

centre section; which in Mk.8 production aeroplanes was filled with a new 95-gallon (432-litre) fuel tank. RA382 was briefly tested by A&AEE pilots in February 1949 before it was lost in a crash, but enough flying was done to show that different flying characteristics were present compared to when the aircraft had had a Mk.4 tail unit fitted. The general flying qualities had improved in that the rudder control and the elevator force required to initiate a manoeuvre were lighter. However, the improved elevator control accentuated the heaviness of the ailerons and the usual warning buffeting or preliminary nose-up change of trim at high Mach numbers (associated with the Mk.4) were absent. Therefore while the aircraft would make a better gun platform there was a greater likelihood of reaching high Mach numbers inadvertently. In other respects RA382's behaviour was similar to the Mk.4.

The prototype Meteor F Mk.8, VT150, in formation with the Gloster E.1/44 'Ace' TX148 on 4th August 1949. The F.8 tail unit design was based on that of the E.1/44. Russell Adams, via Tony Buttler

The first production Meteor F.8, VZ438, posing for the official camera at Moreton Valence in November 1949. ATP 18536A, via Phil Butler

To accommodate the expected extra stresses, yet more strengthening was worked into the Mk.8's undercarriage, and indeed all around the airframe. Many other refinements were incorporated (including an ejection seat) as the variant represented a progressive development of the Mk.4, but the basic 'break-down' of the structure was the same as on the earlier versions. The biggest visible change from previous Meteors was the tailplane itself. Compared to older marks the tips of the tail were squared off and the fin and rudder sported straight rather than curved leading and trailing edges; the under keel surface or tail skid was also gone. The F Mk.8 was to become the most prolific mark of this famous aircraft and the ultimate day fighter version.

Another Mk.4, VT150, was converted into a full F Mk.8 prototype and made its maiden flight from Moreton Valence on 12th October 1948 in the hands of Gloster's famous test pilot Jan Zurakowski. To help prove the new tail arrangement, the old Mk.4 tail was test flown on VT150 by A&AEE during January and February 1949, a move which was also intended to cover the likelihood that a Mk.4 type might be fitted to the first production batch of Mk.8s instead of the E.1/44 (which for a period was a possibility). These tests showed that the Mk.8 in the configuration tested was unacceptable as a fighter aircraft because of the heavy nature of the elevator forces. It was found that under comparable war load conditions the Mk.8 stick force per 'G' (with the old tailplane) was some 4 lb (1.8kg) greater than on the Mk.4 (and rather more in various high weight conditions). This resulted in pilots tiring very quickly when engaged in combat manoeuvres and, indeed, after a few minutes of tail-chasing two hands were required on the stick. However, apart from elevator forces in combat manoeuvres the Mk.8's handling qualities, such as directional behaviour, were found to be generally similar to those of the Mk.4.

VW360 is a Meteor FR.9, identical to the F.8 apart from the nose-mounted oblique cameras fitted for tactical reconnaissance duties.
Gloster Aircraft, via Tony Buttler

An official photograph of a production Meteor PR.10, VS984, taken at Gloster's Moreton Valence airfield on 8th November 1950, before delivery of this aircraft to the RAF. ATP 20125F, via Tony Buttler

A&AEE Boscombe Down tested VT150 with the new tail during the second half of 1949 and, compared to older marks, found a small addition to the Meteor's limiting Mach number together with some other improvements, but there were difficulties with stability after recovery from a spin. For the first time on a Meteor a new clear bubble single-piece cockpit canopy and a Martin-Baker ejection seat (the Mk.1E) were fitted, and these were praised very highly. From an overall flying point of view the F Mk.8 with the new tail was seen as an improvement over the older Mk.4.

Deliveries began on 10th December 1949 when VZ438 arrived at Tangmere to join No 1 Squadron, the last (WL191) flew on 9th April 1954 and the F Mk.8 served as the RAF and RAuxAF's primary single-seat interceptor until 1955, prior to the arrival of the Hawker Hunter. No 245 Squadron had the version on strength from June 1950 until April 1957 and No 616 also received examples making it the only squadron to use Meteor Marks 1, 3, 4, 7 and 8. With worldwide sales well over a thousand were built before the final F Mk.8 was delivered in April 1954. The Mk.8's powerplant was two Derwent 8 engines and in due course production aeroplanes began to receive a new wider-diameter 'deep breather' intake on each nacelle that permitted a greater mass flow. As such these provided another 240 lb (1.07kN) of thrust per engine and the majority of WK and WL-serialled Meteor 8s were to receive them.

Meteor FR Mk.9 and PR Mk.10

There were two more versions of the single-seat Meteor line. The fighter reconnaissance FR Mk.9 differed from the Mk.8 only in having a modified nose, 9in (22.9cm) longer, to take an F.24 camera. There were three glass panels to allow oblique or ahead photography and the F.24 was remotely operated by the pilot. Zurakowski flew the first production machine, VW360, on 22nd March 1950 and the production run was completed in mid-1952. A&AEE tested VW360 in July 1950 and confirmed that the handling characteristics were similar to F Mk.8 VT150 except that there was a fairly large, but not unacceptable, change of longitu-

The 'Reaper' ground-attack prototype was developed by Gloster as a private venture. It featured a strengthened wing for additional under-wing stores and wingtip fuel tanks, on an otherwise standard Mk.8 airframe. Photographed on 31st August 1951.
Russell Adams P.400A/51

dinal trim with speed. Also the elevator was lighter and tightening in turns was encountered at and above about 32,000ft (9,754m). Although mild and insufficient to render the aircraft unacceptable, the self-tightening tendency made the high-altitude general handling borderline. For low-altitude FR duties the aircraft was regarded as satisfactory from the handling aspect subject to the reservations made in regard to the Mk.8 (that is, ailerons too heavy etc). As a reconnaissance platform the Mk.9 was considered to be an improvement on existing aircraft in that category.

For high-altitude strategic reconnaissance the PR Mk.10 had the old long-span Mk.III wing, a Mk.4 tail, Mk.8 centre fuselage and a Mk.9 nose, and two F.52 cameras in the rear fuselage supplemented the F.24; the guns were left out. This variant's development ran parallel with the Mk.9 and Zurakowski flew the first example, VS968, on 29th March 1950. In July this aircraft went to A&AEE and the flight test report noted that its handling characteristics resembled those of the Mk.4 and, were in general, acceptable for this type of aircraft. However, the heavy control forces and poor control harmonisation (the latter caused mainly by the heaviness of the ailerons in comparison with the elevator) were severely criticised. These criticisms were of greater significance than on previous marks because the PR Mk.10 would be called upon more frequently to operate to its limits of load and endurance. A lack of manoeuvrability was serious because it limited

the pilot's power to evade an attack, vital to an unarmed aircraft. Nevertheless, deliveries of Mk.10s began in December 1950.

Ground Attack Private Venture

Another Gloster private venture Meteor was a ground-attack aircraft first proposed in a brochure completed in February 1950. Gloster had identified that a broadening of the Meteor's capability was needed to try and extend its production life and the F Mk.8 fighter formed the basis of the project. Two 100-gallon (45-litre) tip tanks were fitted and alternative loads comprised four 1,000 lb (454kg) bombs (one under each outer wing, two under the fuselage) or eight 95 lb (43kg) rocket projectiles under the centre fuselage; the cannon were unchanged. Other additions included rocket-assisted take-off gear using six 1,500 lb (6.7kN) rockets, each of six seconds duration. Wingspan with the tip tanks was 41ft (12.5m), without 37ft 1½in (11.3m), length 44ft (13.4m) and the estimated all-up-weight was 15,800 lb (7,167kg).

A prototype was built which was unofficially known as the 'Reaper', or sometimes the 'GAF' for ground-attack fighter, and civil registered G-AMCJ. It was painted carmine red and flew from Moreton Valence on 4th September 1950 piloted by Jim Cooksey. Through the next year the machine undertook some extensive development flying and in the following July the colour scheme was switched to silver and the civilian 'B Conditions' identity G-7-1 was given

to the aircraft. In the end no orders were secured for production 'Reapers' although the RAAF pilots in Korea were to use their Mk.8s in the ground-attack role. In 1954 G-7-1 was converted to a T Mk.7, registered G-ANSO and painted larkspur blue; in 1958 it passed to Swedish ownership.

This particular aircraft however, has its place in history as the display machine for legendary test pilot Jan Zurakowski's extraordinary cartwheel manoeuvre seen at the 1951 Farnborough Show. His routine incorporated a cartwheel rotated about the aircraft's neutral axis that was executed at the top of a sustained zoom climb, which itself followed a high-speed dive. The cartwheel began as the aircraft approached the point of stall and fall back. A report in the aviation press, based on Zurakowski's own description, said 'While in a vertical full-power climb speed was lost down to 70mph to 80mph (110km/h to 130km/h), one Derwent was shut down and then the aircraft cart wheeled under asymmetric power. After three-quarters of a turn Zurakowski shut down the second Derwent and the Meteor, having unusually high inertia due to the rock-

Another view of G-7-1, the ground-attack 'Reaper' version, with RPs aboard. Tony Butler

WH453 of No 5 Civilian Anti-Aircraft Cooperation Unit (operated by Short Brothers & Harland at Woodvale) in a standard camouflage scheme, probably photographed in 1959. Shorts also operated the Temperature & Humidity Flight, which shared No 5 CAACU aircraft, although relatively few weather sorties were flown by the Meteors. via Tony Buttler

ets on the wings, carried on to complete one and a half vertical cartwheels, finishing nose down. Thereupon Zurakowski started a spin but after a quarter to a half turn, at 105mph to 115mph (169km/h to 185km/h), control began to be restored'.

Zurakowski explained that one engine was not 'opened up' (as many observers thought was the case) because, whereas thrust could be lost by throttling back in one and a half to two seconds, full power was not forthcoming from the turbojet in less than six seconds. For such a manoeuvre to be achieved it was necessary to have two power units widely spaced. Tip tanks and 24 wing-mounted rockets were also aboard along with relatively little internal fuel, which meant much of the weight was distributed away from the centre of the aircraft to assist the spin. The Meteor was to suffer many in-service accidents which, at times, formed not the best reputation, and it took an exceptional pilot with a deep knowledge of engineering and science to work out this sequence and display it safely. Zurakowski was Gloster's chief development test pilot between 1947 and 1952 and was to contribute much to the Meteor's development.

Compressibility

Mention has been made several times of the phenomenon of compressibility. The Meteor arrived during a period of big advance in aviation technology. Piston-powered fighters had begun to suffer the effects of compressibility (the scientific term for the 'sound barrier') during high speed dives with some pilots unable to recover before hitting the ground, and the potential extra speed of jet aircraft threatened to exacerbate the problem. A build up of compressed air ahead of an aircraft from about Mach 0.7 onwards gave symptoms of stiffening controls with buffet or violent shaking and a strong tendency to either pitch up (which could

pull the aeroplane apart), or enter an ever steeper dive that was extremely difficult to pull out of. Pilots were approaching and entering a transonic condition where some air passing over the aircraft became supersonic and this produced localised and powerful pressure or shock waves which caused the buffeting. The phenomenon was not yet clearly understood but had to be overcome.

The April 1946 AFDS report on the Meteor F Mk.III referred to earlier in this chapter gave a full account of the effects of compressibility on the aeroplane. The aircraft's limiting speed was reached in a 15° dive but, provided the angle of dive was not very steep, ample warning was

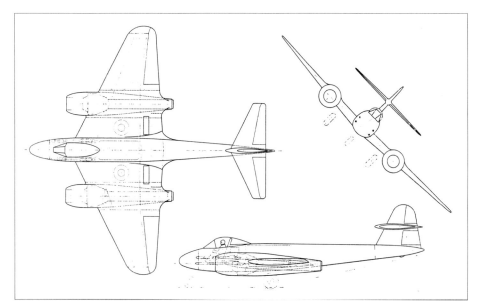

Three-view drawing of Gloster's P.263 Meteor development project. Eric Morgan

given of the approach of the phenomena; also the forward load required on the control column to maintain the dive became very uncomfortable. The tendency for the nose to rise as compressibility was approached was noted as 'a good characteristic of the Meteor III'. The phenomena encountered by AFDS's pilots were:

1. At 500mph (805km/h) indicated air speed (IAS), Mach 0.68 and 4,000ft to 5,000ft (1,219m to 1,524m) altitude, there was severe snaking combined with lateral oscillation. The controls were still effective.

2. At 510mph (821km/h) IAS, Mach 0.72 and 5,500ft to 6,000ft (1,676m to 1,829m), violent snaking and lateral oscillation. The stick was nearly solid but still effective and there was a nose-up tendency.

3. At 528mph (850km/h) IAS, Mach 0.73 and 6,000ft (1,829m), there was violent 'juddering' (vibration up and down) and the stick was also vibrating badly and was entirely ineffective and solid. However, on throttling back the controls became effective again after a short pause.

The report declared that 'directly the first indication of compressibility was experienced, the engines should be throttled back and the aircraft eased gently out of the dive. Use of excessive "G" in recovery will aggravate the compressibility effects and bring on "juddering" at the lower Mach number than under steady flight conditions.' It was noted that marked differences were apparent between individual aircraft, due to dirty aerofoil sections, dents in cowls, and the like, which resulted in differences of as much as 30mph (48km/h) in their critical Mach number. (A specific aircraft's Critical Mach number is the speed at which its controllability is first affected by compressibility; in other words the point at which shock waves first appear.) The limiting speeds for the Meteor III given in the official Handling Notes at this time were 400mph (644km/h) IAS at 20,000ft (6,096m), 360mph (579km/h) at 25,000ft (7,620m), 325mph (523km/h) at 30,000ft (9,144m) and 290mph (467km/h) at 35,000ft (10,668m) and the report concluded that, in war conditions, a pilot would have diffi-

culty in remembering these figures and in watching the necessary instruments.

The diving of Meteor prototypes to high speeds had begun in 1943 and the characteristics of compressibility was evident immediately. The buffet experienced in dives could be very uncomfortable and quite destructive to the airframe, ranging from the removal of rivets to structural damage. Research work continued for some years into the onset of compressibility and on 9th July 1946 test pilot Roland Beamont established that a Meteor F Mk.4 could enter the condition in a shallow descent at low level; Beamont established Mach 0.79 as the new boundary for reasonable control. At Mach 0.83 to 0.84 there would be powerful pitch-down with the elevators giving no help at all, so a dive would have to be ridden out until, below 15,000ft (4,572m), the aircraft's nose could be lifted slowly as the Mach number was reduced with loss in altitude. The Mach number becomes less as the thicker air at low level is reached, even though the air speed might be unchanged.

Experiments at English Electric in 1947/48 established the Meteor's absolute limits of compressibility from sea level right up to its operating ceiling, probably the first time this had been investigated for any specific type of aeroplane. The test aircraft was F Mk.4 EE545 and the results had long-term benefits for English Electric's own supersonic programmes (which led to the Lightning fighter). The Meteor, however, was always subsonic and its nasty response to a high Mach number, termed by pilots as 'getting on the Mach', helped fuel the menace and mystery attached to the sound barrier at that time. At the time EE545 was with English Electric to provide test pilot experience for the Canberra.

Projects

Throughout the 1940s Gloster Aircraft produced plenty of designs for Meteor developments, both with major or minor changes to the structure and layout and/or to the equipment the aircraft would carry. There were versions drawn with a V-tail while the proposals made with a delta wing probably mark the start point for the development of what became Gloster's last fighter, the heavy two-seat Javelin all-weather fighter. On 13th November 1947 drawing P.262 was completed showing a 'Meteor' with a delta-type wing and a slab (one-piece) horizontal tailplane; the powerplant was two Derwent 5 engines. Six days later a version with an alternative fixed tail plus elevators was shown in drawing P.263. Their fuselages, cockpit and armament appear

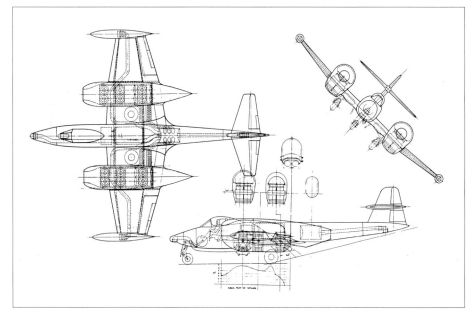

Three-view drawing of Gloster's P.497 VTOL Meteor project. Ray Williams

Gloster P.503 project. Ray Williams

Gloster P.504 project. Ray Williams

to be similar to a Mk.8 but no estimated performance figures are available.

Chapter Seven will describe the research programme undertaken with Mk.4 Meteor RA491 fitted with Rolls-Royce Avon jet engines. In June 1949, during RA491's flight test programme, Gloster submitted a brochure for an RAF interim day fighter Meteor powered by two 6,500 lb (28.9kN) thrust RA3 Avons called P.292. It is listed here because this was a proposal for a production aircraft, not another research prototype, and was offered as a stop-gap pending the arrival of the more advanced Hawker Hunter and Supermarine Swift swept-wing fighters then currently at the design stage. Compared to the standard F Mk.8 this had greatly increased power to go with thinner wings and horizontal and vertical tail surfaces, the wing thickness/chord ratio being reduced from 12% to 10%. The front fuselage and main undercarriage were the same as a Mk.8 but the rear fuselage needed some localised strengthening. Gross wing area was increased from 350ft² to 500ft² (32.55m² to 46.50m²), the empennage was switched to the E.1/44-style tail (which was by now in production for the Mk.8) and the nacelles would be the same as those used by RA491. Finally, fitting spring tab ailerons would improve the rate of roll by 50%. The Avon Meteor's span was 46ft (14.0m), length 47ft (14.3m) and all-up-weight 19,000 lb (8,618m).

The combined effect of all of these changes was an estimated increase in sea level rate of climb from 7,100ft/min to 16,000ft/min (2,164m/min to 4,877m/min), rate of climb at 30,000ft (9,144m) was 8,200ft/min (2,500m/min), time to 40,000ft (12,192m) was reduced from eleven to four minutes, there was a much higher service ceiling of 53,000ft from the previous 42,000ft (16,154m to 12,801m) and the absolute ceiling was 56,000ft (17,069ft). The maximum 3G manoeuvre limit was increased from 33,000ft to 43,000ft (10,058m to 13,106m), the limiting Mach number was up from 0.82 to 0.85, limiting diving speed was increased from 600mph to 650mph (965km/h to 1,046km/h), and the maximum level speed at sea level had risen from 585mph to 640mph (941km/h to 1,030km/h), and at 40,000ft (12,192m) from 520mph to 550mph (837km/h to 885km/h); the sea level speed, which corresponded to Mach 0.84, was the highest at any height. It is unknown how seriously the project was considered at Ministry level but, in the event, the progress with the Hunter and Swift was such than any plans to procure this Meteor proved unnecessary.

In 1960 Gloster proposed some Meteor developments with multiple RB.108s to give full vertical take-off capability. The first of these was Project/Drawing number P.497, dated 8th

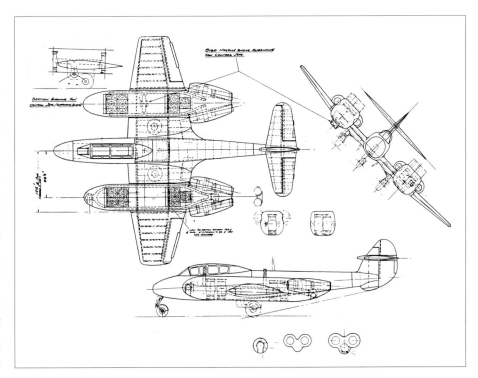

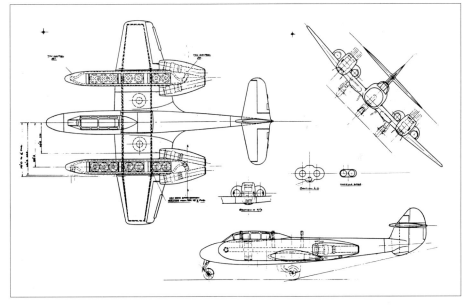

June, which had six 2,100 lb (9.3kN) RB.108s in a large nacelle that replaced the Derwent. These were mounted in three pairs and a network of ducting would have directed vertical thrust for control to the nose, wingtips and fuselage rear. In addition the forward and rear pairs of RB.108s could be tilted backwards to give forward thrust and the front pair could also go forwards 30° for deceleration. A rough estimate of the all-up-weight came out at 16,000 lb (7,258kg), total lifting thrust was 25,000 lb (111.1kN), the forward component 7,000 lb (31.1kN), decelerating component 4,000 lb (17.8kN) and the control thrust at each corner 650 lb (2.9kN).

The P.497 was based on a Mk.8 or 9 airframe but, shortly afterwards, two more ideas followed which would have used a converted T Mk.7. Drawing P.503 (dated 22nd July 1960) had seven RB.108s in each nacelle for lift plus

two conventional engines (at the rear of each nacelle) for forward propulsion. The lift jets were grouped four at the front, three to the back, in such a way that the ducting all around the aircraft in the P.497 could be taken out. This may have simplified the aircraft structure, but the massive nacelles on their own were a very complex arrangement and the aircrew would have had to start up eighteen engines. The follow-on P.504 of 9th August had the seven RB.108s in a line within the nacelles. For both projects the estimated all up weights were 18,680 lb (8,473kg), propulsive thrust 7,520 lb (33.4kN) and total lifting thrust 26,320 lb (117.0kN). None of these ideas were ever close to being turned into hardware and in appearance these were some of the least attractive Meteors, but they were fascinating concepts and would have been exciting additions to this list of testbeds.

Chapter Four

Night Fighters and Target Tugs

Soon after the end of the Second World War the need to supply new aircraft to re-equip the RAF's night fighter force was becoming quite serious. The type currently in service, the piston-powered de Havilland Mosquito, was incapable of dealing with new enemy jet-powered bombers. These bombers were also expected to be carrying nuclear weapons before too long so a new specification, F.44/46, was raised in January 1947 for a Mosquito replacement. However, work on finding a suitable jet fighter to fill the requirement was slow. During this period the introduction of more advanced aerodynamic swept or delta wing shapes, more powerful engines and new weapons such as air-to-air guided missiles brought substantial changes to the overall concept and design of the new fighter aircraft. Consequently F.44/46, which itself was replaced by the upgraded specification F.4/48 in June 1948, was not fulfilled until the arrival of the Gloster Javelin. That aircraft did not fly until November 1951 and the first production example was not airborne until July 1954.

Clearly an interim Mosquito replacement with better performance was needed to fill this time gap pending delivery to the Service of the more advanced F.4/48 and the resulting aircraft was to be based on the Meteor. Gloster's first brochure was written in October 1948 and showed a converted Mk.7 with Derwent 5s which offered a much better performance over the Mosquito. There was a 5ft (1.52m) extension to the basic Meteor nose to house a 28in (71cm) diameter AI Mk.IXB radar scanner

(development of AI Mk.IXB/9B was abandoned in 1949). There was also no cockpit pressurisation and it was necessary to fit the extended wingtips of the Meteor III, giving a span of 43ft (13.1m). Length was 48ft 6in (14.8m), wing area 374ft² (34.8m²), wing thickness/chord ratio 12% at the root and 9% at the tip, the all-up- weight was 15,700 lb (7,122kg) and the estimated top speed Mach 0.82 at 16,000ft (4,877m).

However, Gloster was fully stretched with its commitments to the manufacture of single-seat Meteors and so the night fighter development programme was passed to another company within the Hawker Siddeley Aircraft group, namely Armstrong Whitworth Aircraft (AWA). This company's design team was led by H R Watson. Specification F.24/48 and Operational Requirement OR.265 were issued on 12th February 1949 to cover the new type and stated that a night fighter version of the Meteor Mk.7 would cover the period prior to the production of the F.4/48. It would have an E.1/44-style (Meteor F Mk.8) high tailplane unit and the extended front fuselage would accommodate an AI (airborne interception) Mk.10 radar (an alternative arrangement was also to be prepared to house an AI Mk.17 radar). The windscreen and canopy were to be revised and there would be two crew, the pilot and the navigator/radar operator (nav/radar), seated in tandem in a pressure cabin; ejection seats were not required.

AI Mk.10 was the designation given to the American SCR-720B equipment and there had to be two crew because the radar could not be

operated by the pilot alone, so the base aircraft therefore had to be the Mk.7 trainer. The aircraft's performance had to be comparable with that of the Meteor F Mk.4 and a speed of 435 knots (501mph/806km/h) was acceptable with underwing drop tanks. An endurance of at least two hours was required at 30,000ft (9,144m), and this did not include fifteen minute's combat. Two Derwent Mk.8 engines would supply the power and the armament was still four 20mm Hispano cannon, but the introduction of the nose radar meant that, unlike the day fighters, these had to be moved to the wings. Some pilots who flew night fighter Meteors believed that this new position was less satisfactory than having the guns in the nose.

In the meantime Meteor F Mk.III EE348 had completed some tests with a nose-mounted AI radar and this step may have also influenced the decision to use the Meteor airframe as the interim night fighter. EE348 had been fitted with an American AN/APS-4 set (which became AI Mk.15 in British service), the nosewheel frame providing a strong and solid base on which to mount the complete unit. AN/APS-4 was a self-contained system that just required external power (from the aircraft) and the fitting of a control unit in the cockpit. The gun ports were faired over and the aircraft arrived at the Telecommunications Research Establishment at Defford in September 1945, where it was used to assess the radar's ability to feed data into the gyro gun-sight in the day fighter role. This would never be fully representative of a Service aircraft because EE348 lacked a second crewman to operate the equipment effectively, but the experiments could show if the radar detected targets at greater ranges than the Mosquito and in poor weather. In 1952 this aircraft became a ground instruction airframe.

Armstrong Whitworth Meteor NF Mk.11
A Meteor night fighter mock-up had been completed by the end of 1948 and T Mk.7 VW413 was converted by Armstrong Whitworth at Bitteswell into an aerodynamic test prototype; it was delivered to AWA with F Mk.3 wings already fitted. The aircraft featured a 4ft longer (1.22m) nose but, to save time, the overall modification would use as much existing Meteor

Three-view of Gloster's two-seat night fighter Meteor development project. The drawing, No PL.16, is dated 14th October 1948. Note the cannon mounted outside the engine nacelles.
Eric Morgan

structure as possible. The wings had to be the long-span 43ft (13.1m) type because they were needed to balance the additional weight. Every example of this first night fighter variant had a distinctive fairing on the bottom of the radome to cover the lower bearing bracket carrying the scanner, which protruded outside the line of the lower fuselage. Finally the four cannon were moved just outboard of the nacelles but, overall, the aircraft when fully modified looked similar to the Mk.7 except for the longer nose and new tail (the latter was later adopted by the trainer as well). Cabin pressurisation was supplied by tapping the Derwent 8 compressor to give an equivalent cabin altitude of 24,000ft (7,315m) at 40,000ft (12,192m). The new variant was designated the NF Mk.11 and carried a 180-gallon (818-litre) ventral tank.

The opening of the Korean War in 1950 accelerated the re-equipment of RAF Fighter Command and in December of that year Sir Ralph Cochrane, Vice Chief of the Air Staff, wrote that the Command's chief area of weakness would be a lack of night fighters over the next year and a half. As a result more were ordered which also included night fighter versions of de Havilland's jet fighters, but it was still intended that the majority should be Meteors. Armstrong Whitworth test pilot Bill Else first flew VW413 in its new guise on 28th January 1949 but the Mk.8 tail was not fitted until March.

This last alteration stretched the length of the aircraft by a further 1ft (0.30m) over the old tail, to 48ft 6in (14.8m). In this final form it was flown again on 8th April, this time by AWA chief test pilot Eric Franklin, as aerodynamically representative of the Mk.11. Flight testing revealed that the new elevators were lighter than that previously experienced, which then stressed the heaviness of the ailerons and put both controls rather out of harmony. In flight vibration was found at Mach 0.72 but this did not reach an excessive level.

Brief handling, longitudinal stability and manoeuvre tests with VW413 were carried out

This photograph shows the prototype Meteor NF.11, VW413, which was built by Gloster as a T.7 but with the extended wings of the early single-seaters, and delivered to Armstrong Whitworth for further modification.
Armstrong Whitworth A126, via Phil Butler

by A&AEE at Boscombe Down during the following September and October, the objective being to obtain advance information on the likely flying qualities of the night fighter. The results indicated that the type should possess adequate longitudinal stability for night operations and would meet the requirements of the

The first AWA-built Meteor NF.11 prototype, WA546, is shown in this photograph, taken at Bitteswell. Armstrong Whitworth JF16, via Phil Butler

specification in this respect. However, it was recommended that lighter ailerons should be fitted to improve the lateral control qualities, while the landing characteristics should be investigated further because excessive 'float' was present. It was considered that this 'float' would be a hazard on a normal-length runway at night, so there was an opportunity here to increase the drag in the landing configuration to the benefit of the aircraft overall.

The first of three true NF Mk.11 prototypes was WA546, which made its maiden flight on 31st May 1950 with Eric Franklin as the pilot. The third prototype, WB543, introduced a strengthened centre section, wings and under-carriage. In fact, this aircraft was identical to the production standard except for the radar which, like the second prototype WA547, was AI Mk.17. WA546 carried out much of the radar development testing at Defford and in 1957

was still being used by AWA. The first production aeroplane was WD585 which flew on 19th October 1950 while, as required by the specification, WD586, WD587 became the additional airframes used at Defford to assess the alternative AI Mk.17 radar; this fitting required an even longer nose. WD590 onwards introduced spring-tab ailerons which much improved the aircraft's flying characteristics, the control harmony between ailerons and elevator, and the rate of roll. Service deliveries began on 20th August 1951 when WD599 arrived at Tangmere to join No 29(F) Squadron.

During March and April 1952 Mk.11 WD604 was tested by A&AEE with wingtip tanks, rather than the normal underwing variety, and the handling was found to be satisfactory and similar to those with underwing tanks. Without external wing tanks the handling characteristics of the NF Mk.11 with the standard and modified wingtips (with or without tip fairings) were found to be almost identical. However, the alterations to fit tip tanks could not be put into the production line until about March 1953, which meant that the overall programme would also require the retrospective modification of a

The first prototype Armstrong Whitworth Meteor NF.11, WA546, photographed at the SBAC display at Farnborough in 1950.

This photograph of WD597 shows off the wing planform of the NF Mk.11, which reverted to the long span of the Mk.III. The wing-mounted cannon can also be seen. BAE Systems NN0247

large number of aircraft already delivered to the Service. This would be expensive and so the tip tank proposals were abandoned. WD686 and WD687 were also fitted with AI Mk.17 radars and in this form were the same as the second and third production machines. Mk.11s were used for various trials and included WD743, WD744 and WD745, and WM372, WM373 and WM374, which were all allocated as test airframes for the Fairey 'Blue Sky' air-to-air missile programme. Details of other Meteor night fighter trials aircraft are given in Chapter Seven.

During combat the Mk.11 would dispose of its underwing external fuel tanks but would keep the ventral tank giving a maximum weight of 18,000 lb (8,165kg). Although the aircraft when carrying underwing tanks was cleared (from a strength point of view) at speeds up to 435 knots (501mph/806km/h), on account of possible wing damage the jettisoning of the tanks was restricted to a maximum of 260 knots (299mph/482km/h). In August 1951 AWA completed a review of the Mk.11 programme which noted that extra landing flaps had been flight

Meteor NF.11 WD608 on a pre-delivery test flight. Ministry of Supply, via Phil Butler

Another official air-to-air photo of WD597, the T-shaped aerials under the rear fuselage are for radio altimeters. Armstrong Whitworth NF67, via Phil Butler

Meteor NF Mk.12 WS697, 'N' of No 25 Squadron, photographed on 30th April 1954.
Armstrong Whitworth NF300, via Ray Williams

tested outboard of the nacelles and later production aeroplanes would incorporate them. In addition a variety of AI equipment was available for fitting, including both British and American equipment, and future developments would include a new clear view sliding cockpit hood. In contrast however, service operations would show that around 12% of interception sorties had to be aborted because of technical failures – further improvements were needed.

Meteor NF Mk.12

A big improvement over the wartime-developed AI Mk.10 was offered by the American-designed APS-57 radar, or AI Mk.21 in RAF service, which could detect targets at twice the range of the Mk.10 set – up to 20 miles (32km) for large targets or 15 miles (24km) for Meteor-sized aircraft. In addition the scanner could be directed by the navigator with a joystick, instead of the set of tilt-selectors as used on the older equipment. AI.21 was a modified version of APS-57, with British IFF and strobe unit. It also had an ASV capability and experienced navigators would also find that the Mk.21 set would show runways and hangars quite well, which allowed them to use the equipment as a landing aid. Consequently a Mk.11 Meteor, WD670, was modified for a trial installation which introduced a further 17in (43.2cm) nose extension but also brought the end of the undernose fairing. The extra weight was offset by the addition of new more powerful 3,800 lb (16.9kN) thrust Rolls-Royce Derwent 9 engines which also had an improved relighting facility both for more consistent relighting and an increased altitude where relighting was possible. This new variant was designated NF Mk.12 and WD670 served as the first prototype.

Boscombe Down's pilots got their hands on WD670, with its new nose, during June and July 1952 for some brief handling trials (the aircraft was then still fitted with Derwent 8s). They found a tendency for fin stalling at altitude, which was described as 'a most unpleasant and dangerous characteristic', but the handling both with and without underwing tanks was found to be satisfactory and similar to the Mk.11. There was also some rudder over-balance during sideslip at low altitude, but it was the fin stalling problem that was considered to be unacceptable for Service operations. As a result the second Mk.12 prototype WD687 (another former Mk.11) introduced a modified fin with fillets above and below the tail 'acorn' bullet. This increased the total fin area by approximately 1ft^2 (0.09m^2) and, together with a restriction of 17.5° each way on the rudder travel, eliminated both the fin stalling and rudder overbalance problems; it also gave satisfactory handling. Eric Franklin flew the first production aircraft, WS590, on 21st April 1953 and the first unit to receive the Mk.12 was No 238 Operational Conversion Unit; No 85 Squadron had Mk.12s on strength from early 1954.

Meteor NF Mk.13

A version actually developed before the Mk.12, the NF Mk.13 was a 'minimum-change' Mk.11 adapted for operations in the tropics and it was 450 lb (204kg) heavier than the original because some additional equipment had been fitted. The extra kit was a cold-air ventilating or air conditioning system and a radio compass (the latter indicated by a D/F loop aerial placed beneath the cockpit canopy behind the navigator). Only forty examples of the Mk.13 were completed and all of these were converted

from NF Mk.11s during production. First to fly was WM308, piloted by Joe Lancaster, on 23rd December 1952 and deliveries began at the end of January 1953. The first squadron to convert was No 39 at Fayid in March of that year.

Meteor NF Mk.14

The ultimate Meteor night fighter was the NF Mk.14 which used the same equipment as the Mk.12. Initially however, it may have been intended to fit the American APQ-43 radar into the new type, but by now the Meteor night fighter's future was very short term and so it would not have been worth the design effort to complete such a modification (the nose was also too small to take the dish). The NF 14 also introduced a new clear-vision sliding canopy and showed the same area modifications to the fin. However, contrary to what most published sources have reported, the Mk.14 was the same length as the Mk.12. Modeller John Adams has physically measured examples of both versions to confirm this. He told the authors 'The NF Mk.14 nose looks longer than the Marks 11 or 12 as it has a shorter steeper angled windscreen and the 6in (15.2cm) shorter "big bore" engine nacelles. In fact in service the length of nearly all Mk.14s became shorter at 49ft 8½in (15.14m) when a passive tail warning radar R3697 was fitted, by the removal of the extreme rear fuselage tip and replacing it with a flat waveguide plate which reduced the length by 3½in (8.9cm). Later in its service (as the NF(T) Mk.14) it sometimes occurred that,

when the radomes were re-painted gloss black, the first metal fuselage ring was also painted giving the illusion of a longer radome'.

This variant offered some improvement over the earlier NFs, and for the aircrew inside the view out was much better than the greenhouse canopy of the earlier marks, but the night fighter Meteors would never look as elegant as their single-seat day fighters contemporaries. WM261, the 291st production Mk.11, was used for the trial installation of the sliding hood canopy which helped it to become the proto-type Mk.14. An auto-stabiliser was used to eliminate high-altitude instability and ejection seats were also now available in a night fighter Meteor for the first time. WS722, the first production aeroplane, was flown by Bill Else from Baginton on 23rd October 1953 and deliveries began on 6th November. The first front line to unit to have the Mk.14 was No 25 Squadron which received the type from March 1954. Curiously the existence of both Mks 12 and 14 was not made known to the public until December 1953 and April 1954 respectively, quite some time after their first flights.

When WS848 departed from the line during May 1955 the production run for all variants of the Meteor was complete. The manufacture of all of the night fighters was undertaken entirely by AWA at Baginton and the aircraft did indeed become the RAF's standard night fighter until the arrival of Gloster's follow-on Javelin. Such was the NF Mk.14's popularity within the Ser-

A shot of Meteor NF.14 WS838 in plan view during a flight from RAE Bedford. This shows the long-span wings, long nose, wing tanks and gun position of the night fighter Marks to good effect. RAE Bedford B3105F, via Tony Buttler

The prototype Meteor NF Mk.14, WM261, photographed at Bitteswell on 29th July 1953, showing the amount of fuselage re-work needed to incorporate the sliding cockpit canopy of this version. After use as a photo-ship at English Electric's Warton base, it was transferred to Ferranti and was later civilianised as G-ARCX. Armstrong Whitworth NF199, via Ray Williams

vice it became known as the 'Queen of the Skies' although sources also note that the type could not intercept RAF English Electric Canberra bombers during exercises because they were incapable of reaching their target's altitude. Javelins began to replace the Mk.12s and 14s from 1957 onwards with the last UK-based aircraft being withdrawn in June 1959. After their removal from the front line some aircraft had their radars removed and replaced by UHF radios which, as NF(T) Mk.14s, allowed them to be used further to train navigators for fast jet operations. During 1960 Mk.14 WM261 had a long pointed nose radome fitted by Ferranti to allow it to take part in the 'Red Garter' programme; as such this aircraft, at 57ft 9in (17.6m), became the longest Meteor to fly.

Meteor TT Mk.20

Armstrong Whitworth's involvement with developments of the Meteor, however, did not come to a close with the end of the night fighter production line because in 1956 the NF Mk.11 was turned into a target tug for the Royal Navy. At the time the Fleet Air Arm's piston-powered Fairey Firefly tugs were in need of replacement and, since Mk.11 airframes were becoming surplus due to their substitution in the front line by NF Mk.14s, they were considered to be ideal conversions for the task. Eventually fifty were so modified, either by AWA or by the Royal Navy's Air Yard at Sydenham. Specification TT.179D was drawn up to cover these night fighter conversions.

A wind-driven ML Aviation G-Type winch was mounted above the starboard wing between the engine nacelle and the fuselage, and a tail guard prevented any fouling of the rear control surfaces by the 6,100ft (1,860m) long cable. Two crew were still needed because a winch operator was now seated in the rear cockpit and he was not only responsible for the winch but also the cable cutter which could dispose of the target should an emergency arise. The radar and guns were removed but, because the tug's winch and cable were of similar weight to the deleted equipment, the Mk.20's all-up-

Meteor TT Mk.20 WD767 is shown streaming a drogue target. This aircraft was used for system development and was effectively the prototype TT.20. Armstrong Whitworth NF430, via Ray Williams

This detailed shot of the Fleet Air Arm TT.20 WD706 shows the Del Mar winch installation inboard for streaming drogue targets, and a Del Mar rotating target in the outboard position. The latter was only used for trials conducted with this aircraft and did not enter service. The winch more commonly used was the ML Aviation Type G shown on the Danish aircraft. via Tony Buttler

Drawing from October 1950 showing Armstrong Whitworth's second proposed layout for Sweden of a Meteor night fighter powered by de Havilland Goblin engines. Span was 43ft 0in (13.1m) and length 48ft 6in (14.8m).

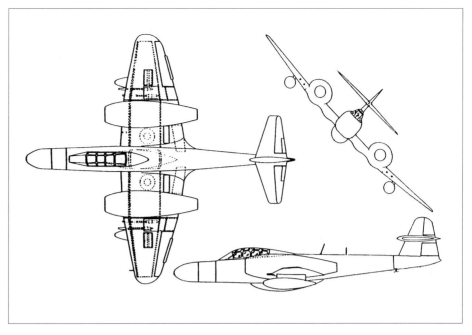

weight and performance were little changed from the Mk.11. Former Mk.11 WD767 became the TT Mk.20 'prototype' and first flew as such on 5th December 1956. From 1970 target tug Meteors were replaced by the Canberra TT Mk.18. (The missing Meteor mark numbers [15, 16, 17, 18 and 19] all relate to unmanned drone conversions, either real or planned, and are described in Chapter Seven.)

Projects

Armstrong Whitworth made at least five proposals for developments of the Meteor NF Mk.11 and these were given numbers in the Armstrong Whitworth project list, something the four versions turned into hardware never received. The AW.60 was to be powered by Armstrong Siddeley Sapphire axial engines, the AW.61 by Rolls-Royce Nene units and the AW.62 was to have de Havilland Goblins. In addition the AW.63 was to be fitted with an APQ-43 radar while the AW.64 introduced staggered side-by-side seating and wingtip tanks.

The AW.62 appears to have been a version drawn in October 1950 specifically for the Swedish Air Force, who had approached AWA about such an aeroplane in September. Also specified were SAAB ejection seats and Goblin engines equipped with reheat and a variable

nozzle. The resulting brochure showed two versions with the engines in different positions – one was very similar to the normal Derwent layout but the second had its nacelles mounted above the wing with the rear spar cranked slightly to allow it to pass beneath the exhaust cone. It was expected that there would be little increase in performance because the greater thrust of the Goblin would be absorbed by the extra weight. However, when it later became clear that substituting the Derwent for the Goblin would not be as difficult as first thought, this

second arrangement was dropped. AWA was to put several months of effort into trying to sell this Goblin-powered night fighter Meteor to the Royal Swedish Air Force, but in the end the NF Mk.51 variant of de Havilland's Venom fighter was the aircraft finally selected.

This photograph shows WD604 fitted with wingtip fuel tanks as a trial installation. Photo taken 26th February 1952. Armstrong Whitworth NF122, via Ray Williams

British Service

Meteor Front Line Units

The Meteor first entered squadron service in July 1944, when the aircraft and several pilots of a tactical trials unit, a joint RAF/Royal Aircraft Establishment formation called 'T' (Tactical) Flight, transferred from Farnborough to RAF Manston and became part of No 616 Squadron of the Royal Air Force as its Meteor Flight, flying the first production Mk.I Meteors, initially chasing V-1 flying bombs over Kent. Within a few weeks No 616 gave up its remaining Spitfires and became completely equipped with Meteors. Thereafter, successive Marks of the Meteor remained in RAF front-line service until the withdrawal of No 60 Squadron's Mk.14s, based in Singapore, in August 1961, while the last drone conversion was only withdrawn from use at RAE Llanbedr with closure of that base in 2004. More than sixty RAF Squadrons flew the Meteor as their primary equipment, and jet-conversion trainer T.7s flew with many more Regular and Auxiliary jet squadrons.

Prior to its equipment with the Meteor, No 616 Squadron had been based at RAF Culmhead in Somerset, equipped with the (quite rare) Supermarine Spitfire Mk.VII high-altitude variant, although when the unit first formed in 1938 it had been an Auxiliary Air Force fighter unit based at Doncaster. The transition to the first jets went quite smoothly, no doubt benefiting from the experience gained by several of the Squadron pilots as members of 'T' Flight. The first operational sorties took place on 27th July 1944, engaging V-1 flying bombs that were being fired towards England from launch sites in northern France. It took a few days before the first successful interception, but on 4th August two V-1s were destroyed, one by the Meteor's guns and the second by flying a Meteor alongside the V-1 and tipping it over with a wingtip (thereby upsetting its gyroscope control and causing it to crash), after the Meteor's guns had jammed. After being re-equipped with the first Mk.III Meteors at Colerne in January 1945, one Flight of No 616 was dispatched to Brussels/ Melsbroek in the hope that combats with Messerschmitt Me 262s might arise, although pilots were forbidden from flying over enemy territory. By March 1945, the whole Squadron

A well-known photo of Meteors from No 616 Squadron at Manston in 1945, on their hardstanding composed of 'PSP' (pierced steel planking). The line-up includes both Mk.I and Mk.III aircraft. The nearest 'YQ-P' is a Mk.III, as is 'YQ-O' (EE234), but 'YQ-W' is Mk.I EE229, and there is at least one more Mk.I further down the line – study the cockpit canopies! IWM CL.2923

had transferred to the Continent, being based at Gilze-Rijen in Holland. With the end of the European war a few weeks later, the unit moved to Lüneberg, and then Lübeck in Germany itself. Here, some of the pilots were able to sample brief flights in captured Me 262s, although no combats between the two types had ever taken place during the war. At the end of August 1945, No 616 Squadron was renumbered as No 263 Squadron, no doubt in preparation for the unit's original number to be available for the re-establishment of the Auxiliary Air Force in peacetime, a few months later. (Only later did the AAF become the Royal Auxiliary Air Force.)

This shot of a Meteor III of No 616 Squadron shows the overall white colour scheme adopted early in 1945 during the severe European winter when snow covered the ground for weeks on end. The temporary white colours covered everything bar the RAF roundels, fin flash and serial number. Although this photo appears to be taken in England, the white colours were soon washed off with the aircraft reverting to their normal camouflage. Tony Buttler

In the meantime, the second Meteor Squadron, No 504, had converted to the Meteor F Mk.III at RAF Colerne in March 1945, but, with the impending end of the war, it remained based in England. No 504 was also renumbered (as No 245) in August 1945, again to release an Auxiliary Squadron number for post-war use.

Other Squadrons to receive the Meteor III in 1945 included No 74 (in June), No 124 (in July, but renumbered as No 56 Squadron in April 1946) and No 222 in October. Thereafter there was some delay in further re-equipment, as the Royal Air Force returned to a peacetime footing, but further Fighter Command units received the Mk.III in 1946. These units were Nos 234 in February (renumbered as 266 in September), 257 in September, 1 and 91 in October and 66 in November. The final units were No 92 Squadron (renumbered from 91 in January 1947) and No 63 in April 1948, the latter as an introduction to its first F Mk.IV, which it received a few weeks later. No 500 Squadron, of the Royal Auxiliary Air Force, was the only RAuxAF unit to fly the Mk.III, which it did from July 1948 to October 1951, being the last Squadron operator of this Mark. The Mk.IIIs were replaced by the Mk.IV (later styled the F Mk.4). The Mk.III aircraft were all passed on to the Advanced Flying Schools and Operational Conversion Units that were responsible for training the post-war jet pilots as Fighter Command expanded with the increasing Cold War threat of the late 1940s and 1950s. Meteor F Mk.III squadrons were deployed thus:

No 1	Tangmere
No 56	Boxted, then Wattisham, Duxford and Thorney Island
No 63	Thorney Island
No 66	Duxford
No 74	Colerne, later Horsham St Faith
No 91	Duxford and Debden, renumbered No 92
No 92	Duxford
No 124	Molesworth, later Bentwaters, renumbered No 56
No 222	Molesworth, later Exeter and Tangmere
No 234	Boxted, later renumbered No 266
No 245	Colerne, later Bentwaters and Horsham St Faith
No 257	Church Fenton, later Horsham St Faith
No 263	Acklington, later Church Fenton
No 266	Boxted, then Wattisham and Tangmere
No 500	West Malling
No 504	Cologne, later renumbered No 245
No 616	Lübeck, later renumbered No 263

The F Mk.4 served with all the post-war units that had flown the Mk.III, namely Nos 1, 56, 63, 66, 74, 91 (soon renumbered as 92), 222, 245, 257, 263 and 266 Squadrons, all in Fighter

EE227 'YQ-Y' of No 616 Squadron photographed at Manston shortly before it was delivered to Rolls-Royce to be converted to have Trent turbo-propeller engines. IWM CL.2926

Meteor III EE401. via Tony Buttler

A line-up of No 257 Squadron Meteor F.4s at Horsham St Faith in 1950. The three nearest aircraft are VW266 'A6-H', VT113 'A6-K' and EE544 'A6-C'. via Phil Butler

A line-up of No 263 Squadron F.4s carrying 1950 roundels at Horsham St Faith. The nearest aircraft is VT240. via Phil Butler

A 'vic' of Meteor F.4s from No 74 Squadron awaiting take-off instructions on the runway at Horsham St Faith in 1950, still wearing the '4D' code of that unit. The nearest aircraft are RA427 '4D-E' and RA439 '4D-F'. via Phil Butler

A mixed bag of Meteor fighters on the runway at Horsham St Faith in 1950. F.8 VZ528 'MR-R' of No 245 Squadron, F.4 'A6-K' of No 257 and an F.4 of No 263, the latter uncoded but wearing the blue crosses on a red background of No 263 Squadron, are all with units of the Horsham St Faith Wing. via Phil Butler

A nice air-to-air photograph of a silver F Mk.4, RA444 'A6-B' of No 257 Squadron. The lion motif on the nose comes from the squadron's badge. Ministry of Defence R-1584, via Tony Buttler

Command. Further units formed with the F.4 included Nos 19, 41, 43, 64 and 65 Squadrons, while Nos 500, 504, 600, 609, 610, 611, 615 and 616 Squadrons of the RAuxAF also received the F Mk.4, these of course including the original 'numbers' of the Squadrons that had introduced the Meteor into front-line service in 1945. The RAuxAF Squadrons were at first units of Reserve Command, albeit under Fighter Command operational control, but were transferred to Fighter Command proper in 1949. The prime role of the Royal Auxiliary Air Force was to reinforce Fighter Command and the 2nd Tactical Air Force (TAF) in time of war, with the de Havilland Vampire units intended for the tactical role and the Meteor squadrons allotted to air defence.

In due time the F.4 version was superseded by the F Mk.8 fighter variant, which was the most widely-used version. All the F.4 squadrons listed above (Regular and Auxiliary) re-equipped with the F.8, except No 266, which had been renumbered as No 43 Squadron in the meantime. In addition, further expansion of Fighter Command meant that Nos 34 and 111 Squadrons reformed with the Mk.8, while Nos 54 and 247 re-equipped with the F.8 in place of Vampires. Nos 601 and 604 Squadrons of the RAuxAF also received the F.8, again replacing Vampires. (The F.8 also later served in small numbers with No 85 Squadron when this transferred from a night-fighter to a second-line target-facilities role in 1963).

The Meteor F.8 was retained as the main equipment of Fighter Command in the defence of the United Kingdom, so did not serve with units permanently based overseas, although units often deployed to Malta and elsewhere for air-firing exercises. Any intentions to equip units in the 2nd Tactical Air Force were quashed by the experience of the Royal Australian Air Force in Korea, where the Meteor 8 was clearly outclassed by the MiG-15. The

A formation of No 41 Squadron F.8s photographed approaching the South coast of England in 1951. Visible are WF700 'H', WA962 'D', WE958 'B', WE867 'S', WE943 'G' and others coded 'A', 'W', 'X' and 'Y'. Russell Adams P466/51, via Phil Butler

WH480 and others of No 41 Squadron in formation, airborne from Biggin Hill in May 1953. The second aircraft is unidentifiable, while the back two are WA929 'W' and WA994 'X'. WH480 is the Squadron commander's aircraft and wears a Wing Commander's pennant below its cockpit. Russell Adams P.187/53

main strength of the 2nd TAF lay in its fighter-bomber Wings of de Havilland Vampire FB.5s, later replaced by de Havilland Venoms. It had relatively few 'pure' fighter units. Thus, following the lessons of the Korean War, day fighter units based in Germany received Canadair-built North American (F-86) Sabres supplied under the Mutual Defence Aid Program (funded by the USA), in lieu of the Meteor. A further batch of Sabres also replaced the Meteors of Nos 66 and 92 Squadrons of Fighter Command, pending the delivery of the first Hawker Hunters to the Royal Air Force.

As with the earlier Marks, the F.8 continued to fly in many secondary roles after its withdrawal from front-line service in 1957. The Mark had already served with many Station Flights, Sector Flights and as the individual mount of some senior officers. Other aircraft served with units such as the Armament Practice Stations at Acklington in Northumberland and at Sylt in

North Germany (and others in the Middle East and Far East Air Forces). One of the final users was the Royal Air Force Flying College at Manby, which even flew an aerobatic team with silver, 'yellow-banded' F.8s. The F.8 had for many years been used as a tug for the 'banner' type gunnery targets used for air-firing exercises on all front-line fighter units. Most Meteor F.8 squadrons would have had two or more aircraft with a 'hook' attached to the rear of the belly fuel tank which were routinely fitted to and used by the Mark in service. (Underwing fuel tanks were also a standard fitment, but were only used on the single-seat Meteors during long-range deployments, such as en route to armament camps overseas, being removed for general day-to-day flying). The towrope for the banner was looped around the 'hook' before

take-off, and if the pilot maintained tension on the rope the banner followed the aircraft into the air. At the end of the exercise the hook was unlatched over the runway at base, allowing the banner to fall to the ground. The banner, usually white or yellow, also had an aiming spot and a vertical line in a contrasting colour (giving rise to the unit marking of the APS at Acklington, see page 143), and carried a weighted bar at its front end to ensure that the banner stayed vertical whilst being towed. Since the standard 'modification' to tow banners was fitted to many Squadron Meteors, it is probably erroneous to term such machines an 'F(TT) Mk.8', although this designation is often applied to aircraft used in the role in later years.

The specialised photographic reconnaissance versions, the Fighter Reconnaissance

A line-up of No 610 Squadron Meteors on their hardstanding at Hooton Park on 21st June 1953, with two T.7s and eight F.8s visible. All are silver with the unit's black and white 'sawtooth' markings, and black anti-dazzle panels on the noses of the F.8s. Several have the Squadron badge on their engine nacelles. Phil Butler

WF774 Meteor T.7 'K' of No 66 Squadron, with RCAF Sabres in the background, seen here in an overall silver scheme, with the blue-outline markings of No 66 Squadron either side of the fuselage roundel. via Phil Butler

WF714 and other Mk.8s of No 500 (County of
Kent) Squadron, Royal Auxiliary Air Force,
photographed on 18th May 1953.
Russell Adams P.244/53

WH253, seen here as 'R' of No 600 Squadron,
RAuxAF, shows off the red-and-white triangle
markings of its Biggin Hill-based unit.
via Phil Butler

Meteor T.7 WF785, 'K' of No 610 Squadron, Royal
Auxiliary Air Force, taxying out at Hooton Park in
1953, wearing the black-and-white 'saw-tooth'
markings of that unit and without the yellow
T-bands. Phil Butler

Meteor F.8 WK807 'W' of No 600 Squadron on an aerobatic sortie in March 1955. Later this aircraft moved to the Western Sector Flight at Woodvale, and was eventually converted to a U.16.
via Tony Buttler

(FR) Mk.9, and the Photo Reconnaissance (PR) Mk.10, were produced in smaller numbers than the fighter versions. The FR Mk.9 was intended for low-level tactical reconnaissance and shared the four 20mm cannon armament of the F.8 version, while the PR Mk.10 was unarmed. The FR.9 entered service with No 2 Squadron in the 2nd TAF in December 1950, and also flew with No 79 Squadron in Germany. No 2 had previously flown Spitfire PR.19s, while No 79 was reformed to fly the Meteor after a period in abeyance. Both units later received the Swift FR Mk.5 to replace the Meteor. The FR.9 was also flown by No 8 Squadron at Khormaksar, Aden, and No 208 Squadron at Kabrit in the Suez Canal Zone, the latter moving to Malta after the British withdrawal from Egypt.

Meanwhile the PR.10 served with No 541 Squadron at Buckeburg in the 2nd TAF (after converting from its previous Spitfire PR.19s in the UK) from June 1951, together with No 13 Squadron in the Middle East and No 81 at Butterworth (later Tengah) in the Far East Air Force. A Flight of No 2 Squadron received the

Meteor F.8 WH505 'A' of No 611 Squadron, photographed outside the Squadron's 1917 'Belfast' hangar at Hooton Park on 20th September 1952. Note the air raid sirens on the hangar roof! R A Scholefield

The Meteor night-fighter versions commenced with the Mark 11, introduced into service by No 29 Squadron in July 1951. It was also the last Fighter Command squadron to operate this Mark, retaining it until November 1957. The Meteor shared the night-fighter role with the Vampire NF Mk.10 (and later the Venom NF Mk.2 and NF Mk.3), so not all the Wings in Fighter Command had a Meteor NF unit. In 1954, the Fighter Command Squadrons were:

No 29	Tangmere
No 85	West Malling
No 141	Coltishall
No 151	Leuchars
No 264	Linton-on-Ouse

NF Mk.11s also served with the night-fighter squadrons of the 2nd Tactical Air Force in Germany, namely, Nos 68 and 87 at Wahn and Nos 96 and 256 at Ahlhorn.

No 68 was renumbered as No 5 Squadron in 1959, and No 256 became No 11 Squadron at the same time. Such re-numberings were common practice as the size of the Royal Air Force reduced (a practice still prevalent today), with the object of retaining the continuity of Squadron numbers for the more famous units.

The NF Mk.13, of which only forty examples were built, was identical to the Mk.11 apart from having tropical equipment fitted, for service in the Middle East. The Mark 13 served only with Nos 39 and 219 Squadrons, based in the Suez Canal Zone at Kabrit. With the British withdrawal from the Canal Zone in 1955, No 219 was disbanded and No 39 moved to Luqa, Malta. No 219 had operated

PR.10 in Germany, but only for a brief period, pending the arrival of No 541.

The scale of RAF use of the Meteor is amply demonstrated by this Mark-by-Mark listing, with over thirty squadrons flying the Mark 8 over the years:

Mk.I	616
Mk.III	1, 56, 66, 74, 91/92, 124, 222, 234, 245, 257, 263, 266, 500, 504, 616
Mk.4	1, 19, 41, 43, 56, 63, 64, 65, 66, 74, 92, 222, 245, 257, 263, 266, 500, 504, 600, 609, 610, 611, 615, 616
Mk.8	1, 19, 34, 41, 43, 54, 56, 63, 64, 65, 66, 72, 74, 85, 92, 111, 222, 245, 247, 257, 263, 500, 504, 600, 601, 604, 609, 610, 611, 615, 616
Mk.9	2, 8, 79, 208
Mk.10	2, 13, 81, 541
Mk.11	5, 11, 29, 68, 85, 87, 96, 125, 141, 151, 256, 264, 527
Mk.12	25, 29, 46, 64, 72, 85, 152, 153
Mk.13	39, 219
Mk.14	25, 33, 46, 60, 64, 72, 85, 152, 153, 264

A photo of WH505 of No 611 Squadron, taken at Hooton Park on 28th August 1954, by now in camouflage, but still fitted with the metal-framed hood. Phil Butler

Meteor F.8 WK713 still wearing its No 222 Squadron chequerboard markings at 12 MU Kirkbride while awaiting the scrapman on 1st April 1959. Phil Butler

Meteor T.7 WA743 'L' of No 610 Squadron, dropping off a passenger at Liverpool-Speke on 19th July 1953. Phil Butler

Mk.11s for a period prior to the Mk.13 becoming available.

The Mk.11 Meteor was replaced in turn by the NF Mk.12 and then the NF Mk.14. These later versions featured more up-to-date Airborne Interception radars. The Mk.12 entered service with Fighter Command in 1954 and served with these Squadrons:

No 25	Tangmere, later West Malling, replacing Vampire NF.10
No 29	Leuchars (in parallel with Javelins for a short period)
No 46	Odiham. Formed on the Mk.12
No 64	Duxford (replacing Meteor F.8s on change of role)
No 72	Church Fenton (replacing F.8s on change of role)
No 85	West Malling (replacing NF.11)
No 152	Wattisham. Formed on the Mk.12
No 153	West Malling. Formed on the Mk.12

The Mk.14 was similar to the Mk.12 apart from the introduction of the completely revised clear-vision cockpit canopy. It served alongside the Mk.12 in Nos 25, 46, 64, 72, 85, 152 and 153 Squadrons, and also with the following units:

No 33	Leeming – renumbered from No 264 Squadron in September 1957
No 60	Tengah, Singapore (change of role from Venom FB.4, October 1959)
No 264	Linton-on-Ouse, replacing the NF.11, until renumbered as No 33 Squadron.

The service of the Meteor NF.14 with No 60 Squadron in the Far East marked the final 'front-line' use of the Meteor, the type only being withdrawn at the end of August 1961. Since the Mk.12 and 14 Meteors were equipped with the same type of radar, they were operationally interchangeable, so most units flew a mix of the two versions.

The drone Marks of Meteor, the drone U Mk.15 and U Mk.16 versions, and the target-towing TT Mk.20, did not enter RAF Squadron service. The drone versions served with the Guided Weapons Trials Wing of the Royal Aircraft Establishment (RAE), mainly at Llanbedr in North Wales. The RAE and its successors is not part of the Royal Air Force, being an element of the Ministry of Supply, and its successor, the Ministry of Defence (Procurement Executive). Some details of RAE activities are given in Chapter Seven.

The TT.20 was, at first, mainly intended for service with the Royal Navy's Fleet Air Arm (FAA), particularly with the 'Fleet Requirements Units' which provided target-towing services, radar targets, and other forms of mock attacks on Royal Navy vessels to enable them to practice air-defence skills. The TT.20 therefore served with the FAA's No 728 Squadron at Hal Far, Malta, and the Fleet Requirements Unit based at Hurn in Dorset. The latter unit was civilian-manned by Airwork Ltd, and operated several types of naval aircraft, including the Meteor T.7 and TT.20. Thereafter, the RAF did use the TT.20, both in the Far East with No 1574 (TT) Flight in Singapore, and with the civilian-manned Civilian Anti-Aircraft Cooperation Units in England, including No 3/4 CAACU at Exeter and No 5 at Woodvale. Other examples flew

Meteor T.7 WA689 'T' of No 600 Squadron. via Phil Butler

Meteor T.7 VZ649 'E' of No 616 Squadron.
via Phil Butler

war or other emergency might well take their place in the front-line, which is why they received codes similar to those of operational Squadrons.

Not all Meteor units used these two-letter codes, some being formed, or re-equipped, with Meteors only after the scheme had been replaced by individual coloured markings to represent each Squadron. These colourful unit markings of the main RAF Squadrons that flew the Meteor appear on pages 140-143 of this book. The two-letter Squadron identities that they replaced had been used for security purposes ever since the 'Munich Crisis' of 1938, surviving into the early years of the 'Cold War'. The markings in many cases revived those used prior to 1938 (or even during the First World War), while others related to the squadron's official badge, or other titles or associations arising from the unit's history.

Other Meteor Units
In the early days of its RAF service, quite aside from its key role at the heart of the United Kingdom's air defence, the Meteor was chosen to make attempts on the World Air Speed Record. The first attempts were made in November

with experimental establishments, such as the A&AEE at Boscombe Down and the Royal Aircraft Establishment at Farnborough.

Bases normally had a Wing of two day fighter Squadrons, usually supplemented by a night-fighter Squadron. At the peak of its strength, in January 1954, the F.8 force was deployed thus:

Nos 1 and 34	Tangmere
Nos 19, 72 and 609	Church Fenton
Nos 41, 600 and 615	Biggin Hill
Nos 43 and 222	Leuchars
Nos 56 and 63	Waterbeach
Nos 64 and 65	Duxford
Nos 66 and 92	Linton-on-Ouse
Nos 74 and 245	Horsham St Faith
Nos 111, 601 and 604	North Weald
Nos 54 and 247	Odiham
Nos 257 and 263	Wattisham
No 500	West Malling
No 504	Wymeswold
Nos 610 and 611	Hooton Park
No 616	Finningley

The many codes used by the OCU (see table on opposite page) arose from its large size, much larger in strength than a single Squadron. OCUs had a 'war role', and in the event of

Meteor FR.9 VZ593 'Q' of No 208 Squadron, with a line-up of other squadron aircraft at Idris in April 1951. via P H T Green/G R Pitchfork

Use of Meteor Marks by Squadrons

Squadron	Mark	Period
No 1	F.III	Oct 1946 to Aug 1947
	F.4	Jun 1948 to Sep 1950
	F.8	Sep 1950 to Jun 1955
No 2	FR.9	Dec 1950 to May 1956
	PR.10	Mar to Jul 1951
No 5	NF.11	Jan 1959 to Aug 1960
No 8	FR.9	Jan 1958 to Apr 1961
No 11	NF.11	Jan 1959 to Mar 1962
No 13	PR.10	Jan 1952 to Aug 1956
No 19	F.4	Jan to Apr 1951
	F.8	Apr 1951 to Dec 1956
No 25	NF.12 &14	Mar 1954 to Mar 1959
No 29	NF.11	Jul 1951 to Nov 1957
	NF.12	Feb 1958 to Jul 1958
No 33	NF.14	Sep 1957 to Jul 1958
No 34	F.8	Aug 1954 to Dec 1955
No 39	NF.13	Mar 1953 to Jun 1958
No 41	F.4	Jan to Apr 1951
	F.8	Apr 1951 to Jun 1955
No 43	F.4	Feb 1949 to Sep 1950
	F.8	Sep 1950 to Sep 1954
No 46	NF.12 &14	Aug 1954 to Mar 1956
No 54	F.8	Apr 1952 to Mar 1955
No 56	F.3	Apr 1946 to Sep 1948
	F.4	Aug 1948 to Dec 1950
	F.8	Dec 1950 to Jun 1955
No 60	NF.14	Oct 1959 to Sep 1961
No 63	F.3	Apr to Jun 1948
	F.4	Jun 1948 to Jan 1951
	F.8	Dec 1950 to Jan 1957
No 64	F.4	Dec 1950 to Mar 1951
	F.8	Mar 1951 to Mar 1957
	NF.12	Aug 1956 to Sep 1958
	NF.14	Dec 1956 to Sep 1958
No 65	F.4	Dec 1950 to Apr 1951
	F.8	Feb 1951 to Feb 1957
No 66	F.III	Nov 1946 to May 1948
	F.4	May 1948 to Jan 1951
	F.8	Dec 1950 to Dec 1953
No 68	NF.11	Mar 1952 to Jan 1959
No 72	F.8	Jul 1952 to Feb 1956
	NF.12 &14	Feb 1956 to Jun 1959
No 74	F.III	Jun 1945 to Mar 1948
	F.4	Dec 1947 to Oct 1950
	F.8	Oct 1950 to Mar 1957
No 79	FR.9	Nov 1951 to Aug 1956
No 81	PR.10	Dec 1953 to Jul 1961
No 85	NF.11	Sep 1951 to Apr 1954
	NF.12 &14	Apr 1954 to Oct 1958
No 87	NF.11	Mar 1952 to Nov 1957
No 91	F.III	Oct 1946 to Jan 1947.
	F.IV	Jan 1947 (renumbered No 92)
No 92	F.III	Jan 1947 to May 1948
	F.4	May 1948 to Oct 1950
	F.8	Oct 1950 to Feb 1954
No 96	NF.11	Nov 1952 to Jan 1959
No 111	F.8	Dec 1953 to Jun 1955
No 124	F.III	Jul 1945 to Apr 1946 (renumbered No 56)
No 125	NF.11	Apr 1955 to Jan 1956
No 141	NF.11	Sep 1951 to Sep 1955
No 151	NF.11	Apr 1953 to Sep 1955
No 152	NF.12 &14	Jun 1954 to Jul 1958
No 153	NF.12 &14	Mar 1955 to Jul 1958
No 208	FR.9	Mar 1951 to Jan 1958
No 219	NF.11	Oct 1952 to May 1953
	NF.13	Apr 1953 to Sep 1954
No 222	F.III	Oct 1945 to Jul 1948
	F.IV	Dec 1947 to Sep 1948
	F.8	Sep 1950 to Dec 1954
No 234	F.III	Feb 1946 to Sep 1946 (renumbered No 266)
No 245	F.III	Aug 1945 to Mar 1948
	F.4	Nov 1947 to Jun 1950
	F.8	Jun 1950 to Mar 1957
No 247	F.8	Apr 1952 to Jun 1955
No 256	NF.11	Nov 1952 to Jan 1959
No 257	F.III	Sep 1946 to Mar 1948
	F.4	Dec 1947 to Oct 1950
	F.8	Oct 1950 to Mar 1955
No 263	F.III	Aug 1945 to Mar 1948
	F.4	Dec 1947 to Nov 1954
	F.8	Oct 1950 to Apr 1955
No 264	NF.11	Nov 1951 to Nov 1954
	NF.14	Oct 1954 to Sep 1957
No 266	F.III	Sep 1946 to Apr 1948
	F.4	Feb 1948 to Feb 1949
No 500	F.3	Jul 1948 to Oct 1951
	F.4	Jul 1951 to Jan 1952
	F.8	Nov 1951 to Mar 1957
No 504	F.4	Oct 1949 to Feb 1952
	F.8	Feb 1952 to Mar 1957
No 541	PR.10	Dec 1950 to Sep 1957
No 600	F.4	Mar 1950 to Feb 1952
	F.8	Nov 1951 to Mar 1957
No 601	F.8	Aug 1952 to Mar 1957
No 604	F.8	Aug 1952 to Mar 1957
No 609	F.4	Dec 1950 to Jun 1951
	F.8	Jun 1951 to Mar 1957
No 610	F.4	Jul 1951 to Mar 1952
	F.8	Mar 1952 to Mar 1957
No 611	F.4	May 1951 to May 1952
	F.8	Dec 1951 to Mar 1957
No 615	F.4	Sep 1950 to Sep 1951
	F.8	Sep 1951 to Mar 1957
No 616	F.I	Jul 1944 to Feb 1945
	F.III	Jan to Aug 1945 and Jan 1949 to May 1951
	F.4	Apr to Dec 1951
	F.8	Dec 1951 to Mar 1957

Squadron Codes

Squadron	Code	Squadron	Code	Squadron	Code
No 1	'JX'	No 222	'ZD'	No 609	'PR'
No 43	'SW'	No 234	'FX' (and as No 266)	No 615	'V6'
No 56	'ON' & 'US'	No 245	'MR'	No 616	'YQ'
No 63	'UB'	No 257	'A6'	No 226 OCU	'HX', 'KR', 'UU', 'XL'
No 66	'HI' & 'LZ'	No 263	'HE'	Armament Practice Station,	
No 74	'4D'	No 500	'S7'	Acklington	'WH'
No 91	'DL' (and as No 92)	No 504	'TM'		

Meteor PR.10 WB178 'D' of No 13 Squadron.
via P H T Green/Bill Morton-Hall

One of Russell Adams' favourite 'vertical climb' angles, this time FR.9 WB139 taken in 1951. Russell Adams P285/51, via Phil Butler

1945, and at that time were led by Gloster Aircraft, with support from Rolls-Royce and the Ministry of Aircraft Production. Two production Meteor IIIs (EE454 and EE455) were chosen and given a high-speed paint finish. In addition, their armament was removed and the gun ports faired over. Most importantly they had the long engine nacelles of the type being developed for the Meteor Mk.4. The first aircraft (EE454) was named 'Britannia', while the second aircraft was not named but was painted a bright yellow overall and referred to as 'the Yellow Peril'. The two aircraft were flown by Group Captain H J Wilson (a test pilot at RAE Farnborough) and Eric Greenwood (Chief Test Pilot of Gloster Aircraft). The attempts were flown over a three-kilometre course at Herne Bay, Kent. The course had to be flown once in each direction to compensate for the effects of the wind. On 7th November 1945, the two aircraft achieved average speeds of 606.25mph (975km/h) and 603mph (970km/h) in their timed runs over the course. The flights by Wilson in EE454 qualified as the World Air Speed record, overtaking the figure achieved on 26th April 1939 by an Messerschmitt 'Me 109R' (in reality the Me 209V1) by a substantial margin, the Messerschmitt having reached 469mph (751km/h).

In 1946, the RAF, having in the meantime taken delivery of the definitive Meteor 4, thought that they could improve on the earlier attempt and a special 'High Speed Flight' was formed at Tangmere to carry out this task, in July 1946. The title High Speed Flight had previously been used for the RAF unit that had competed in the Schneider Trophy races between 1927 and 1931, resulting in an outright win of that Trophy in 1931. This time the aircraft chosen were EE548, EE549 and EE550. They were known as 'Star Meteors', once various modifications had been incorporated. Once again guns were removed, gun ports faired over, and the dorsal radio masts were removed. Special attention was given to all drag-inducing gaps in the structure, including locking the airbrakes closed, and filling in all the irregularities with filler and wax to obtain the best possible finish.

On 7th September 1946 a new record was established in EE549 by Group Captain E M Donaldson, the Officer Commanding of the Flight. This raised the record speed to 616.8mph (987km/h). The measured 3-kilometre course lay between Worthing and Littlehampton in Sussex. The margin of a greater than 1% increase in speed above the previous record was sufficient for its official recognition by the Fédération Aéronautique Internationale.

Meteor FR.9 WL256 in camouflage at the Hawarden Battle of Britain open day on 15th September 1956. Phil Butler

Meteor PR Mk.10 WB157 on static display during the Battle of Britain open day at RAF Hawarden on 15th September 1956. The camera ports in the nose are blanked off to avoid damage to the optically flat panels. Phil Butler

The High Speed Flight was then disbanded, but the record-breaking Meteor went on to be included in the inventory of the Royal Air Force Museum.

The Meteor equipped a number of units in Flying Training Command, which was responsible for training the large numbers of fighter pilots needed to man the many front-line squadrons required during the Cold War. These units comprised Advanced Flying Schools (AFSs) which provided jet training for pilots who had received their 'wings' on piston-engined trainers (typically training on Percival Prentices, followed by North American Harvards), or Operational Conversion Units (OCUs), where the graduates from AFSs received training more specific to their operational role. In each type of unit, pilots would receive dual training and supervisory checks on the Meteor T Mk.7, and fly solo tasks on the F.4 (or the F.8 or other operational type that they were destined to fly in the 'front-line'). The main Meteor training units included:

No 205 AFS	Middleton St George
No 206 AFS	Oakington
No 207 AFS	Full Sutton
No 209 AFS	Weston Zoyland (later re-designated No 12 Flying Training School)
No 211 AFS	Worksop
No 215 AFS	Finningley
No 226 OCU	Molesworth, later Stradishall (Meteor day-fighters)
No 228 OCU	Leeming (Meteor night-fighters)
No 238 OCU	Colerne (Meteor night-fighters, training radar operators)

The Meteor T.7 also served with other Advanced Flying Schools, including Nos 202, No 203, No 208 and No 210, all of which were primarily equipped with Vampires.

The T.7 also served with several more Operational Conversion Units. These included No 229 (OCU for Vampire, Sabre and Hunter pilots), No 231 (OCU for English Electric Canberra pilots), No 233 (OCU for Vampire and Hunter pilots) and No 237 (OCU for Meteor FR/PR pilots).

The T.7 was also used by the Fleet Air Arm for jet conversion training and for instrument rating practice. Initial service with No 702 Squadron at Culdrose in 1949 actually preceded its entry into full RAF use. (702 Squadron was the Royal Navy's Jet Evaluation and Training Unit at the time). The T.7 also served with No 759 Squadron at Culdrose from 1952, No 728 (FRU) Squadron at Hal Far, the Airwork-operated Jet Conversion Unit at St Davids in 1955, and the similarly operated Fleet Requirements Unit at Hurn, as well as with many Fleet Air Arm Station Flights and communications units.

After withdrawal from front-line service, a number of NF.14 Meteors were refurbished for use at Nos 1 and 2 Air Navigation Schools (succeeding Vampire NF.10s previously used). Their task was to give jet aircraft navigators practice at low-level high-speed navigation – at a level where electronic aids could not compete with the 'Mk.1 eyeball'. The aircraft used were liberally plastered with Day-Glo patches or stripes over their camouflage, and in some cases were repainted a silver/Day-Glo colour scheme. They were often referred to as NF(T) Mk.14, reflecting their change in role, although this is believed not to have been a change in 'official nomenclature', unless any reader can confirm otherwise. NF.14s also served with the two night-fighter Operational Conversion Units, No 228 at Leeming and No 238 at Colerne.

WD644, 'W' of No 141 Squadron, is seen here in external storage after being withdrawn from service. via Tony Buttler

Pilot's Comments

The following comments from 'Wing Commander' give a feeling of what it was like to be an RAF fighter pilot during the service of the Meteor.

'You asked me to write a few notes on the Meteor. I am sure you will have access to all the "nuts and bolts" detail of the various Marks, so I will confine myself to my experiences with several of them. Looking back now, they had so many inadequacies and so many people died in them (490 fatal crashes in peacetime, almost as many as in the Battle of Britain) but at the time we loved it and did not appreciate the full picture.

'I was lucky to fly rather more Meteors than the average Squadron pilot, because during my first squadron tour I did the Pilot Attack Instructor's course at the Central Gunnery School, preparatory to my second tour as a Gunnery Instructor at the UK Armament Practice Station at RAF Acklington. Every Fighter Squadron did an annual three-week visit. I was there to improve their skills and got to fly their aircraft as well as our own. Then, as a Staff officer on my third tour, I was expected to cadge four hours per month flying time wherever I could, and Meteors were easier to borrow than those aircraft with which I was less familiar – if at all.

'My log book shows that I flew 44 single-seat F.4s, 70 F.8s, 25 two-seater T.7s, 14 two-seater Meteor NF.11s and two NF.13s – nearly five hundred flying hours in 155 individual Meteors.

'After training on the de Havilland Tiger Moth and North American Harvard, I qualified for my wings in June 1949 and was posted to fly Spitfires. Then, when about to report after leave, I found my course was cancelled – no more Spitfire pilots needed. How I regret that now! I was sent to fill in time on No 222 Squadron, pending a Meteor course. Lots of coffee and Orderly Officer duties! All the other Meteor squadrons had their aircraft painted with coloured checks – only 222 Squadron retained the Second World War code "ZD" followed by an aircraft letter. I did get one ride in a Meteor 7 to whet my appetite, and I recall the odd funeral and the sight of many Meteors in the salvage yard – par for the course at the time.

'On the train journey to No 203 AFS at Driffield on a "pre-Beeching" local line, a goods train passed in the opposite direction. It had endless open wagons, like a coal train, but these were filled with crashed Meteors. At the airfield there were many more remains of Meteors around the field – they had not been cleared as the salvage yard was already full. Not a good start!

'A line-up of six (or was it eight) two-seater Meteor T.7s was a great sight, and a relief. You will recall that fighter pilots were not usually favoured with dual-controlled aircraft. Harvard to Meteor was a huge leap forward, but luckily Glosters had developed the trainer version on

their own initiative and the Air Ministry "saw the light" and ordered it, otherwise there would have been far more accidents.

'We had ground school and signed that we understood the systems, then flying began. Forty to forty-five minutes was a normal sortie at medium height without a ventral tank, but on my second flight (engine handling, stalls, slow flying), we only managed thirty-five minutes.

'Flying was so smooth in a Meteor, and so fast, but the visibility was so wonderful without the gunsight. Training was hard, one was so busy. By the fourth flight we were on to single-engined flying, critical speeds and single-engined overshoots. After many accidents on this exercise, later the engines were only throttled back instead of one being shut down, but every pilot had to use a very strong leg to determine the minimum speed to maintain height and direction. Always the same engine because the other one provided the pumps. Then a trip on circuits and another on instrument flying, followed by a circuit check by the Squadron Commander (who had just come off flying boats) and it was time to go solo at under five hours on type.

'Ground/Flight switch to GROUND (external battery), high pressure and low pressure cocks ON, throttles closed. Low pressure pump on for selected engine, wind up the starter solenoid by pressing the starter button for two seconds. The engine slowly accelerates to idling speed, but the jet pipe temperature has to be watched. If it reaches 600°C, the engine has to be shut down by closing the HP cock. Resonance can accompany this, and excess fuel has to be drained before any re-attempt (it rarely happened). One quickly learns the right balance. Usually the jet pipe temperature (JPT) will settle down at about 500°C, and instruments will show the vacuum pump and generator to be working. Now do the same for the other engine. With engines idling at about 3,500rpm, do the cockpit checks, release the brakes and taxi out. Throttle response is slow. Frequent throttle adjustment should be avoided. Line up and brake. Release brake and open the throttles slowly and smoothly to 14,550rpm. Ease the nosewheel off at 80-85 knots (148-158km/h) – not high as the tail might touch. Fly it off at 125 knots (232km/h), brake quickly and retract the undercarriage. This has to be up and locked by 175 knots (324km/h). Safety speed for engine failure on take-off is about 165 knots (308km/h) with no rudder trim in place. If airborne below this speed and an engine fails there is a dire emergency!

'If all is well let the speed increase (in a gentle climb) to 290 knots (537km/h) and maintain. RPM may build up to 14,700 but JPT should not

Meteor NF.14 WS755 'B' of No 152 Squadron at Hooton Park for the Battle of Britain Day display on 15th September 1956. Phil Butler

WD779, 'E' of No 256 Squadron, is seen here during spares recovery prior to scrapping. The photo was taken at No 12 MU, Kirkbride, on 1st April 1959. Phil Butler

exceed 680°C. 30,000ft (9,144m) is achieved in about five minutes and 40,000ft (12,192m) in ten minutes. Control response is poor over 30,000ft. Speed can be built up to 0.78 Mach, but no further nose-down trim should be used over 0.76 Mach. This necessitates a lot of stick forward force. Snaking, buffeting wing drop or even a nose down trim might occur, but usually does not.

'To conserve fuel, stay at height as long as possible, then close the throttles and descend at 0.7 Mach. In moist conditions cockpit icing is likely at low level, but melts within a few minutes (if one has time to spare).

'The Meteor handled wonderfully most of the time and was a very popular aircraft, particularly the single-seat versions. The engine could "blow out" with rough use of throttle at height, so we did that on my eighth dual flight. This exercise was also later dropped from the syllabus for safety reasons, but simple engine cutting and re-lighting procedures continued, with single-engined landings. There was some formation flying and lots of simulated and actual instrument flying. This was just as well, as we

Meteor NF.14 WS841 'X' of No 264 Squadron at Hawarden for the Battle of Britain Day display on 15th September 1956. Phil Butler

Meteor NF.11 WD765, coded '5' of the Empire Test Pilot School, photographed at RAE Farnborough on 6th September 1957. The ETPS was then based at Farnborough, before moving back to Boscombe Down in 1968. Phil Butler

A nice formation shot of a T.7, F.8 and TT.20 taken on a flight over Singapore. The F.8 is WL180, the TT.20 is WM246 and the T.7 WH218. These were among the last Meteors in RAF service. via Phil Butler

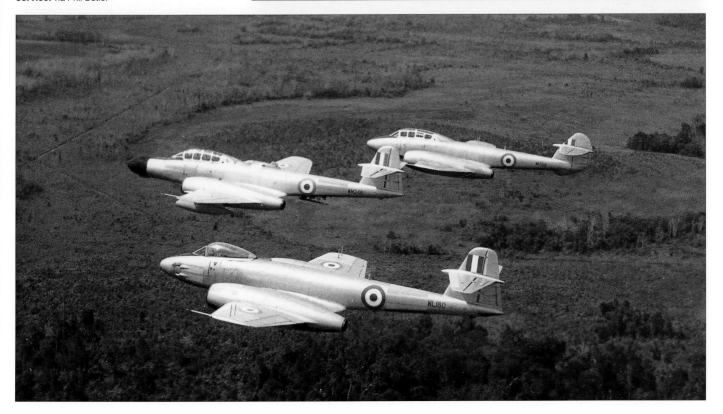

Meteor T.7 WH218 of the Target-Towing Flight, RAF Seletar. In silver topsides, with the diagonal black/yellow undersides of a target-tug.
via Phil Butler

This shot of WS842, coded 'B', shows an NF.14 in use as a low-level navigation trainer at an Air Navigation School, with liberal application of Day-Glo over the original camouflage. This example served with both No 1 and No 2 ANSs.
via Tony Buttler

were being pushed to complete the course by the Chief Flying Instructor.

'Visibility was poor on my first solo, perhaps worse than I met for the first year on Meteors. Some pilots, busy in the office when downwind, even called "finals" on an adjacent disused airfield. There was not a lot of difference between the two-seater Meteor 7 and the single-seat Mk.4, except for the fixed gunsight which obstructed the forward view and made it harder to rub a thumb-hole in the windscreen ice after a quick descent. We did not like the hood on the Meteor 7 and the lightweight canopy on the Meteor 4 seemed more secure. With the Meteor 4 we enjoyed, for the first time, flying a single-seat fighter, alone. It was a huge step from the tailwheel and large obstructing engine and propeller of the Harvard to the nosewheel, great visibility, jet engine, and speed of the Meteor. We had arrived, but there was still much to learn.

'Most of us passed the course. We were pushed out at thirty hours to make way for others, instead of the forty hours scheduled. Next, No 226 OCU, Stradishall, to learn how to shoot. First a sector recce – Stradishall is in the middle of East Anglia which is flat, one had no navigation aid and one tried to resist calling up the tower for a steer. We went off in pairs to practice gunsight ranging and the cine range line and deflection. A recorder camera, half the length of a video, sat on top of the gunsight and reduced the view. After four solos a ride in another T.7 for

a demonstration of parallel and opposite quarter attacks, then six more solos to practice these, followed by another dual to demonstrate the drogue pattern for a live firing attack, solo.

'Then, "Go to your Squadrons. Sorry, we can't spare you more than eleven hours of the forty scheduled, you can pick up the rest on the Squadron." I learned quite a lot on that brief course. Quarter attacks are always easy to misjudge, even as experienced fighter pilots, and opposite quarter attacks almost impossible. I did only a few opposite quarter attacks after that. Firing the guns was a novelty. The Meteor was a stable gun platform and the harmonisation so easy with guns beside the knees.

'Now for the real world. Down to No 222 (Natal) Squadron at Thorney Island. I think they only had eight Meteor 4s and one dual T.7. Serviceability was not good, but we managed about twenty hours per month. More asymmetric work, aerobatics, affiliation with sector control, dusk and night flying. Also a cross-country flight to Cheltenham, Cranwell, Hatfield and back in an hour.

'In March 1950 we occasionally had four serviceable aircraft and I could learn about battle formation – how to fly wide to cover each other and cross over in turns to avoid any loss of position. There was no spare throttle to catch up at altitude – something else that requires practice. Close formation is important too, or how else do several aircraft get down in bad weather? Then

low flying, navigation, pairs cine, and my first cine attack on a Boeing B-50 bomber. One closes very fast and the break reversal is within a couple of seconds of impact. Also many more practice interceptions and minor exercises.

'On bigger Exercises, with special efforts to raise more aircraft, we flew as a Wing with 56 and 63 Squadrons. All lining up together on the runway by staggered pairs, taking off at ten-second intervals and entering cloud fairly quickly. Pairs leaders flew accurately and the wing leader called any turns in cloud. It was interesting to see all the pairs almost in line "on top". Bad instrument flying would be readily apparent.

'On my very first big formation, sector called that they had a target, and I thought that some bomber was about to get a fright. The fright was mine, as two Wings met head on and then it was one grand battle. My leader had said that he would have my guts for garters if I lost him, so now there were aircraft all over the sky, all Meteors. So much going on, but I was relieved to be able to maintain contact with my leader. It was so hot that my flying suit got quite wet. I don't think I was much help, but I was learning.

'Just before we left Thorney Island, 56 and 63 Squadrons moved out for another big Exercise and we were joined by a Belgian and a Dutch Meteor squadron. They had only just received their Meteors and had not flown at night. The inevitable happened – a Wing scramble at dusk. Appreciating a difficulty, the Wing leader broke off early and we were almost all together approaching the airfield. Fortunately there was a good moon and Thorney Island and the coast were easily recognisable. I remember overshooting twice as unlit aircraft were blanking off runway lights, distance unknown. Few foreigners had found their navigation light switches and you could not tell if the lights were on. We all got down safely, but a Belgian was astray on the headcount. He had landed across the stream on a short unlit runway into moon and had finished up on the mudflats!

'It was surprising that we did not have more Meteor accidents at Thorney Island. One enterprising pair had a thrilling demonstration routine, including passing inverted overhead, one span apart, at the top of a loop, several times. Another individualist included a slow fly-by, yawing each way rapidly. He was stopped when too many rivets popped. Only a couple of years later were we warned to avoid yawing the Meteor as several had crashed because of it. Actually the Meteor always yawed as the undercarriage was lowered, this was easily cor-

EE455 is the Mk.IV test aircraft 'Forever Amber' (painted yellow overall), which together with EE454 'Britannia', was used for the World Speed Record attempts at Herne Bay in November 1945. These two aircraft were from the F.III production batch, but were completed as F.IVs. via Phil Butler

Meteor T.7 WF844 of the Royal Air Force Flying College at Manby, in the standard scheme of silver overall and yellow 'T'-bands on the rear fuselage and outer wings. Photograph taken at Liverpool-Speke on 3rd November 1957. Phil Butler

Meteor T.7 WH223 in a later colour scheme with orange Day-Glo paint on its nose, wingtips and fin/rear fuselage. Phil Butler

rected, but was possibly more dangerous when coming in fast at low level, chopping the power at the runway caravan and using no more power for a complete circuit and landing, levelling only momentarily as the gear came down and on touchdown.

'One incident gave a clue to the frequent Meteor fatalities. OC (Officer Commanding) 63 Squadron, a pre-war tied-together aerobatics ace, always stood awkwardly as a result of an accident which had left his legs with little bulk. On a high-level flight he had suffered oxygen failure and came-to very close to the sea in a vertical dive. He pulled a great amount of "G", popping many rivets, but maintaining vision as his blood had nowhere to go – he was his own "G-suit". Clearly we all needed better oxygen masks and G-suits – but we never got them on Meteors. We lost two pilots at Thorney Island in the three months I was there, both unexplained.

'In June we moved to Leuchars in Scotland. The threat was increasing and the Scottish Auxiliary Squadrons needed support. Our weekends were relocated. Almost immediately we flew down to Acklington, Northumberland, for our annual armament summer camp. Flag targets towed by Martinets at 100 knots or thereabouts, and sprogs like me being given a demonstration in a de Havilland Mosquito (interesting, but no dual gun-sight and a seat on the wing-spar). I did eleven air-firing sorties in the Meteor 4, achieving two ducks and a best of 15.8%. Quite a good score at the time. Great judgement was required to fly a good air-to-air pattern. One positioned about three-quarters of a mile out, parallel and a few degrees ahead. Turning in to achieve the right angle to the target path at (I think) about 600 yards (549m), then pulling very tight one should achieve about 30° angle off at about 300 yards (274m). A quick burst and break violently over the flag (in case it comes off). Never fire below 15° or there is a danger of shooting down the tug aircraft. Two hundred rounds fired from two guns in four of five correct passes. Ammunition is colour-tipped and there is much competition between pilots, and many unexpected ducks, or so one thinks until the Pilot Attack Instructor analyses the films. Even the most experienced frequently got it wrong.

'Back to Leuchars and in September my first flight in a single-seat Meteor F.8. Now this is different – a comfortable seat, further back from the instruments, which can EJECT. Now, at last, a better way of leaving a Meteor but it was not yet complete. At least in the Meteor 4 we had a dinghy in case of ditching or baling out into a cold North Sea. No dinghy in the F.8 because it had not yet been produced. We had to fly with rolled-up blankets as a substitute. Leg restraint had not been thought of either, so anyone ejecting was almost guaranteed back and leg injuries. But we did get bonedomes (I think), a heated windscreen and spring tabs on the

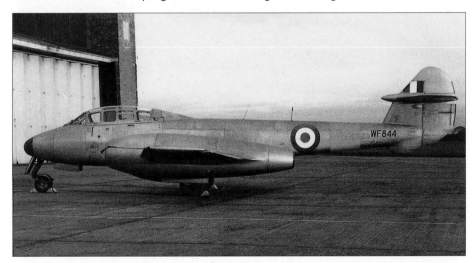

ailerons. What luxury! Much lighter handling and a bit faster – everyone's favourite Meteor.

'The threat was growing. Many more pilots arrived and many more Meteor F.8s. Instead of No 222 being a gentle flying club, it now had twenty-two Meteor 8s and thirty pilots. All Squadrons went this way. The Auxiliary Squadrons were called up and flew Meteors or Vampires instead of Spitfires.

'We soon got our dinghies and thought we had a wonderful aircraft, there was plenty of friendly rivalry. Anyone not keeping a good look out was quickly "bounced" and on No 222 we got our landing rate down to twelve touch-

EE354 'XL-H' of No 1335 (Meteor) Conversion Unit at Molesworth shortly after the end of the war in Europe. This unit later became No 226 OCU. IWM. CH.16363

A formation of Meteor T.7s from the Central Flying School, photographed in 1953. Three of the aircraft wear the CFS Pelican badge on their noses. Russell Adams P.368/53 via Tony Buttler

WH301, seen here at Blackbushe on 3rd September 1957. This aircraft was serving with the RAF Flying College at Manby, and thus wore training colours: that is, silver overall with yellow bands. Phil Butler

downs in twenty-four seconds – then someone wrote off the approach lights and we had to ease off. We did air-to-ground firing on 10-foot-square targets, ensuring that the angle was right to avoid ricochets and being close enough for the harmonisation.

'Larger formations were often used. We regularly "snaked" up through cloud as before and snaked down too if the cloud base allowed. Sometimes the visibility was poor below, which added to the excitement, as did really bumpy clouds. If the weather was so poor that a QGH ("Controlled Descent through Cloud") talk-down and Ground Controlled Approach (GCA) was necessary, only the leader of the whole formation spoke to Air Traffic Control, the rest followed in pairs on ten second delays. If GCA was necessary, the interval was slightly greater and the leader of each pair would get a couple of directions before pairs touched down. Hairy, but it worked.

'In July 1951 I went on a Pilot Attack Instructor's course at the Central Gunnery School at Leconfield, near Hull. Twenty-five more flights in the Meteor F.4 on cine and live air-to-air firing, plus one dual trip on the Meteor T.7 to try very high quarter attacks on bomber targets. Rapid speed increases and very fine judgement of the break-off.

'On 3rd August air-to-ground firing, rockets and dive-bombing started. The night before the Chief Instructor casually asked if anyone had not flown a Vampire. I put my hand up and was thrown a set of Vampire Pilot's Notes – "you can have twenty minutes familiarisation before we start". I stretched it a few minutes and started dive-bombing the same day and rocketing on the next. My first bomb landed just at the foot of the cliff below the quadrant tower. They said it must have been a dud as they did not see any smoke near the target. The error was not surprising. Cloud cover over the range was about three-eighths and I had to judge the time to wing-over for my 60° dive – I popped out of cloud to see every rivet on a Meteor that should not have been there. I expressed an expletive as I pressed the button on the throttle. That would have transmitted on a Meteor, but released a bomb on a Vampire! Rocketing, dive-bombing and air-to-air firing took twenty-six Vampire flights in eight days, then it was back for another fifteen flights of cine quarter attacks in the Meteor 4 in difficult situations, and suddenly I

WL180, photographed in the Far East late in its life, silver overall with 'stick-on' Day-Glo stripes. via Tony Buttler.

A formation of three F.8s of the Royal Air Force Flying College based at Manby, late in the type's career when the College provided an aerobatic team for air displays. Air Ministry PRB 23960, via Tony Buttler

was a PAI (Pilot Attack Instructor). Then back to the F.8 and 222 Squadron. Very busy now, but three months later I was posted down the road to Acklington as a Staff PAI.

'Perhaps to go solo and instruct on the Mosquito? No such luck. But just as good, they now had three pre-production Boulton Paul Balliol trainers. A nice little aircraft, powered by a single Merlin (my closest to a Spitfire), but with an Austin 7 cockpit. That is, side-by-side seating, each with a gun-sight and room for golf clubs behind. It had airbrakes too and would turn on a sixpence. Unlike the Meteor, it was necessary to use rudder in turns and it had great torque on take-off. Not perfect for gunnery duals, but the best yet. Several months later I had an engine failure at 15,000ft (4,572m) over the sea, dead sticked it on the airfield and was able to park it in the usual spot thanks to a steerable tail-wheel, which avoided use of brakes to taxi as Meteors and Vampires did. OC Flying thought I was showing off…

'We had an Airspeed Oxford for convenience, a Meteor T.7, Meteor F.4, Meteor F.8 and a Vampire FB.5 to keep our hands in. They made an interesting Christmas photo, but I stalled out in the Meteor 8 as the Oxford turned my way. There was hardly any difference between the Oxford's maximum speed and my minimum, we were at 1,000ft (305m).

'Squadrons of day and night fighters, Vampire and Meteor equipped, visited for three weeks. I was the host of one of the two sections, each taking a Squadron. I scored the target flags, assessed the films, pointed out the errors and flew their aircraft as well as our own. Most were Meteor F.8s but night fighter Squadrons either had the Meteor NF.11 or the Vampire NF.10, neither of which I liked. The NF.11 Meteor was incredibly heavy fore-and-aft, but as light as a Meteor 8 laterally. Radar in the nose prevented fuselage guns, so these were mounted in the wings, up to 26ft (7.9m) apart. The normal round Belt Feed Mechanism would not fit so a new flat BFM was used, resulting in a stoppage rate of one. There is nothing more frustrating than only firing only one round. Later, better links improved the stoppage rate, but with guns so far apart, harmonisation and shooting range was critical. Firing one side only was interesting.

'The Vampire NF.10 night-fighters were a tight squeeze and only used after an Egyptian order for fifty was embargoed. They only had an old-fashioned 3°22' fixed ring sight instead of the customary 2° gyro gunsight.

'My great regret was when a Canadian Squadron of F-86 Sabres came I had the best dispersal but OC Flying decreed that they

Five generations of Fighter Command equipment, showing a formation of Hurricane II LF363, Spitfire PR.19 PM631, Meteor F.8 WL181, Hunter F.6 XJ715 and Lightning F.1 XM190 'G'. All are being flown by pilots of No 111 Squadron, with the Hunter in the 'Black Arrows' overall black scheme. The Meteor did not serve with No 111 Squadron but appears to be wearing the unit's marking for this photo shoot in 1962.
Air Ministry PRB 23828, via Tony Buttler

pilot hopes to see his target before he is seen. There was a Frenchman on my Day Fighter Leaders' course who was always the first to see the target. In those days a speck of dust on the windscreen focussed eyes short when there were no distant clouds.

'Then in November 1953 it was time to move on. A Staff Weapons post at Air Headquarters (AHQ) Malta beckoned. Homing torpedoes and all that, plus some fighter weaponeering. As a Staff Officer one was expected to keep in flying practice by cadging whenever the opportunity occurred. This led me to the naval Hawker Sea Fury, the Percival Pembroke light transport, the Australian Vampires and the 39 Squadron Meteor NF.13. The latter was not very different in handling to the NF.11 – heavy fore-and-aft, light laterally.

'Only those who flew with the Australians in Korea flew the Meteors in action. It was not good. My nearest experience was when I cadged a Meteor 8 from the Malta Target-Towing Flight in 1956. They had no tasks that day, so I found two tow pilots about to fly. They said they were going to do close and battle formation practice and looked a little sheepish when I asked to tag along. We flew North without deviation for longer than I had expected. But I twigged when our leader hung around the coast of Sicily. Etna was supposed to be erupting, but was not. Curiosity overcame our leader as he took us on a wide circuit of the volcano. Then followed a closer, lower, circuit, followed by a low pass over the top. Etna objected and threw up a great belch of rocks. The sky seemed full of them, but miraculously none of us were hit. Imagine the accident report!

'I flew another old Meteor T.7 in December 1958, but that was my last Meteor flight. By then I was flying proper fighters, properly-equipped Hunters and still improving. G-suits, leg restraints, pressure breathing oxygen, low-level ejection and proper helmets – so much that we should have had on Meteors, but even the Hunter did not have navigation aids.

'Yes, I enjoyed the Meteors, but I did not know any better at the time. I had an engine failure once just after take-off, but all was OK and no other problems. I think many crashes were caused by lack of oxygen, it caught out young and old. Some old, bold, aviators rushed off low level and ran out of fuel, not appreciating the new technology. Meteor squadron life was great – bags of booze! Great competition between Squadrons and Wings, of which there were many at that time.'

would go to the other section. My friend enjoyed the F-86, I was jealous. We were impressed when they arrived with individual sonic bangs on the airfield (not then prohibited) and we soon realised how far behind our lovely aircraft were. About this time the Australians flew Meteor 8s in Korea and they proved inadequate at high and low level against MiGs. We were learning and out of date.

'In late 1952 our Balliols were replaced by the new Vampire T.11 – a long overdue aircraft. The early ones only had access through a tiny sunshine roof and the emergency hydraulic system handle could not be stowed without completely undoing all seating harness. Both improved later. Good aircraft for gunnery duals and instrument flying. Our target-towing aircraft were Hawker Tempests when I arrived, but these were later changed to Meteor F.8s. The tow aircraft were better, but the towropes were limited to 180 knots, as they broke at 200 knots. We also used winged targets in addition to the 30ft

x 6ft (9.1m x 1.8m) flag targets. The winged ones crashed spectacularly on return but pilots did not fly into them as regularly as the flags, which had a heavy weight to keep them vertical.

'The only respite from air-to-air firing, which I enjoyed, was during Exercises in which us staff and tug pilots joined in. Some were exciting, there were some close shaves and I particularly remember intercepting an American Convair B-36 bomber. Huge! We had to set our gunsights on 70ft (21.3m) and used our range control on the tailplane! None of us believed our gun-sights and no one got near, on any Squadron. Exercises were great fun but one could be sat strapped in and ready to go for long periods and some were embarrassed by an urgent need to be elsewhere. What to do? I also remember one occasion when climbing to intercept an incoming Republic F-84, still being reported well above and ahead. I did not see it, diving steeper than I was climbing, until I just saw the back end of it, just missing me. A fighter

Foreign Service

One wonders if the British Air Staff and Gloster designer George Carter ever imagined when the F.9/40 Meteor was first conceived that it would be built in such prodigious numbers both for the RAF and the many air forces covered in this chapter. It is believed that some of the information given in this chapter is being published, in English at least, for the first time. Note that further serial number details are given in Appendix One.

Argentina

Argentina purchased one hundred Meteor F Mk.4s in May 1947, of which fifty were diverted from RAF contracts (in order to speed up delivery) and fifty were new-build aircraft. The aircraft were numbered I-001 to I-100. The 'I' indicated 'Interceptor', changing in 1959 to 'C' for 'Caza' (Fighter). After initial pilot training at Moreton Valence and shipment of the aircraft to the Argentine, the Meteor entered service with Regiment 4 de Caza Interceptora (R4Caz) of the Fuerza Aérea Argentina, based at Tandil, towards the end of 1947. The second unit to receive the type was Regiment 6 (R6Caz). Following a reorganisation in 1951, these units became Grupos 2 and 3 de Caza.

The Argentine Meteors saw action only in short-lived coups or revolutions in 1955, when both sides flew Meteors. During the first attempted coup Meteor I-063 shot down a rebel North American AT-6 of the Argentine Navy on 16th June 1955; during the same period, six Meteors flown by escaping rebels landed in Uruguay to seek asylum, I-064 being written off in a forced landing. In a later insurrection on 19th September of the same year I-079, being flown by a rebel pilot, blew up in the air while being flown with petrol in its tanks – although the Derwent could run on petrol, this required adjustments to the fuel system which had not been made. I-079 was one of four Meteors being flown by the rebels. During the same revolution, Meteors flown by loyalist pilots attacked two Argentine Navy destroyers under rebel control, severely damaging one of them.

After their return to a more peaceful routine, in 1959 the Meteor units were re-designated Grupos de Caza Bombardeo (Fighter-Bomber Groups), by which time the Meteors were based at Moron. The surviving Meteors remained in service until the end of 1970.

Australia

The first RAAF Meteor was a Mk.III, EE427 delivered for evaluation in June 1946. It was

C-001, an F.4 of the Fuerza Aérea Argentina. via Phil Butler

C-005, an F.4 of the Fuerza Aérea Argentina, in camouflage, with shark's teeth markings on the underwing tank. via Tony Buttler

renumbered A77-1 after its arrival in Australia, but had a relatively short life with the Aircraft Performance Unit at Laverton, being written off in a heavy landing in February 1947.

With the start of the Korean War in June 1950, RAAF participation as an element of the United Nations' forces demanded the acquisition of jet aircraft to replace the North American Mustangs which were at that time the RAAF's 'front-line' equipment. By 1951 the Chinese had joined the North Korean forces in the conflict, supplementing the obsolete North Korean aircraft with their own Mikoyan MiG-15 swept-wing jet fighters.

Australia was unable to acquire swept-wing North American F-86 Sabres due to the USAF needing all that could be manufactured for its own re-equipment, so the RAAF had to acquire the Meteor instead. This resulted in the delivery of ninety-four F Mk.8s to serve with No 77 Squadron, together with nine T Mk.7s for conversion training. All were diverted from RAF contracts.

No 77 Squadron RAAF was based at Iwakuni in Japan with its Mustangs, and the first Mete-

Meteor F.8 EG-226 of the Belgian Air Force, at the end of a line-up at the Avions Fairey factory, where it was assembled. via Phil Butler

Meteor F.8s being assembled in the Avions Fairey factory at Gosselies in Belgium in April 1952. The nearest aircraft is EG-224, the first to be produced. via Phil Butler

Avions Fairey (becoming ED-13 to ED-32). Finally, a further eleven ex-RAF T.7s were received (ED-33 to ED-43).

As the build-up of NATO air forces continued in the early 1950s, the Belgian Air Force received much larger numbers of the Meteor F.8, a total of 217 being delivered. These included five diverted from the RAF, 67 assembled by Avions Fairey as Gosselies from Gloster or Fokker components and 145 built by N V Fokker at Schiphol. Serial numbers were EG-1 to -145 (Fokker-built), EG-146 to -150 (ex-RAF), EG-151 to -180 assembled by Avions Fairey from Fokker components, EG-201 to -223 (ex-RAF) and EG-224 to -260, assembled by Avions Fairey from Gloster-made components. The Mk.8s served with the following Squadrons:

No 4	Beauvechain	'SV'
No 7	Chievres	'7J'
No 8	Chievres	'OV'
No 9	Chievres	'S2'
No 22	Bierset	'IS'
No 24	Sylt	'XO'
No 25	Brustem	'VT'
No 26	Bierset	'JE'
No 29	Brustem	'MS'
No 33	Brustem	'K5'
No 349	Beauvechain	'GE'
No 350	Beauvechain	'MN'

These squadrons were organised in Wings on the RAF pattern (and were part of the 2nd Allied Tactical Air Force). No 1 Wing consisted of the Beauvechain units, No 5 covered the Sylt squadron, No 7 was at Chievres, No 9 at Liege-Bierset and No 13 at Brustem (later moving to Koksijde). No 24 Squadron at Sylt was later downgraded to a Target-Towing Flight (using the code 'B2') at Sylt, in north Germany, which was one of the armament practice bases used by the Belgian Air Force for air-firing over off-shore ranges.

Many of the above squadrons were later re-equipped with Hawker Hunters. Nos 349 and 350 Squadrons commemorated the service of Belgian-manned RAF squadrons with these numbers during the Second World War.

Later twenty-four Meteor NF.11s were delivered for the night-fighter wing at Beauvechain, replacing de Havilland Mosquito NF.30s with Nos 10 and 11 Squadrons (codes 'KT' and 'ND', respectively). The NF.11s were replaced by Avro Canada CF-100s in 1959.

After the Belgian Air Force Meteors had been retired, a number of surplus ones were purchased (mostly by the contractor Cogea), possibly with the intention of using them on

ors were shipped direct to Japan on board the British aircraft carrier HMS *Warrior* in February 1951. After the squadron pilots finished their jet conversions, the unit moved to Kimpo in South Korea in June 1951. Being outclassed by the North Korean (Chinese) MiG-15s, the Meteors were mostly flown on ground-attack sorties, although a small number of MiG-15s were shot down by No 77, albeit that the Squadron lost a much greater number of Meteors in air-to-air combat, from ground fire, or from accidents. The first MiG 'kill' was claimed by Flying Officer Bruce Gogerly on 1st December 1951, but the main task of the Squadron came to be ground-attack using cannon fire and 60 lb (27kg) Rocket Projectiles (the HVAR type – High Velocity Air Rocket – provided from American stocks). After the war ended, the surviving Meteors were shipped to Australia, and continued to fly with No 77 Squadron at Williamtown, New South Wales. Some of the reserve aircraft from No 77 joined the de Havilland Vampire-equipped No 75 Squadron at the same base. As these two Squadrons began to receive Australian-built North American Sabres, the Meteors were released to serve with the Citizens Air

Force units, Nos 22 and 23 Squadrons at Richmond and Amberley. After their retirement from the Citizen (reserve) units in 1960, fifteen Meteors were converted to drones in Australia, by Fairey Aviation at Bankstown. One Meteor NF.11, the former RAF WM262, flew with an RAAF serial number (A77-3), after being used for 'Blue Boar' missile trials at Woomera, only to crash in 1955.

Belgium

Belgium received forty-eight Meteor F Mk.4s, with deliveries commencing in April 1949. These were given the serial numbers EF-1 to EF-48 and they initially equipped No 349 (code GE-) and 350 (code MN-) Squadrons at Beau-vechain. Some Mk.4s later served with No 4 Squadron (code SV-) and a short-lived 'Auxiliary' squadron.

The first F.4s had been preceded in service by three T.7s, ED-1 to ED-3, delivered in 1948, while a further nine T.7s followed in 1951 as the Belgian Air Force began to receive a much larger number of Meteor F.8s. As the F.8s were delivered, the F.4s were withdrawn and twenty of them were converted to T.7 standard by

Meteor NF.11 OO-ARZ after sale by the Belgian Air Force to COGEA. Although the civilian contractor bought a number of surplus Meteors, this was the only one to be painted in a full civilian colour scheme. via Phil Butler

Belgian Air Force EN6 photographed at Ostend Airport after its withdrawal from military service. The civilian registration OO-ARS can be seen on the fin in the original print. via Phil Butler

Meteor F.8s EG-224, -225 and -227, awaiting delivery from the Avions Fairey works at Gosselies, where they had been assembled from Gloster Aircraft components. via Phil Butler

Meteor FAB 4399 of the Brazilian Air Force, showing the rocket rails for launching unguided HVAR projectiles. 4399 was an 'additional' aircraft built up from spares and salvaged components in Brazil. Military Aircraft Photographs

Fighter Aviation Group) After their shipment to Brazil, assembly of the Meteors began in May 1953 and they served mainly in a tactical role until 1966, when the F.8s were withdrawn at the end of their fatigue lives. Although the Meteor had been purchased with the interceptor role in mind, Brazil was unable to acquire the radar infrastructure to enable this to be put into practice, so the units trained in the tactical role, including the use of HVAR rockets. Some of the TF-7s lasted rather longer in the training role, the last one being withdrawn in October 1971.

Canada

One F.4 (VT196) was loaned for jet engine reheat experiments, as detailed in the 'Engine Testbeds' section. In reality it was on loan to the Canadian National Research Council, the organisation funding the afterburner development being carried out at A V Roe Canada. VT196 was not the only Meteor to serve on the strength of the RCAF, since three Mk.III Meteors were also taken on RCAF charge. These were EE282, EE311 and EE361. EE311 was specifically loaned to Turbo Research Ltd to give the RCAF some jet experience, while the other two were in Canada for trials. Various

A Meteor III, EE311, during winterisation trials in Canada. via Tony Buttler

government contracts (on which Cogea already flew other ex-military aircraft). In the event, although some were sold in the Congo, most were scrapped. The aircraft were:

OO-ARO (EN-18)   OO-ARV (EG-178)
OO-ARP (EN-21)   OO-ARW (EN-5)
OO-ARQ (EN-16)   OO-ARX (EN-5)
OO-ARR (EN-2)   OO-ARZ (EN-19)
OO-ARS (EN-6)   OO-GEV (EN-20)
OO-ART (EG-164)   OO-GEZ (EN-23)
OO-ARU (EG-162)

Brazil
The Brazilian Air Force (Força Aérea Brasileira) acquired its Meteors in 1953. At the time Brazil was short of convertible currency, preventing it from buying North American F-86 Sabres or other American aircraft. The deal to acquire the Meteor was only possible because the British government agreed to accept supplies of Brazilian cotton to the value of the contract, in lieu of pounds or US dollars. The order covered ten T.7 Meteors (designated the TF-7 in Brazil) and sixty F.8s (designated F-8 in Brazil). All of these were new aircraft, although the T.7s had been intended for delivery to the RAF as WS142 to WS151 before being reassigned to Brazil. The final five F.8s had been built for Egypt but never delivered because of arms embargoes placed on deliveries to countries in the Middle East.

The Brazilian Meteors served with three main units, GAVCA 1°/1°, GAVCA 1°/14° and GAVCA 2°/1°. (GAVCA = Grupo de Aviação de Caça –

Meteors 261, 262 and 263 of the Royal Danish Air Force, possibly on their delivery flight.
Gloster Aircraft Company DM/2/A, via Phil Butler

other RAF Meteors were temporarily based in Canada for cold-weather trials at the Winter Experimental Establishment, Namao, but of these only F.4 RA421 was taken on RCAF charge for a short period of time in 1948, the others remaining on RAF strength.

Denmark

In 1949, the Danish government ordered twenty Meteor F.4s, which were at first delivered to the 3rd Air Flotilla of the Danish Navy at Karup in October of that year. At the time, the Danish Army and Navy had separate air arms, but these were amalgamated into an independent Royal Danish Air Force (Kongelige Danske Flyvevåbnet) on 1st October 1950, at which point the 3rd Air Flotilla became No 723 Squadron. The F.4s also flew with No 724 Squadron at Karup, until this unit re-equipped with the F.8.

Meteor F.8 487, of the Royal Danish Air Force, on the runway at Moreton Valence shortly before delivery to Denmark. Russell Adams P121/51, via Tony Buttler

Royal Danish Air Force Mk.8s (499, 495, 488, 498 and 500) photographed on 4th June 1951, at which time camouflaged Meteors were a rarity, the RAF only changing to camouflage in 1954.
Russell Adams P.254/51

Royal Danish Air Force NF.11 501, photographed air-to-air on 12th November 1952. Armstrong Whitworth NF155, via Ray Williams

Royal Danish Air Force TT.20 508 is shown in this shot, taken at Karup, with the M L Type G target winch prominent on the starboard wing, inboard of the engine. RDAF, via Phil Butler

Another shot of 508, barely distinguishable from an NF.11 from this angle, apart from the towing gear visible below the fuselage roundel. via Ray Williams

During 1950 a batch of nine Meteor T.7s was ordered to equip an Operational Training Unit and the Flying School, while twenty F.8s were ordered to replace the F.4s and were delivered during 1951 to re-equip No 724 Squadron. The F.4s then joined the T.7s in the Flying School.

Early in 1952, twenty NF.11 night fighters were ordered, these aircraft being diverted from an RAF contract (whereas all the previous Danish Meteors had been built against Danish contracts). The NF.11s (Nos 501 to 520) were delivered between November 1952 and March 1953 and equipped No 723 Squadron, in place of the F.4s. When their service came to an end, six NF.11s were returned to Armstrong Whitworth Aircraft and converted to TT.20 target-tugs for continued service. Four of these aircraft were later sold to Svensk Flygtjänst, the Swedish contractor that took over the provision of targets for the Danish armed services, as described under 'Sweden'.

Ecuador

In May 1954 the Ecuadorean government ordered twelve Meteor FR.9s to equip a squadron of the Fuerza Aérea Ecuatoriana, these being ex-RAF aircraft refurbished by Glosters. Deliveries were made later in 1954-55, the aircraft being numbered 701 to 712 inclusive. The Meteors remained in service with Escuadrón de Combate 2111 at Taura until the late 1970s, when they were replaced by SEPECAT

Jaguars. A number of examples still survive in museums in Ecuador.

Egypt

The Royal Egyptian Air Force ordered the first batch (of three) of Meteor F.4s in 1948, and, after several interruptions because of arms embargoes, eventually received twelve aircraft. Unusually, seven of these F.4s came from the Armstrong Whitworth production line, with export contracts normally being fulfilled by Glosters. Three new Meteor T.7s were also delivered. Similar embargoes interfered with

This photograph shows Meteor FR Mk.9 712 of the Ecuadorian Air Force, on a test flight before delivery. The camera ports are covered by temporary panels. Russell Adams P515/54, via Phil Butler

deliveries of Meteor Mk.8s, of which twenty-four were on order at one point. The embargoes resulted in the diversion of most of the intended new aircraft to other customers. Eventually, a batch of twelve new Egyptian F.8s was completed at Moreton Valence, only to be interrupted by another embargo after four of them

Two Egyptian aircraft, F.4 1401 and T.7 1400, during a sortie over Gloucestershire in 1950. Russell Adams P16/50D, via Phil Butler

had been ferried to Egypt. The balance of eight new aircraft were actually then diverted (ironically) to Israel and Brazil. After further delays, the balance of eight aircraft was made up of refurbished ex-RAF aircraft, which were delivered in 1955, together with three ex-RAF T.7s, and six NF.13s, also ex-RAF.

During the Suez campaign in 1956, one of the NF.13s intercepted and damaged an RAF Vickers Valiant bomber, but little else is known of the Meteor's service in what was, by then, the Egyptian Air Force (no longer 'Royal'). The Meteors were replaced by Soviet-supplied aircraft in 1958.

France

The first French Meteors were two Mk.4s, both of them ex-RAF. The first was F-WEPQ (previously EE523 and later F-BEPQ), supplied for evaluation in 1948, while the second was RA491, the former MetroVick Beryl testbed, after it had been modified by Air Service Training Ltd at Hamble to test-fly the SNECMA Atar axial-flow turbojet in France.

Meteor T.7 MK7-228 of the French military, photographed at Toulouse-Blagnac in 1964. It served with the EPNER, the French military test pilot and test engineers school (École du Personnel Navigant d'Essais et de Réception) based at Istres. The EPNER badge appears below the forward cockpit glazing.
Military Aircraft Photographs

French Air Force NF11-25, photographed at Bitteswell on 6th May 1953. Armstrong Whitworth NF185, via Ray Williams

NF14-747 was an ex-RAF aircraft (WS747) which passed to the French Air Force for use on experimental work. via Tony Buttler

The next delivery was of the two embargoed Syrian T.7s (Syrian nos. 91 and 92). These were followed in turn by eleven more T.7s to carry out pilot conversion training for the night-fighter unit Escadre de Chasse (EC) 30. Then followed nine NF.11 versions to undertake work as equipment testbeds at the Centre d'Essais en Vol (CEV) at Melun-Villaroche and thirty-two NF.11s to equip EC.30 at Tours, replacing that unit's Mosquitoes. The EC.30 NF.11s were replaced in turn by Sud-Ouest Vautour IINs in 1957/58, with some of the Meteors then going to the night-fighter training unit (CITT 346) at Merignac. The first twenty-five NF.11s were delivered from January 1953 onwards, while the sixteen to make up the balance of the EC.30 aircraft followed during 1954 – the latter sixteen being delivered after RAF service, while the original twenty-five NF.11s were diverted from RAF contracts and never served with the RAF. The NF.11s were numbered 'NF11-1' to 'NF11-41', while the T.7s were 'F1' to 'F11'.

Following these acquisitions, small numbers of further aircraft were received. These included an ex-RAF T.7 delivered to the CEV as F-BEAR in April 1955 (believed to be a conversion trainer for the CEV fleet of NF.11s). F-BEAR crashed after take-off at Melun on 28th February 1957. The remaining deliveries were all night-fighter versions. First were two ex-RAF NF Mk.14s, WS747 and WS796, which were delivered to the CEV later in 1955, becoming 'NF14-747' and '-796'. The CEV then received two surplus RAF NF Mk.13s in June 1956. Much later, in 1974, six surplus TT Mk.20s were sold to France, all being ferried with the markings 'F-ZABD'; these were required as sources of spares and did not fly again after delivery. The large CEV fleet, gradually reducing through attrition, was not entirely retired until the late 1980s.

Israel

The Meteor was acquired by the Israeli Defence Forces/Air Force (IDF/AF) because the United States declined to provide military materiel to Israel during the first years of the country's independence. An uneasy political situation led to Britain, as an arms supplier to both Israel and the hostile surrounding Arab countries, trying to balance supplies of arms so as to give no state an overwhelming advantage. Many arms embargoes were enforced, resulting in arms orders being cancelled or deferred until tense situations had relaxed.

The Meteors delivered in 1953 were the first jet fighters acquired by the Israeli Air Force. The first delivery comprised four T.7 trainers and eleven F.8 fighters. The fighters were similar to

Two Israeli F.8s photographed during take-off, probably during their delivery flight – note that underwing fuel tanks are fitted. Russell Adams P21/54, via Phil Butler

Meteor T.7 I-1 of the Royal Netherlands Air Force, photographed at Moreton Valence on 17th January 1949 shortly before delivery to Holland. This aircraft was originally the Gloster demonstrator, G-AKPK. Gloster GM63, via Tony Buttler

Meteor F.8 I-94 of the Royal Netherlands Air Force, as delivered in silver overall and the code '7E-1' of No 327 Squadron. Flash Aviation, via Coen van den Heuvel

Two views of Belgian and Dutch Meteors being assembled in the Fokker factory at Schiphol.
Via Tony Buttler

those of the RAF apart from being fitted to fire American HVAR type rocket projectiles (which apparently they could obtain). All these were new aircraft, although they included three originally ordered by Egypt that had been embargoed. They entered service with No 117 Squadron, which also operated the FR.9 versions received later.

In 1955, as part of the 'balancing act' between Israel and the Arab states, seven refurbished RAF FR Mk.9s and two more T Mk.7s were delivered to Israel, concurrently with orders for similar aircraft supplied to Egypt and Syria. In the following year, six ex-RAF NF Mk.13 night fighters were assigned to Israel, but because of the impending Suez crisis, three of these aircraft were embargoed, with their delivery delayed until after the war. The NF 13s served with No 119 Squadron. Meanwhile five more examples of the T Mk.7 were received from Avions Fairey, converted from Belgian F.4s and fitted with Mk.8 tail units; these aircraft were delivered after the UK had declined to supply further T.7 aircraft.

Netherlands

The Royal Netherlands Air Force began to acquire Meteor F.4s in June 1947, when the first contracts were placed with Gloster Aircraft. The first deliveries were made to the Fighter School at Twenthe in 1948, with further aircraft going to Nos 322 and 327 Squadrons at Soesterberg and Nos 323 and 326 Squadrons at Leeuwarden. The first 34 aircraft (I-20 to I-54) were new machines built for the Dutch, but they were later supplemented by ex-RAF aircraft numbered I-55 to I-80. The F.4 Meteors also served with Nos 324, 325 and 328 Squadrons. The Dutch had also ordered T.7 versions to serve with the Fighter School, the first batch (numbered I-1 to I-20) included the Gloster demonstrator G-AKPK (which became I-1), six new aircraft and thirteen ex-RAF examples.

By the time the F.8 was chosen to replace the F.4, with further expansion of the RNethAF, it had been decided that licence production for the Belgian and Dutch air forces would be undertaken by N V Fokker at Schiphol, with the licence being signed in July 1948. This resulted in 155 Meteor F.8s being built for the Dutch as I-101 to I-255, with five ex-RAF aircraft being delivered as I-90 to I-94. The remainder of the Fokker production was delivered to Belgium, either directly or as kits of parts for assembly by Avions Fairey. The Mark 8s saw service with the following Squadrons:

No 322	Soesterberg	'3W'
No 323	Leeuwarden	'Y9'
No 324	Leeuwarden	'3P'
No 325	Leeuwarden	'4R'
No 326	Leeuwarden	'9I'
No 327	Soesterberg	'7E'
No 328	Soesterberg	'8S'

Gloster Meteor 79

The Squadron markings were in continuation of the style of unit markings used by the RAF during the Second World War, the Squadron numbers also commemorating Dutch-manned RAF units from the same period. The Meteor Mk.8 was replaced in Dutch service by the Hawker Hunter, from 1956.

New Zealand

The RNZAF received Mk.3 EE395 for evaluation in January 1946. It was renumbered as NZ6001 and served with the Jet Propulsion Unit at Ohakea, which was formed to give RNZAF pilots jet experience. The aircraft was placed in storage during 1947. In September 1950 the Meteor was flown to Hobsonville where it became instructional airframe INST 147 before being scrapped in 1957.

South Africa

The SAAF received one Meteor Mk.III, EE429, on loan from the RAF, for evaluation purposes. EE429 was returned to the RAF in 1949.

Sweden

Although the Royal Swedish Air Force, the Flygvapnet, had considered purchasing versions of the Meteor, particularly night-fighter variants, none were acquired, the air arm relying instead on home-produced SAAB jets and versions of the de Havilland Vampire and Venom. The first Meteors to fly in Sweden were two T Mk.7s, purchased by Svensk Flygtjänst AB, to carry out target-towing duties under contract for the Swedish military services. The two aircraft were registered SE-CAS and SE-CAT, both of them being ex-RAF machines refurbished by Gloster Aircraft, respectively ex-WF833 and WH128. These two were delivered in 1956 and served with a number of ex-Fleet Air Arm Fairey Firefly target-tugs that had been purchased from Fairey Aviation at the same time.

In January 1959 SE-CAT was written-off in an accident and Svensk Flygtjänst AB was then able to buy the Gloster demonstrator G-ANSO as a replacement. This was registered as SE-DCC and was delivered in September 1959 after it had its Mk.8 type tail unit replaced by the normal Mk.7 type. SE-DCC survives in the museum at Ugglarp, while SE-CAS is preserved at the Flygvapenmuseum Malmen at Linkoping.

Finally, Svensk Flygtjänst acquired four TT.20 Meteors from the Royal Danish Air Force. These had been modified from NF.11s previously delivered to Denmark. The aircraft were registered in Sweden as SE-DCF, -DCG, -DCH and -DCI, previously RDAF numbers 512, 517, 508 and 519, respectively. Svensk Flygtjänst had contracts to carry out target-towing duties for the Danish military as well as for Sweden.

Syria

As with Meteors supplied to Egypt and Israel, deliveries to Syria were disrupted by intermittent arms embargoes, arising from attempts by the United Nations and the arms suppliers to defuse the potential for Arab-Israeli conflicts, while retaining 'influence' by controlling their supplies of spare parts. Another imperative of the time was the perceived need to keep Soviet influence in the area to a minimum, although this policy eventually failed.

Twelve Meteor F.8s diverted from RAF contracts and two new-build T.7s were taken over by Syrian pilots at Moreton Valence after orders had been placed in January 1950. The order had been delayed because of an embargo imposed during 1951. The Mk.8 were delivered, starting in December 1952, but the T.7s were still at Gloster's works, where they had been used for pilot conversion, when a new embargo was enforced. The two T.7s were then delivered to France instead. Although it has been reported that two ex-RAF T.7s were delivered to Syria at a later date, we have been unable to trace any evidence to support this report.

In 1956 further deliveries were made to Syria, comprising seven Meteor F.8s, two FR.9 and six NF.13s. All of these were surplus RAF aircraft. No details are known of Syrian service, although supplies of Soviet aircraft types soon replaced all previous equipment in the Air Force.

Meteor NF Mk.13 '476' of the Syrian Arab Air Force, photographed at Bitteswell on 1st July 1954. Armstrong Whitworth NF366, via Ray Williams

Engine Testbeds, Trials Aircraft, Drones and Civilian Meteors

Engine Testbeds

The earlier chapters have given some details of specific aircraft which were used for trials and testing, but many more Meteors were used in this type of work. Jet engine manufacturers employed quite a number of Meteors as testbeds. The Meteor had quite a robust airframe and was therefore suitable for flight-testing engines that were much more powerful than its normal Rolls-Royce Derwents, which each normally developed 3,500 lb (15.6kN) of static thrust. With the most powerful power plants, such as the Armstrong Siddeley Sapphire offering potentially 7,000 lb (31.1kN) of thrust each the airframe would have been overstressed if full power was applied in level flight, but this did not prevent the use of full thrust in a steep climb. Equally, many tests involved taking performance measurements, or checking engine behaviour, at less than full power and still gave the opportunity for obtaining data that could never be measured in a test cell on the ground.

Of course the first Meteor testbeds were all of the original F.9/40 prototypes as described in Chapter Two and it is worth listing them again for reference. DG202 flew with Rover-built W.2B/23 engines, DG203 flew at different times with Power Jets W.2/500 and W.2/700 engines. DG204 had Metropolitan-Vickers F.2 engines and would have been joined by DG210, which

was, however, never completed. DG205 was the Rover W.2B test aircraft and DG206 and DG207 were completed with Halford H.1 engines, while DG208 had the Rolls-Royce W.2B/23 and DG209 flew with Rolls-Royce W.2B/37 Derwents. Of the production Meteor Mk.Is, normally Welland-powered, EE215 was used for engine trials with its original Wellands at RAE Farnborough and then from May 1946 for some reheat experiments at Power Jets at Bitteswell after being fitted with W.2/700 engines. The NGTE was formed out of the former Power Jets company, after the latter had ceased engine design and development in 1946.

One pioneering engine development theme to involve the Meteor was the research undertaken into afterburning. Afterburning (or reheat) involves the injection of vapourised fuel into the high-temperature efflux from the turbine, resulting in ignition and further expansion of the exhaust gases and increased thrust, albeit at the expense of a much-increased fuel consumption. Use of the technique was postulated as early as 1943, when a programme of research by RAE into a full-scale jet exhaust reheat system was instigated by the Ministry of Supply. This was reported in two RAE Technical Notes, written in February and June 1944 respectively, under the title *Thrust Boosting of a*

Another official photograph, showing EE223/G fitted with Rolls-Royce Derwent engines in place of the Wellands normally installed in the Mk.I. It is believed this photograph was taken at Rolls-Royce's Church Broughton airfield. ATP 15023B, via Tony Buttler

Simple Jet Propulsion Engine. These experiments were begun using Whittle W.1A No 3 which was rated at 1,000 lb (4.4kN) thrust and then, after the results had shown that the concept held good prospects, the effort was transferred to a Rolls-Royce Welland (W.2B/23) installed in EE215.

In mid-1944 some urgency was given to the reheat research by the opening of the bombardment of London by German V.1 flying bombs and it was at this point that the decision was made to try and apply the principle of reheat to the Meteor, which resulted in the initial trials with EE215. It was proposed that the speed of Meteor Mk.Is could be boosted by afterburning when they were being used to chase the unpiloted V.1 missiles over southern England. However, the early repulse of the V.1 attacks reduced the gravity of the situation and the research settled down to a steadier rate of progress. Performance tests with EE215 at maximum reheat conditions at various heights were compared with the standard aircraft and a

The Meteor I EE227/G after conversion to test the Rolls-Royce RB.50 Trent turbo-prop engines. Photograph taken at Hucknall in September 1945. IWM MH.6425

gain in true airspeed of 46mph (74km/h) was obtained at all altitudes up to 12,000ft (3,658m), together with an apparent 65% increase in fuel consumption. The effect of reheat on the rate of climb was a marked increase of 46%, but during 'dry' running (that is, with reheat switched off) the extra weight and drag of the installation apparently pushed the speed to below normal F Mk.I levels. This series of tests, which lasted some thirty flights, was concluded by the transfer of work to Power Jets Ltd. Meteor I EE221 was another early production aircraft to be used to test a reheat system, also with W2/700 engines.

In truth the initial trials undertaken with Mk.I Meteors had shown that, from an operational viewpoint, the early reheat systems suffered from numerous installation and functional defects. Eventually a new system was fitted to

Mk.III EE291 using its Derwent I engines which had been considerably cleaned up and simplified; if found successful, it was intended to fit it to operational aeroplanes as a means of increasing the thrust of the engines for short emergency periods. EE291 was allotted to Power Jets at Bitteswell in April 1945 for this next series of trials and the early results obtained with the equipment were encouraging. With the reheat in operation an increase of 23mph (37km/h) was realised at 5,000ft (1,524m) against the figure for the aircraft in its standard condition. It was also observed that reheating could be maintained in a climb up to 27,000ft (8,230m) although at a considerably reduced intensity above 14,000ft (4,267m).

A component failure necessitated the installation of a new pair of engines of an 'improved design', however, the performance of both of

these units with reheat was found to be inferior to the first pair – the level speed increase was now a mere 5mph (8km/h). A crash terminated this investigation on 21st July 1945 (EE291 was being displayed to Power Jets' employees during an event at the company's Whetstone works in Leicestershire when it was lost). Nevertheless, enough had been learnt to show that, although the new system was undoubtedly more reliable in operation than that fitted to the Mk.Is, individual engines needed to be adjusted in order to obtain the optimum performance. The first public demonstration of reheat was given at Farnborough in September 1949 by Meteor Mk.IV RA435 during the annual flying display. In the event no Meteor service aircraft was to be fitted with reheat but this research laid the foundations for its adoption by later generations of combat aircraft.

Another Mk.I, EE223, received W.2B/37 Derwents and was used for 'intensive flying trials' by Rolls-Royce, before being sold to Power Jets Ltd in November 1945. Maximum level speed trials recorded with EE223 flown during February and March 1945 showed that, with the W.2B/37 running at 16,850rpm and at an aircraft all-up-weight of 11,900 lb (5,398kg), a speed of 465mph (748km/h) was reached at 16,000ft (4,877m) and a combat level speed

An air-to-air shot of the Trent Meteor. Real Photographs, via Tony Buttler

Another angle on the Trent Meteor, showing the additional finlets on the tailplane needed to counteract the prop-wash. ATP 14091D, via Phil Butler

Meteor 4 RA435 showing its rearwards-extended engine nacelles during its time as a testbed for Derwents fitted with re-heat (afterburning). This photo was taken during the 1949 SBAC Display at Farnborough. Tony Buttler

over the height range sea level to 25,000ft (7,620m) of between 458mph and 465mph (737km/h to 748km/h). This aircraft was struck off charge on 28th April 1946 and was superseded on Derwent intensive flying trials at Rolls-Royce (from July 1945 to June 1947) by Mk.III EE339. This aircraft also went to the National Gas Turbine Establishment as an instructional airframe. Later it returned to the RAF, where it served with No 500 (RAuxAF) Squadron.

The number of research and development projects that were under way required several further Meteors to be delivered to Rolls-Royce, including EE360 for development of the Derwent Mk.V (for the Meteor F Mk.IV) from December 1945, which in the process effectively made it the prototype Mk.IV. It finished its life as instructional airframe 6867M. EE517, another production Mk.IV, was also used for Derwent Mk.V development at Rolls-Royce from May 1946. RA435 and VT196 were also involved in Derwent V development, but these examples were then transferred to work on afterburner development.

Perhaps the most interesting example of an engine testbed was Mk.I EE227 which, after front-line service with No 616 Squadron, was sent to Rolls-Royce in March 1945 to be fitted with Rolls-Royce RB.50 turbo-prop engines, making it the first 'prop-jet' in the world to fly. The RB.50 was named the Trent, not to be confused with the present-day Trent which is an unrelated turbofan engine designed for wide-bodied airliners. Here the original Trent was a Derwent turbo-jet engine fitted with a gearbox to drive a propeller and gave 1,000 lb (4.4kN) of thrust plus 800hp (597kW) shaft horse power. A complete unit with an airscrew was hangar-tested for the first time in March 1945, the blade diameter being restricted by the Meteor's undercarriage which was 6in (15.2cm) longer than standard. To go with the new powerplant, EE227 also had more ballast in the nose which replaced the guns and their ammunition; however, it proved impossible to get EE227's weight below 13,865 lb (6,289kg).

The first flight was made at Church Broughton on 20th September 1945 with Eric Greenwood in the cockpit and EE227 immedi-

ately displayed the shortest take-off yet seen by a Meteor. After the first flight the leading half of the tailplane had two small fins fitted near to the tips to help correct some directional instability generated by the increased torque of the propellers. Capt Eric Brown also flew EE227 and recorded that the aircraft was easier to taxi than the pure jet Meteor because a more positive response was available from the propellers.

The climb was good and the time taken to reach the service ceiling was near identical to the Meteor fitted with Derwent II power units. There was also less directional snaking compared to the standard jet-powered fighter. Top speed was 440mph (708km/h) at 10,000ft (3,048m) and, compared to pure jet engines, fuel consumption was very low and the throttle could be slammed fully open without trouble.

Meteor 4 RA435 shown after conversion to test an early afterburner system on the Rolls-Royce Derwent. This testbed was demonstrated at the 1949 SBAC Show at Farnborough. Rolls-Royce H3338, via Phil Butler

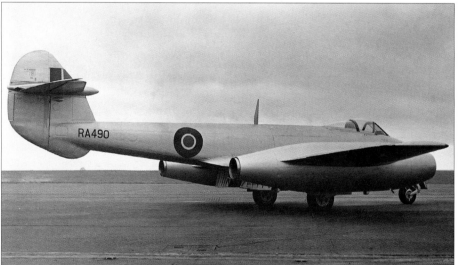

The Beryl Meteor, RA490, showing the later installation of the MetroVick engines, this time not slung under the wings. ATP 17024C, via Tony Buttler

The Beryl Meteor, RA490, photographed at RAF Pershore, showing the large nacelles needed for the MetroVick Beryl engines. via Phil Butler

Another view of the Beryl Meteor RA490. Phil Butler

The landing speed was higher than normal but this was a by-product of the higher weight.

In fully fine pitch the airscrews acted like giant airbrakes resulting in nose-down pitch and the original diameter of 7ft 11in (2.4m) was later reduced to 4ft 10⅛in (1.5m), with the range of pitch also drastically reduced. As such the Trent now produced 1,400 lb (6.2kN) of thrust and 350hp (261kW) shaft horse power. EE227 was used by A&AEE for dummy deck-landing trials, in addition to general prop-jet development at Rolls-Royce during the period April 1945 to October 1948; after 1948 it was only used for engine ground running. Altogether this programme supplied plenty of data for the turbo-prop development programmes that followed.

The array of Meteor airframes adapted for use as engine testbeds also included the following:

EE480   Allotted for tests of the W.2/700 engine at Power Jets Ltd, Bitteswell, from 9th May 1946 until December 1949. This aircraft later became an instructional airframe as 6983M.

RA435   This aircraft was originally delivered to Rolls-Royce for Derwent V development

RA490, the former Beryl Meteor, after conversion to a deflected-thrust testbed with Rolls-Royce Nene engines, photographed at Farnborough in July 1955. F G Swanborough, via Peter Green

work which began in August 1947. It was later flown with afterburners, extended rear nacelles and variable nozzles, flying as such on 10th June 1949 although the reheat was not used in flight until later that month. It was shown at the 1949 SBAC Display. It was returned to the RAF at St Athan in December 1951 to become instructional airframe 7131M.

RA490   Used to test the Metropolitan-Vickers Beryl, in this case the F.2 Series 4 which was a development of the engine flown previously in the F.9/40 prototype DG204. The latter had required underslung nacelles because the F.2 could not fit between the wing spars but on RA490 a modified wing centre had inverted U-sections in both front and rear spars which could accommodate different engines with sufficient ground clearance. The engines were installed at Glosters in 1948 and aircraft was shown at the 1948 SBAC Display by MetroVick. RA490 then went to NGTE at Bitteswell in January 1949 for engine development work, after Metropolitan-Vickers' gas turbine interests had been transferred to Armstrong Siddeley. With the Beryl RA490 could attain 40,000ft (12,192m) in 7.5 minutes. This aircraft was later reassigned for 'jet deflection' experiments (see later).

RA491   The first suggestion to fit a pair of 6,500 lb (28.9kN) Rolls-Royce AJ.65 (Avon) axial engines into a Meteor airframe was made in 1945. The estimated performance figures showed a sea level top speed of over 615mph (990km/h), 565mph (909km/h) at 30,000ft (9,144m), time to that height 2.2 minutes and ceiling over 53,000ft (16,154m). It was Air Vice Marshal J N Boothman who made the initial enquiry about the concept and the Ministry of Aircraft Production said that it would like to go ahead with an experimental installation. However, on 10th December 1945 Boothman declared that 'attractive as the proposition is to us, I cannot but think this is merely putting new wine into old bottles'. He felt such a move would keep the Meteor in the first line as a high performance aircraft for some considerable time but added that the whole problem of a new interceptor should be viewed from the angle of fitting similar or more powerful engines in a completely modern design, following the Meteor standard of size and general arrangement.

Eventually, in December 1948, F Mk.4 RA491 arrived at Rolls-Royce direct from the production line to have two 6,000 lb (26.7kN) thrust RA.2 Avons installed; this modification also required a strengthened centre wing. The nacelles had to be 25% bigger than the usual form and Bill Waterton first flew the aircraft on 29th April 1949 as the first aircraft to be powered purely by Avons (although development engines had

flown in a mixed powerplant Avro Lancastrian). It was also the most powerful Meteor flown so far and in April 1950 it acquired 6,500 lb (28.9kN) RA3s. In practice, with these units, RA491 reached 40,000ft (12,192m) in 2.7 minutes and 50,000ft (15,240m) in 3.65 minutes.

RA491's career was spent mostly with Rolls-Royce although it also served with the National Gas Turbine Establishment at Bitteswell from May to July 1950. It was shown at the 1950 SBAC Display at Farnborough and it was provisionally allotted as instructional airframe 6879M for intended use at Cranwell. However, it was dispatched instead to Air Service Training (AST) at Hamble in 1951 and was later sold to France via AST and used to test that country's SNECMA Atar axial turbo-jets. It was delivered to France in December 1952, after the 5,181 lb (23.0kN) thrust Atar 101.B2 units had been installed at Hamble.

VT196   This aircraft, initially a standard Meteor F Mk.4, was flown by Rolls-Royce for Derwent V development at Hucknall from July 1948. The Derwent Mk.V was the normal power plant for the Meteor 4. However, the aircraft was later fitted with afterburners for basic research into re-heat technology which pushed the engine's thrust up to 4,400 lb (19.6kN). In July 1953 VT196 was dispatched to Canada for further trials with the Schmidt afterburner. Here it was on loan to the Canadian National Research Council, but during this period it was officially on charge with the Royal Canadian Air Force. The CNRC trials appear to have been completed in June 1955, being related to the development of afterburners for the Avro Orenda axial-flow turbojet, which (in non-afterburner form) was used in the Avro CF-100 and the later Marks of the North American Sabre jet fighter built in Canada by Canadair Ltd. VT196 was then returned to England and converted to a U Mk.15 drone. This aircraft's career actually lasted fifteen years and probably encompassed more variety than any other Meteor.

VZ517   This Meteor Mk.8 was delivered to Rolls-Royce Ltd for Derwent 8 development work (for the standard engine fitted to the

Meteor Mk.8) from 1950, initially to deal with some surging problems. It was then turned over to Armstrong-Siddeley Motors Ltd at Bitteswell for trials with that company's 8,000 lb (35.6kN) thrust Screamer rocket motor from July 1953, making its first flight with the rocket mounted in a re-stressed ventral fuel tank on 17th September 1953 and remaining in use as such until December 1955 (some sources state that flight clearance was only given in December 1955). The Screamer was a controllable-thrust rocket engine intended for application to mixed-power-plant fighter aircraft then under development and it was intended to be the powerplant for the Avro 720 fighter, which was ordered in prototype form only to be cancelled in favour of the Saunders-Roe P.177. VZ517 was sent to RAF Halton in April 1956 for ground instructional use as 7322M, after the Screamer project was cancelled during the previous month.

VZ608   Another aircraft delivered to Rolls-Royce at Hucknall, in March 1951, for further development of Derwents with afterburners. From June 1953 it was used for reverse-thrust experiments, still with Derwents. Then in June 1955 VZ608 had a Rolls-Royce RB.108 jet-lift engine installed in the fuselage behind the cockpit in the main fuel tank bay for some vertical take-off experiments, but it still retained the Derwents. The conversion was undertaken by F G Miles Ltd and the aircraft flew with the lift jet in place, but without being lit, on 18th May 1956. The RB.108 was finally started in the air on 23rd October; it was usually not lit until after take-off but it was found that the maximum available vertical thrust was sufficient to keep VZ608 at its correct altitude. From September 1962 VZ608 was in use for ground-erosion experiments (still with the RB.108 installed) until struck off charge in 1965. It survives as an exhibit at the Newark Air Museum.

WA820   Two 7,600 lb (33.8kN) thrust Armstrong-Siddeley Sapphire axial engines were installed in F Mk.8 WA820 during March 1950 at Gloster's Moreton Valence works, although it did not fly until 14th August 1950. The installa-

The Avon Meteor, RA491, photographed at Moreton Valence after conversion by Rolls-Royce – it returned to Gloster's airfield for investigation of airframe vibration after its first flight at Hucknall. Russell Adams P23/50, via Phil Butler

WA820, the Sapphire Meteor, photographed at the 1950 SBAC Display. The round marking on the nose is the Hawker Siddeley Group logo. Note the enlarged tail 'bumper' to prevent the rear of the engine nacelles striking the ground during nose-high landings. via Phil Butler

The Sapphire Meteor, WA820, photographed over the Bristol Channel while on a flight from Moreton Valence. Russell Adams P15/50D, via Phil Butler

tion made this the most powerful Meteor of all and it required substantial airframe strengthening to accommodate so much power; in particular, because the wing front spars had to arch over the Sapphires they had to be heavily reinforced – the engines could not be underslung since this would have needed an abnormally long undercarriage. WA820 was shown at the 1950 and 1951 SBAC Displays with these engines in place and was mostly used by the engine manufacturer, being based at Bitteswell from March 1951 to April 1952. It was also flown at the Central Fighter Establishment, West Raynham, simulating the climbing performance of a rocket-powered fighter in May/June 1952. After these flights it returned to Armstrong Siddeley Motors at Bitteswell in July 1952, until being retired to RAF Halton as an instructional

The Soar Meteor, WA982, in flight at the time of the 1954 SBAC Display – the aircraft could maintain height on the power of the Soars alone. The Soar engine was intended to power missiles, but was cancelled in 1956.
Rolls-Royce HN1654, via Phil Butler

A view of a Rolls-Royce RB.93 Soar turbojet on the port wingtip of the testbed (WA982) flown by Rolls-Royce. The shot was taken at Hucknall.
Rolls-Royce HN1235 via Tony Buttler

airframe in April 1954 as 7141M. On 31st August 1951 R B Prickett, a test pilot working for Armstrong-Siddeley Motors, took WA820 from a standing start to 39,373ft (12,000m) in 189.5 seconds, a new time-to-height record.

WA982 Use as a testbed for the small Rolls-Royce RB.93 Soar jet made this the first four-engined Meteor, with its normal Derwents still in place together with Soars on each wingtip. The aircraft arrived at Hucknall in November 1952 for the installation of these expendable engines, which were primarily intended for target and missile applications, and in this form it was demonstrated at the 1954 SBAC Display at Farnborough. After finishing its Rolls-Royce career in March 1956 (when the RB.93 was cancelled) and being stored, it went to the NGTE in March 1957 for a short time, before being passed to Flight Refuelling Ltd later in 1957 for conversion to U Mk.16 drone standard.

The second 'four-engined' Meteor was the French NF Mk.11 'NF11-3' which was converted to test two SFECMAS 1,323 lb (5.9kN) thrust S-600 ramjet engines mounted in pods outboard of the Derwents. This modification was made in 1954 and in the following year the

S-600s were replaced by the larger 2,513 lb (11.2kN) thrust S-900 version.

Jet Deflection

In July 1952 RA490, previously the flight testbed for the MetroVick Beryl axial-flow turbojet, was reallotted for jet deflection experiments. It was transferred to Westland Aircraft for a conversion where Rolls-Royce Nene engines were installed. The machine was used for early jet deflection trials at Westlands and from August 1954 these continued at RAE Farnborough and then Bedford until 1957. In this configuration the aircraft had enormous engine nacelles which stretched more than 8ft (2.44m) ahead of the wing – they were designed by the National

Gas Turbine Establishment. Such large nacelles were necessary because the 5,000 lb (22.2kN) thrust Nene Mk.3 engines were installed entirely ahead of the wing, with only the jet pipe extending through the spar 'banjo' that had enclosed the smaller original engine. Jet deflection angle was 60° and ballast had to be loaded into the rear fuselage to counteract a substantial nose heaviness, despite the fact that the guns, ammunition and armour had been removed. In addition, to ensure adequate lateral stability, a Mk.8 Meteor tail was used together with Trent Meteor type finlets. Finally, an outer wing from a PR Mk.10 gave RA490 a span of 44ft 4in (13.5m), which was the largest of any Meteor.

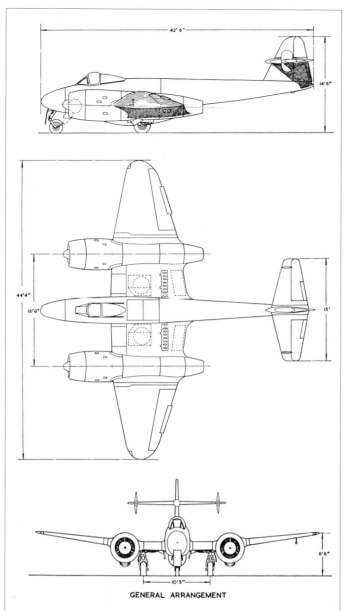

GENERAL ARRANGEMENT

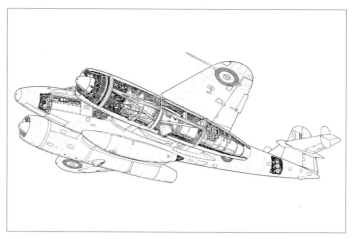

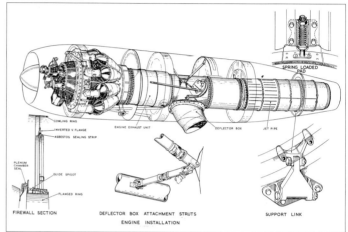

Left: **Westland three-view drawing of RA490 converted for jet deflection experiments with Rolls-Royce Nene engines.** Fred Ballam, Westland Archive

Top: **Detailed drawing of RA490 with the jet deflection installation.** Fred Ballam, Westland Archive

Above: **Engine nacelle detail on the jet deflection Meteor.** Fred Ballam, Westland Archive

Below: **The deflector box and part of the exhaust unit on RA490's nacelle.** Fred Ballam, Westland Archive

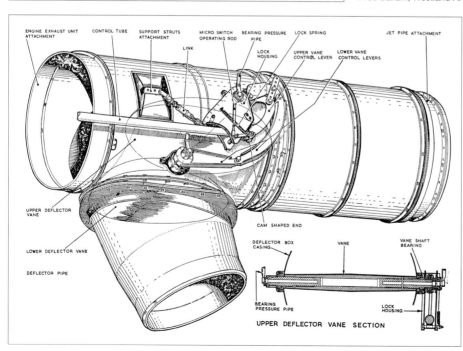

The Nene engines had normal jet pipes but vanes in one of the sections could be redirected to divert the exhaust gases downwards through a 'deflector box'. (See diagram opposite) This series of experiments was related to the parallel work on the vertical take-off 'Thrust Measuring Rigs' being carried out at Rolls-Royce (otherwise known as the 'Flying Bedstead'). The Meteor installation was a success and the lowest full-power airspeed achieved was 75mph (121km/h), 11.5mph (18.5km/h) less than that usually recorded by a standard aircraft. The fate of this aeroplane once its task was complete was to be used for fire-fighting training at Thurleigh, from April 1957. In the end jet deflection was not generally adopted because of the penalty it gave in weight.

Ejection Seat Testbeds

The first crew ejection seats were actually developed in Germany (for example, on the Heinkel He 219A piston-engined night-fighter),

A Meteor III, EE416, in transition between a camouflaged and a silver scheme. This was one of a number of Meteors used by Martin-Baker Aircraft for experimental work on ejector seats, with an additional (ejector) seat behind the normal pilot's position. Martin-Baker Aircraft via Tony Buttler

This photograph shows Martin-Baker's ejection-seat 'live dummy' Bernard Lynch, seated in EE416 at Chalgrove. Martin-Baker Aircraft, via Tony Buttler collection

This photograph shows WA634, originally built as a T.7 but extensively modified to allow testing of Martin-Baker ejection seats. The T.7 tail unit has been removed in favour of the F.8 type, the cockpit has been modified with an open rear seat, and the upper fuselage behind the cockpit has been reinforced to accept frequent blast damage from rocket-assisted seat firing. via Tony Buttler

but they were also developed quite independently by James Martin of Martin-Baker Aircraft Ltd. The first experiments were conducted using a Boulton Paul Defiant 'turret fighter', with the ejection-seat installed in the position of the turret, behind the pilot. The aircraft concerned was DR944, with the first live firings (using a dummy) being made on 24th June 1946. This Defiant was probably the last of its type to remain airworthy, and was retired in 1948. The need for an aircraft able to operate at speeds more representative of jet aircraft had already led to the selection of the Meteor as the type to succeed the Defiant as a trials airframe, and indeed the first firing (with a 'live pilot' as opposed to a dummy) was made only a month after the test with the Defiant, on 24th July 1946.

The first aircraft used was the Meteor F Mk.III EE416, which had the trial seat installed behind the normal pilot's cockpit. Since then a total of four Meteors have been used for flight trials of Martin-Baker ejection seats. EE416 began its life as standard Mk.III aircraft, but was fitted with various trial seats in a second cockpit installed behind the normal pilot's position (in place of the ammunition bay). The final three began their lives as T Mk.7s, but all three had Mk.8 tail units fitted, with the seats being mounted in a modified enclosure in the rear seat position. All these Meteors had strengthening applied to the area of the fuselage behind the ejector seat position to protect the structure from the blast effects of the seat being fired. This was an even more necessary requirement when the later, rocket-assisted, seats were being tested.

The Meteors attached to Martin-Baker over the years were as follows:

EE416   from 6.11.45 to 8.7.59 –
         sold as scrap to R J Coley
EE479   from 1.3.46 to 6.12.49
         (conversion never completed)
WA634   from 24.7.52 until 6.9.62 – now on
         display in the Cosford Aerospace
         Museum as part of a Martin-Baker exhibit
WA638   from 30.3.58, still in use

WA686 used for ground trials only, to assess effects of firing rocket-assisted seats on the fuselage structure

WL419 from August 1963, still in use

In addition, Mk.3 EE415 was allotted to Martin-Baker Aircraft from 6.11.45 to 22.11.49, when it was returned to Gloster Aircraft. It was used for air-to-air photography of seat firings from EE416.

Other companies have also been invited to develop crew-ejection mechanisms, and this led to other Meteors being loaned to these concerns for their trials. The first company involved was ML Aviation Ltd at White Waltham, near Maidenhead, which utilised a modified Meteor III, and then a Mk.IV, to test its 'lightweight' seat. The ML design was used in a number of British prototype aircraft, but development ceased in 1951 after the loss of a prototype aircraft in which the seat was believed to have malfunctioned.

Mk.III EE246 15.10.45 to 21.11.49.
Mk.IV EE519 27.3.51 (after modification by Martin-Baker from November 1950).

Folland Aircraft Ltd obtained a licence to produce the seat developed by SAAB in Sweden, which had been designed for the SAAB J21R and J29 fighter aircraft. The reason for the choice of this seat was the space constraints imposed by installation in the Folland Midge and Gnat series of light fighters. The SAAB seat design was subject to further development by Folland, necessitating the use of two Meteor T.7 aircraft for live firing trials. These trials continued after the Folland flight test unit at Chilbolton was closed down and trials were transferred to Dunsfold in February 1961.

WA690 22.10.57 to 12.5.61 (to A&AEE for further ejection seat trials)

WF877 29.4.54 to 30.11.65

Prone-Pilot Experiments

The Meteor used for prone-pilot trials was the final Mk.8 produced by Armstrong Whitworth Aircraft (AWA) – WK935. This was allotted to AWA for conversion during manufacture and featured a lengthened nose, with a second pilot lying prone in the forward part of the nose. The existing F.8 cockpit was retained, since this aircraft was always flown with a safety pilot in the normal cockpit, but a Mk.14 fin was fitted to compensate for the additional nose area. The objective of the conversion was to assess the merits of the prone-pilot position as a means of increasing pilot resistance to G-forces and the tendency to 'black-out' during high-speed manoeuvres. Earlier experiments had been conducted using the Reid & Sigrist RS.4 Bobsleigh VZ728 (itself converted from the prototype RS.3 Desford twin-piston-engined trainer, G-AGOS).

The Meteor made its first flight on 10th February 1954, and trials continued at Farnborough under the auspices of the Air Ministry's Institute of Aviation Medicine. Although these trials indicated that pilots in the prone position were more resistant to G-force loading, there were other operational problems which led to

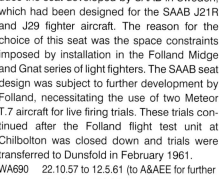

A view of the prone-pilot position on the experimental Meteor WK935. G R Wrixon, via Tony Buttler

WK935, the final F.8 built by Armstrong Whitworth, was modified before completion to have an additional pilot in a prone position ahead of the normal cockpit. This was part of an RAE project to examine ways of reducing 'G' loadings on pilots during high-speed manoeuvres. This aircraft is now in the Cosford Aerospace Museum. Armstrong Whitworth Aircraft NF368, via Ray Williams

Meteor F.4 VZ389, one of the Flight Refuelling trials aircraft (the nose-mounted refuelling probe is scarcely distinguishable in this shot).
via Tony Buttler

WA826, 'F' of No 245 Squadron which, although a front-line squadron, was the trials unit for developing in-flight refuelling techniques with tankers provided by Flight Refuelling Ltd. Here WA826 is seen linking up to a tanker in 1952.
Russell Adams

further development being abandoned. These included difficulty of the pilot in observing to his rear (most important for a fighter pilot) and the tiring effect of operating the controls for any length of time when compared to those of a conventional aircraft. The prone-pilot Meteor was demonstrated at the SBAC Show at Farnborough in 1955 and the flight trials continued until 1956, after which the Meteor was put into store. During 1959 WK935 was sent to No 12 MU at RAF Kirkbride in Cumbria for major inspection and overhaul, but we have been unable to trace records of any further tests being carried out. The aircraft was put in storage at RAF Maintenance Units until being handed over to the Air Historical Branch in 1964, and it is now preserved at the Cosford Aerospace Museum.

Flight Refuelling Development

In-flight refuelling had been championed by Sir Alan Cobham from the 1920s, with experiments being carried out both by the Royal Aircraft Establishment at Farnborough and by Sir Alan's own company, Flight Refuelling Ltd. These experiments had included trials in refuelling commercial Imperial Airways' Short C-Class flying boats in transatlantic operations before the Second World War, and further trials with Avro Lancastrians of British South American Airways Ltd in the immediate post-war period. Flight refuelling was even considered early in the development of the de Havilland DH.106 Comet jet airliner, even to the extent of limited flight trials with aircraft of Flight Refuelling Ltd.

However, military applications of in-flight refuelling as a 'force multiplier' or to facilitate long-range military deployments later came to the fore, and almost inevitably came to involve the Meteor. Flight Refuelling Ltd already operated two Avro Lancasters as tanker aircraft, and later used Avro Lincoln and English Electric Canberra aircraft on loan from the Ministry of Supply for the further development of equipment and techniques. It was also necessary to use 'receiver' aircraft to complete the development of the full system, and this led to the employment of three Meteors, in turn a Mk.III, a Mk.4 and a Mk.8 as 'full-time' trials aircraft based at Flight Refuelling's Tarrant Rushton airfield in Dorset. The aircraft were:

Mk.3	EE397	1.4.49 to 14.3.50
Mk.4	VZ389	9.9.49 to 29.1.51
Mk.8	WE934	14.5.53 to 24.1.61

The first 'link-up' with a Lancaster tanker was made by EE397 on 24th April 1949, while VZ389 first operated with an Avro Lincoln on 20th March 1950. The Mk.8 was retained at Tarrant Rushton after its use for these trials was complete and, when it was no longer needed, joined the programme of conversions to drone Mk.16, which was also undertaken by Flight Refuelling Ltd.

The Meteor F Mk.8 also figured in a more extensive operational trial during 1951 in which a number of standard F.8s belonging to No 245 Squadron, a front-line Fighter Command unit, were given in-flight refuelling capability. To this end they were fitted with refuelling nose-probes and internal fuel-system modifications to act as receiver aircraft. Twenty Meteor 8s were converted by Flight Refuelling for this large-scale trial, the majority of them going on to fly with No 245 Squadron at its Horsham St Faith base. They included VZ476, VZ477, VZ507, VZ528, VZ543, WA823, WA826, WA827, WA829, WA830, WA832, WA834, WA836 and WA837 (it is possible that the other intended conversions were cancelled). As well as the Lincoln (RA657), a Boeing YKB-29T Superfortress (45-21734) of the United States Air Force was used as the tanker aircraft during the trials – the latter enabling three Meteors to be refuelled at once from wingtip as well as fuselage-mounted hose units.

These trials were successful, but flight refuelling was not adopted for the Meteor force, the experience being applied to later types of front-line fighters and bombers, namely the Gloster Javelin, English Electric Lightning and the V-bombers, together with the Fleet Air Arm's de Havilland Sea Vixen, Supermarine Scimitar and Blackburn Buccaneer. The technique is of course still widely used at the present time, with all major aircraft in front-line service being equipped to receive or dispense fuel (or in some cases both).

The Griffith Wing

As part of the Royal Aircraft Establishment's programme of empirical research, various investigations had been made of using the laminar-flow aerofoil designed by Professor A A Griffith. The intended benefit was the use of boundary-layer suction from the top surface of the wing, with the object of removing slower-moving and turbulent air from the wing surface and thereby reducing drag. It was hoped that the reduction in drag would at least balance out the drag effect of the thicker wing needed for the suction 'plumbing'. The concept had been tried on a Hawker Hurricane Mk.II, Z3687, which had been modified by Armstrong Whitworth Aircraft for trials at RAE and which was flown from Farnborough between 1946 and 1948. The intention was to use a Meteor to carry

WM374, seen here with Fireflash missiles fitted on its wingtips, was one of several NF.11s specially modified for missile trials. This photo was taken on a flight over Cardigan Bay, but three aircraft (WM372 to WM374) were later shipped to Australia for further trials at Woomera. via Tony Buttler

out similar experiments at higher speeds and this resulted in the acquisition of Mk.III EE445 for modification.

The Griffith wing demanded a very smooth surface and Armstrong Whitworth had devised a special method of construction to achieve this, which was thus employed on EE445. The suction slots were placed in both wing surfaces at 75% chord and they were arranged to coincide with the gap between wing and aileron. These were then ducted to the engine compressors which sucked away, through the holes, the air boundary layer that was stuck to the wing's surface. As a result the ailerons were especially large and naturally rather 'heavy'. Rolls-Royce adapted its Derwent I engine to fit into this system, calling it the Derwent III, and it was also designed to blow this air out through slots over the ailerons to help improve lift and control.

EE445's first flight in this new form was made by Armstrong Whitworth's test pilot Eric Franklin on 21st January 1947 but any additional flying was curtailed until 25th March by the very severe winter weather experienced that year. Further improvements were made to the system and then EE445 was delivered to Farnborough on 3rd October and the assess-

ment programme lasted until December 1948. Overall the results disappointed because the increase in lift did not reach the estimated figures, but the boundary layer suction data that was collected proved beneficial to another research programme that followed with Armstrong Whitworth's two AW.52 flying wing aeroplanes. After completing the investigation EE445 was consigned for scrap on 1st July 1950.

Missile Trials Aircraft

A number of Meteors were involved with the firing of experimental air-to-air missiles (AAM), or in the development of missile systems. This work included acting as a 'target' whilst being pursued by other aircraft carrying infra-red (or other) homing devices, or photography of the actual firings from the launch aircraft. Meteors were also involved in the development of aircraft radar gun-sights.

The main aircraft used for missile trials was the Mk.11 night fighter, since the work required the carriage of various types of electronic equipment that was more easily accommodated in its lengthened nose. Thus Mk.11s WD743, WD744 and WD745 were allotted to Fairey Aviation for 'Blue Sky' trials and were ini-

tially based at Cranfield where the necessary modification work was carried out. These three aircraft were in use from late 1952 until May 1959 in relation to these trials. 'Blue Sky' was the codename for the Fairey-built AAM that later entered limited RAF service as the Fireflash. It was used by the Supermarine Swift Mk.7 jet fighter for assessment purposes and a trial installation was also tested on Hawker Hunter Mk.4 XF310. Two other Meteor 7s, WF781 and WA738, are believed to have been employed by Fairey Aviation at Cranfield as photographic chase aircraft. A third aircraft, a hybrid Mk.7, WL375, that was fitted with an FR.9 nose section, was used by No 6 Joint Service Trials Unit (JSTU) at RAF Valley in February 1957. After Fairey's Cranfield site was closed, some of these aircraft were moved to Manchester's Ringway airport, close to the Heaton Chapel factory where the missile work was centred. Another aircraft involved in the 'Blue Sky' programme was F.8 WA778, which participated in 'sighting trials' for the system at RAE Farnborough from 1953 to 1955.

Three Meteor 11s, WM372, WM373 and WM374, were employed on 'Blue Jay' trials in Australia. 'Blue Jay' was the codename for the de Havilland Firestreak AAM, which was later fitted operationally to the Gloster Javelin, de Havilland Sea Vixen and English Electric Lightning. All three Meteors were shipped to Australia in 1954/55 and based at Edinburgh Field, from where they conducted missile trials over the Woomera rocket range. WM374 was painted glossy white overall for the Woomera trials and was lost on 24th May 1958, whilst the other two survived to be struck off charge in March 1960.

A further Mk.11, WM232, was fitted with additional electronic equipment, painted black overall, and employed as a target for the 'Blue Jay' infra-red (IR) homing head by de Havilland Propellers at Hatfield from 1953 to 1958. In addition WD604, which had previously been a trials aircraft at Armstrong Whitworth for the wingtip fuel tank installation described in Chapter Four, was also involved in 'Blue Jay' trials at Hatfield after its tip-tanks had been removed. DH Propellers were also developing 'Red Top', a later-generation IR missile, for which a Meteor Mk.12, WS635, served as a target aircraft during its development programme from 1958 to 1962. The Air Department of the Telecommuni-

Meteor NF.11 WM232 in an all-black colour scheme. This aircraft was used for missile trials by the de Havilland Propeller Co at Hatfield, mainly as a target for the Blue Jay homing head. via Tony Buttler

cations Research Establishment (TRE), based at RAF Defford, employed Mk.11 WM180 for general 'homing eye' and camera development work from 1953. By 1958 this task had been formally redefined as 'homing head for guided weapons'. In October 1955, TRE was re-titled the Royal Radar Establishment (RRE) and its flying operations were moved to the adjacent airfield of Pershore.

Yet more Meteors were used in trials of the unguided aerial 2in (5.1cm) rockets, carried in underwing pods, which preceded the real guided weapons into service. The aircraft used for these trials, commencing in 1951, were Mk.8s WE966 (which went to ML Aviation at White Waltham to be modified for the trials) and WE919, which was used by DH Propellers at Hatfield for similar duties, before becoming a 'target' during 'Blue Jay' trials. The unguided weapons were eventually deployed on the Hunter, Sea Vixen, Buccaneer, SEPECAT Jaguar and Hawker-Siddeley Harrier.

Meteors were also involved in the trials of 'Red Dean', a very large air-to-air missile that was under development by Vickers-Armstrongs until its cancellation in 1956. These aircraft included Mk.11 WD686 flying with RRE. WD686 had previously been at A&AEE Boscombe Down where it was involved in trials of 'Green Cheese', an anti-submarine warfare weapon. After 'Red Dean' was cancelled it was transferred to RAE Bedford where it was used for gust research, remaining there until 1967. Vickers-Armstrongs was also developing 'Blue Boar', a TV-guided stand-off bomb for the V-Bomber Force. This programme involved the use of Meteor Mk.11s WM262 and WM295, which were delivered to Vickers at Wisley during 1953. The weapon was cancelled during

1954, by which time WM262 had been shipped to Australia to take part in the trials at Woomera. After the cancellation WM295 was transferred to the RRE at Defford (and later Pershore) for Airborne Interception (AI) radar development work.

Radar Research

The main centre for airborne radar research was of course the RRE mentioned already. Apart from its work on aerial-weapon guidance systems, for which some examples are given above, the RRE worked on all types of military radars, so its aircraft fleet covered AI radars fitted to night fighters (and later to all fighter types), warning systems fitted to bombers to advise their crews that they were being 'illuminated' by enemy radars, radar-ranging gunsights, and guidance systems for surface-to-air guided weapons (SAM).

From 1952 Meteor NF.11s WD686 and WD687 were given the task of developing AI Mk.17 at TRE, Defford, with the latter aircraft also being assigned to test AI Mk.18. Mk.11 WM295 and NF Mk.14s WS832 and WS838 were also used for AI research at the RRE (the re-named TRE). WS838 was later moved to the A&AEE at Boscombe Down, and finally to the RAE at Bedford. Meteor 11 WD790 was another early delivery to TRE, where it was used for development of the 'Red Garter' tail-warning radar for the V-Bombers. In 1958 WD790 left RRE to move to Ferranti Ltd at Edinburgh, where it was employed as a target for the 'Red Brick' radar being developed for use with the Bristol Bloodhound SAM. Its work continued as a target for 'Indigo Corkscrew', the tracking radar for the Bloodhound and English Electric's Thunderbird missiles. This Meteor was

returned to RRE as a testbed for radars being developed for the Panavia Tornado programme, before ending its days as a 'manned' target at RAE Llanbedr.

Finally, single-seat Meteors serving at TRE/RRE, included F.8s WA775 and WA904, which were used to test the radar-ranging gunsights intended for the Hawker Hunter. WA775 then went on to carry out operational trials of the sight at A&AEE Boscombe Down, RAE Farnborough and the Central Gunnery School at RAF Leconfield.

Other Trials Aircraft

The availability of the Meteor led to its use as a testbed for many other items of equipment which came into service on later types of aircraft, after successful trials had been carried out at Service establishments on the Meteor. Quite apart from general systems development work (some examples of which are given in the Table below), tests of particular interest included the fitting of 30mm Aden cannon to F.8 WK660 at Glosters in 1952. Trials of the cannon on this aircraft included its shipment to Canada for tests at the Central Experimental & Proving Establishment, Namao, in cold weather conditions. (The CEPE in Canada has been used by the British services for 'winterisation' testing of new aircraft and equipment for many years). After WK660's return from Canada, firing trials continued at RAE Farnborough until 1956.

Meteor U Mk.15 RA479 'E' is shown at its base of Llanbedr, an outstation of the RAE Ranges Division, where work with drone targets was centred in the UK. This version was also used in Australia. via Phil Butler

Meteor U.15 RA420, taken at Llanbedr, showing the wingtip cameras used to monitor missiles fired at the aircraft when used in unmanned mode. via Phil Butler

Another set of experiments was conducted on WH371, which was used by Flight Refuelling Ltd in 1952 for tests with braking parachutes at Tarrant Rushton. After these company tests were completed, the aircraft went to RAE Farnborough early in 1953 for further trials with the parachute system. Braking parachutes later became a standard fitment of aircraft from the later Marks of Hawker Hunter onwards.

One of the more unusual trial tasks was the laying of smoke screens. These tests were conducted using Mk.4 EE522. After its equipment fit at ML Aviation, White Waltham, in 1948/49, EE522 was sent to the National Gas Turbine Establishment at Farnborough early in 1950. The trials continued until 1956 at RAE and the Radar Research Establishment, and included demonstrations of the system to the 2nd Tactical Air Force in Germany. Another unusual series of trials at RAE Farnborough was carried out using Meteor T.7 WL405, during which a pilot flew the aircraft while relying completely on TV pictures as his external reference. The aircraft was always flown with a 'safety pilot' who used normal visual references. These trials continued from 1962 to 1968, at which point Blackburn Buccaneer XN923 was substituted for the Meteor.

Meteors were also used for many other more mundane research tasks, both at the RAE Farnborough and at various other aircraft and equipment manufacturers. Another RAE aircraft was Mk.11 WD634 which was the trials aircraft for 'Violet Picture' (a UHF homer device) at Farnborough from February to June 1958. Another long-term Farnborough resident was FR Mk.9 WX979 which was flown on reconnaissance camera development from September 1952 to February 1958, again by the RAE. These trials included work on the F.95, GX.90, FX101, F.100, F.97 Mk.2, and F.99 camera types.

A line-up of Meteors at the RAE airfield of Llanbedr, showing Meteor U.15s VT196 'U', VZ415 'A' and another (possibly VT282) coded 'Z', together with T.7 WA662 'K', used as a 'shepherd' to monitor unmanned aircraft during the development of their control systems. This shot was taken in 1959 or 1960.
Short Brothers & Harland J.8.6945F, via Phil Butler

This shot shows Meteor U.16 WH372 'H' at Llanbedr. UK-based U.16s used a red colour scheme with yellow topsides, and were usually identified by a code letter in yellow on their fins. WH372 was delivered to RAE Llanbedr in 1961 and was still in use in 1969. via Phil Butler

Meanwhile Westland Aircraft had looked after two aircraft that had been used by their subsidiary company, Normalair Ltd, for pressurisation and oxygen systems development for some years; these were Mk.4 EE545 from 1946 to 1948, followed, after a gap, by Mk.11 WM252 from 1952 to 1956. Fairey Aviation, as well as involvement in missile development, used Mk.4 EE455 for the development of powered flying controls from 1953 onwards. Another user was Ferranti Ltd at Edinburgh/Turnhouse which was much concerned with the development of radar and weapon-sighting equipment. The latter firm used several types of aircraft, but these included Meteors VW470 (T.7), WD670, WD782 and WD790 (NF.11) and WM261 (the prototype NF.14).

Meteor U.16 WH284, photographed at Tarrant Rushton in 1960 before delivery to RAE Llanbedr, where it was 'lost on operations' on 7th November 1960. via Phil Butler

Meteor U.16 WK870, wearing the code '655' from its time with No 728B Squadron, the Fleet Air Arm unit based at Hal Far, Malta, that provided drone targets for missile trials conducted in the Mediterranean. This photo was taken after WK870 arrived at Llanbedr for further service with the RAE Ranges Division. The extended nose which was a feature of the U.16 version is well shown here. via Phil Butler.

Meteor Unmanned (Drone) Conversions

The Meteor was chosen as a suitable high-speed target aircraft for the trial firing of various ground- and air-launched guided missiles, the piston-engined targets previously used (the Fairey Firefly U Mk.8 and U Mk.9) no longer being fast enough to represent the targets which the missiles were designed to destroy. It was therefore decided, after autopilot and other equipment trials had been carried out at RAE Farnborough, particularly on T.7 VW413 at RAE, to place contracts with Flight Refuelling Ltd at Tarrant Rushton for a number of conver-

sions of Meteor F.4 fighters that had been retired from front-line service. In all, ninety conversions were made to the new U Mk.15 version, under two separate contracts. The prototype U.15 conversion was RA421 which made its initial flight on 11th March 1955. These modified aircraft were at first given an overall silver colour scheme, but could be distinguished from the F.4 by a small black radome on top of the fuselage, some distance behind the cockpit. They were also usually fitted with wingtip-mounted cameras and were soon also distinguished by an overall red colour scheme,

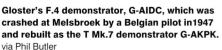

wlth yellow top-sides. Those flown in Australia had the top-sides in white rather than yellow.

In 1955 the first conversions were shipped to Australia, where they were used in connection with the Weapons Research Establishment (WRE) at Woomera, although it was summer 1957 before they began to fly as drone targets. In fact, the first of the unmanned flights in Australia was made on 7th May 1957, the Meteor involved reportedly being destroyed by a Fireflash missile. Further deliveries were made to the Royal Aircraft Establishment Ranges Division outstation at Llanbedr in North Wales where they were to be flown over the Cardigan Bay firing ranges as missile targets. However, the first formal delivery to Llanbedr did not take place until January 1957 and the first drone flight did not occur until 17th July 1958. Some other Meteor U.15s were delivered to the Royal Navy's No 728B Squadron at Hal Far in Malta and used as targets during missile trials with RN ships in the Mediterranean. The first of these flew to Llanbedr on 20th May 1959 in order to enable the Fleet Air Arm personnel to carry out their initial training on the equipment available at the RAE outstation. Fourteen U.15s

were used at Hal Far, of which ten were shot down by missiles, the remainder being lost due to control malfunctions.

The aircraft delivered to Australia were used by the Air Trials Unit at Woomera. In April 1958 the ATU split into Nos 1 and 2 Air Trials Units, RAAF, which flew the aircraft as a service to a succession of numbered Joint Services Trials Units (JSTU), the latter tasked with the development and proving of the different specific weapon systems. The aircraft flown by the Air Trials Units, which included the drones and a number of other Meteor testbeds, were all on the strength of the Royal Australian Air Force, although most retained their British serial numbers. The JSTUs were usually British-manned units, with personnel from whichever of the British services were involved. For example, No 13 JSTU, which evaluated 'Red Top', had both RN and RAF participation, while No 16 was largely manned by the Royal Artillery, since it was concerned with the British Army's English Electric Thunderbird ground-to-air anti-aircraft missile. The two RAAF Air Trials Units were based at Woomera and Edinburgh Field, respectively. This arrangement continued until

1967, when the RAAF handed over the target service (including the remaining Meteors) to civilian contractor Short Bros & Harland Air Services, which also operated the Llanbedr operation for the RAE in North Wales.

In fact a proportion of the flying still involved proving of the drones as a viable system, and they were also used for 'shepherding' target aircraft and on other piloted tasks during the trials. The same applied to the drones held at Llanbedr, where in the latter years of use electronic systems were developed to enable the missiles to 'miss' the target aircraft by a predetermined distance, enabling the drone aircraft to be recovered undamaged while obtaining photographs of the missile's performance. This ensured the survival of the last few Meteor Mk.16 drones (below) until the end of their airframe fatigue lives.

With further trials being needed and the supply of Mk.4 Meteors running low, drone conversions of the F.8 Meteor were then initiated as the Mk.16, also carried out by Flight Refuelling Ltd at Tarrant Rushton in Dorset. The drone conversions were initially designated 'U' (Unmanned) Marks, but this changed to 'D' for Drone during the service life of the Mk.16. Meanwhile the Mk.16 had been followed by the U Mk.21, similar to the U.16 but with different electronic telemetry equipment for operation in Australia at WRE Woomera. It is believed that the Mks 17, 18 and 19 were reserved for drone conversions of the Meteor night-fighter variants, but no night fighters were converted to this condition. Flight Refuelling converted one F.8 to U.21 standard, and then modified seven existing U.16s to the U.21 configuration. All of these were shipped to Australia, although one (WL136) was later returned to serve at Llanbedr as a U.16. In Australia Fairey Aviation converted fifteen RAAF Mk.8s to U.21 or U.21A standard, using kits of parts supplied by Flight Refuelling Ltd. After service at Woomera, a single Australian U.21 (A77-876) was shipped back to the UK in July 1971, modified to U.16 standard (reverting to its allotted RAF serial number, WK800) and became the last U.16 in service, only being retired to the museum at Boscombe Down on 11th October 2004 with the impending closure of the airfield at Llanbedr at the end of that month. Details of the serial numbers for the drone conversions are given in Chapter Eight.

The first Meteor U.16 to be delivered to Llanbedr for drone work was WH284, which arrived in June 1960, although there had been earlier visits during the type's development fly-

ing period. Meanwhile, other U.16s had been shipped to Australia for use over the Woomera range and the Royal Navy was about to receive Meteor U.16s to supplement the U.15s flown by No 728B Squadron at Hal Far, Malta. The first two of the latter were received in October/November 1960, but all four of these U.16 aircraft were later returned to Llanbedr for use by the RAE. It is reported that fifty-nine U.15, U.16 and U.21 Meteors were destroyed by weapons in WRE trials, while a further twenty-two crashed due to malfunctions.

The equipment fitted in a drone included the remote radio control gear and automatic pilot and wingtip pods which housed cameras for filming the missiles flight path. Additional structural modifications to the Mk.16 included a streamlined 30in (76.2cm) nose extension which housed the remote control equipment. This version could be flown as a normal aeroplane with a pilot overriding the remote control gear, or as a remotely controlled machine but with a pilot aboard for monitoring purposes, or purely as a drone with no pilot on board.

The 'Ground-Attack Meteor' G-AMCJ, seen at the 1950 SBAC display. Visible are the wingtip tanks, underwing bomb and the Rocket-Assisted Take-Off Gear distributed around the fuselage behind the wing. Later this was converted to the 'Reaper' and flown with the B Conditions markings G-7-1, in which form it was tested at A&AEE Boscombe Down. Military Aircraft Photographs

Civilian Meteors

The following Meteors have appeared on the British civil register.

G-AIDC   Mk.4   Registered 14.8.46 to Gloster Aircraft Co Ltd. Cancelled 10.5.48, after being damaged at Melsbroek in May 1947. Major parts incorporated into G-AKPK.

G-AKPK   Mk.7   Registered 9.1.48 to Gloster Aircraft Co Ltd. Cancelled 22.11.48 'sold abroad'. To Royal Netherlands AF as I-1.

A nice air-to-air shot of the T.7 demonstrator G-AKPK in formation with Mk.4 VT170. The legend on the T.7's fuselage reads 'GLOSTER METEOR MkVII ROLLS-ROYCE DERWENT V ENGINES'. BAE Systems PLC NN0028

G-AMCJ   Mk.8   Modified as 'Private Venture Attack Fighter'. Registered 19.6.50 to Gloster Aircraft Co Ltd. Cancelled 1.2.51. Sold to Royal Danish Air Force (as 490), However this did not occur, a new aircraft going to Denmark as '490'. Modified to the 'Reaper' ground-attack fighter and flown under 'B Conditions' as G-7-1.

A detail view of G-AMCJ, showing the RATOG fitted to achieve short take-off runs at full load, together with under-fuselage bomb and rockets. Gloster Aircraft, via Tony Buttler

G-7-1   Mk.8   Modified from G-AMCJ and first flown on 9.8.51. After company trials it was also flown at A&AEE Boscombe Down (trial firings of rocket projectiles) from 12.8.52 to 15.10.52. Later converted to Mk.7 G-ANSO but retaining the Mk.8 tail.

G-ANSO   Mk.7 (with Mk.8 tail)   Previously the 'Reaper' private venture ground-attack fighter, fitted with T.7 nose. Registered 12.6.54 to Gloster Aircraft Ltd. Cancelled 11.8.59 'Stockholm, Sweden'. Sold as SE-DCC.

G-ARCX   Mk.14   Previously WM261. Registered 8.9.60 to Ferranti Ltd, although not flown as such until 21.1.63. Withdrawn from use in February 1969. Preserved at Museum of Flight, East Fortune.

G-ASLW   Mk.14   Previously WS829. Registered 12.9.63 to Rolls-Royce Ltd. Cancelled 6.11.69 as 'destroyed'. Sold to Target Towing Aircraft Ltd, although never registered to them, and crashed off the Cape Verde Islands on 6.11.69 while on an illicit flight to the Biafran civil war.

G-AXNE   Mk.14   Previously WS804. Registered 28.8.69 to Target Towing Aircraft Ltd. Cancelled 14.3.77 as 'presumed withdrawn from use'. Had been abandoned at Bissau, Portuguese Guinea, en route to Biafra in 1969.

G-JETM   Mk.7   Previously VZ638. Registered 10.8.83 to Brencham Ltd, later to Aces High Ltd. To P G Vallance Ltd, and at Vallance's Gatwick Aviation Museum. Still officially currently registered.

G-LOSM   Mk.11   Previously WM167. Registered 8.6.84 to Berowell Management Ltd, later to Aviation Heritage Ltd. Currently registered.

G-METE   Mk.8   Previously VZ467. Registered 5.11.91 to Air Support Aviation Systems Ltd and later T J Manna (Kennet Aviation). Cancelled as sold to Australia on 26.10.01 and registered there as VH-MBX ('MBX' abbreviating 'Meatbox', the familiar name of the Meteor in RAF and RAAF service).

The larkspur blue-painted Gloster demonstrator G-ANSO on the ground at Moreton Valence during 1954. Russell Adams P279/54, via Phil Butler

G-7-1, the Meteor Private-Venture ground-attack version, with wingtip tanks, but unencumbered by the selection of bombs and rocket projectiles frequently seen in views of this aircraft. Russell Adams P.342/51, via Phil Butler

Chapter Eight

In Detail

Despite its revolutionary powerplant, the Gloster Meteor's structure followed the accepted manufacturing practice of the time and was reasonably conventional. Consequently the aerodynamics of the airframe were pure piston era and the controls were still manually operated when later and faster types would, by necessity, require powered controls. Overall the Meteor was a twin-engined single or two-seat jet-powered aircraft with a low position wing and a tricycle undercarriage. The fuselage was long and slender and the wing tapered on the leading and trailing edges from the engine nacelle outwards to form a well rounded tip; the wings appeared to extend through the nacelles. A vertical tail was fitted with the horizontal tail located high on the vertical fin. Most of the following relates to the long-span F Mk.4 version – the changes introduced for individual variants are listed in their relevant chapters

although a brief description for the NF Mk.11 is given at the end.

Fundamentally all-metal stressed-skin construction was employed throughout the Meteor airframe and mainplanes and the fuselage was built from three main units – the front section together with the nosewheel, a centre fuselage complete with the wing centre section, nacelles and main landing gear, and finally the rear fuselage which brought the tail unit with it. Each of these primary sections, which were also again sub-divided into further sub-units, could be built up individually and completed ready for assembly as the finished airframe. Apart from solving numerous production problems this system also greatly facilitated the ease of breakdown for transport, shipment or major repairs.

The fuselage was built around four longerons, the extremities of which in each

case acted as the main attachment points for the assembly of these main units to each other. The front fuselage was built up from a stiff internal box-like structure around which was attached, externally, a lighter contour-forming framework and skin. The cannon were mounted between the outer and inner structure and the latter was built up from heavy gauge diaphragms attached to the four longerons and stiffened laterally by three bulkheads. The front bulkhead also formed the attachment base for the nosewheel supporting structure, the centre bulkhead also served to divide the front fuselage into the forward pilot's compartment and rearward magazine compartment, whilst the

Detail cutaway drawing of a Gloster Meteor F Mk.IV taken from a 1947 manufacturer's brochure.

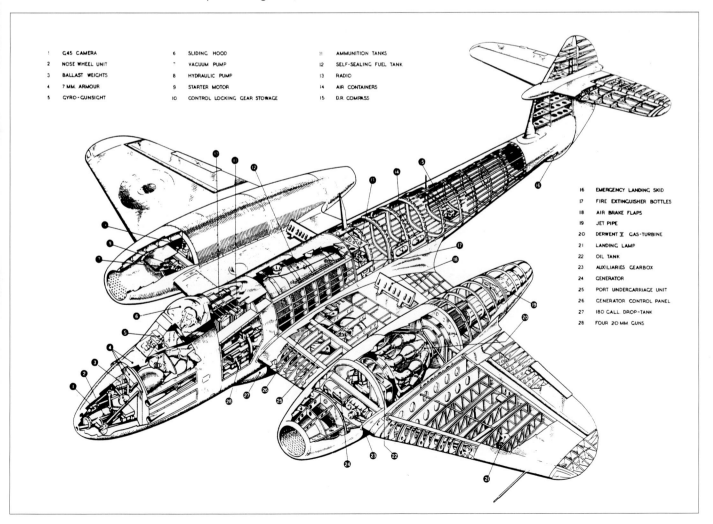

1	G45 CAMERA	6	SLIDING HOOD	11	AMMUNITION TANKS
2	NOSE WHEEL UNIT	7	VACUUM PUMP	12	SELF-SEALING FUEL TANK
3	BALLAST WEIGHTS	8	HYDRAULIC PUMP	13	RADIO
4	7 MM. ARMOUR	9	STARTER MOTOR	14	AIR CONTAINERS
5	GYRO-GUNSIGHT	10	CONTROL LOCKING GEAR STOWAGE	15	D.R. COMPASS

16	EMERGENCY LANDING SKID
17	FIRE EXTINGUISHER BOTTLES
18	AIR BRAKE FLAPS
19	JET PIPE
20	DERWENT V GAS-TURBINE
21	LANDING LAMP
22	OIL TANK
23	AUXILIARIES GEARBOX
24	GENERATOR
25	PORT UNDERCARRIAGE UNIT
26	GENERATOR CONTROL PANEL
27	180 GALL. DROP-TANK
28	FOUR 20 MM GUNS

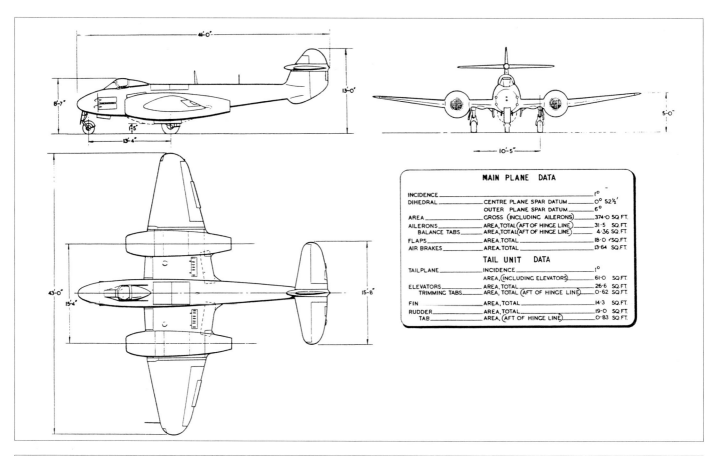

MAIN PLANE DATA

INCIDENCE		1°
DIHEDRAL	CENTRE PLANE SPAR DATUM	0° 52½'
	OUTER PLANE SPAR DATUM	6°
AREA	GROSS (INCLUDING AILERONS)	374·0 SQ.FT.
AILERONS	AREA,TOTAL (AFT OF HINGE LINE)	31·5 SQ.FT.
BALANCE TABS	AREA,TOTAL(AFT OF HINGE LINE)	4·36 SQ.FT.
FLAPS	AREA,TOTAL	18·0 SQ.FT.
AIR BRAKES	AREA,TOTAL	13·64 SQ.FT.

TAIL UNIT DATA

TAILPLANE	INCIDENCE	1°
	AREA,(INCLUDING ELEVATORS)	61·0 SQ.FT.
ELEVATORS	AREA,TOTAL	26·6 SQ.FT.
TRIMMING TABS	AREA,TOTAL(AFT OF HINGE LINE)	0·62 SQ.FT.
FIN	AREA,TOTAL	14·3 SQ.FT.
RUDDER	AREA,TOTAL	19·0 SQ.FT.
TAB	AREA,(AFT OF HINGE LINE)	0·83 SQ.FT.

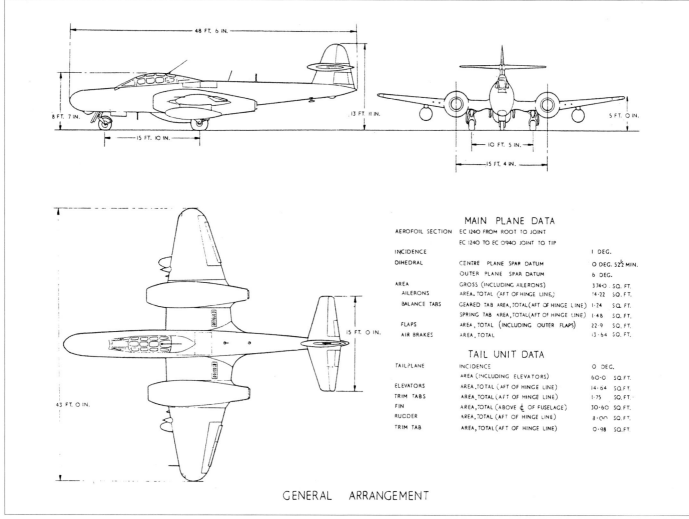

MAIN PLANE DATA

AEROFOIL SECTION	EC 1240 FROM ROOT TO JOINT	
	EC 1240 TO EC 0940 JOINT TO TIP	
INCIDENCE		1 DEG.
DIHEDRAL	CENTRE PLANE SPAR DATUM	0 DEG. 52½ MIN.
	OUTER PLANE SPAR DATUM	6 DEG.
AREA	GROSS (INCLUDING AILERONS)	374·0 . SQ.FT.
AILERONS	AREA, TOTAL (AFT OF HINGE LINE)	14·22 SQ.FT.
BALANCE TABS	GEARED TAB AREA,TOTAL(AFT OF HINGE LINE)	1·24 SQ.FT.
	SPRING TAB AREA,TOTAL(AFT OF HINGE LINE)	1·48 SQ.FT.
FLAPS	AREA, TOTAL (INCLUDING OUTER FLAPS)	22·9 SQ.FT.
AIR BRAKES	AREA, TOTAL	13·64 SQ.FT.

TAIL UNIT DATA

TAILPLANE	INCIDENCE	0 DEG.
	AREA (INCLUDING ELEVATORS)	60·0 SQ.FT.
ELEVATORS	AREA,TOTAL (AFT OF HINGE LINE)	14·64 SQ.FT.
TRIM TABS	AREA,TOTAL (AFT OF HINGE LINE)	1·75 SQ.FT.
FIN	AREA,TOTAL (ABOVE ℄ OF FUSELAGE)	30·60 SQ.FT.
RUDDER	AREA,TOTAL (AFT OF HINGE LINE)	8·00 SQ.FT.
TRIM TAB	AREA,TOTAL (AFT OF HINGE LINE)	0·98 SQ.FT.

GENERAL   ARRANGEMENT

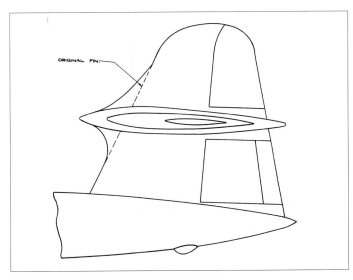

Opposite page:
Above: **Three-view general arrangement drawing of the long-span Meteor Mk.IV.**

Below: **Armstrong Whitworth drawing of the Meteor NF Mk.11 night fighter.** Eric Morgan

This page:
Above left: **Drawing of the modified Mk.12 tail fin compared with the original Mk.11 style, with additional fillets above and below the tail 'acorn' bullet.**

Above right: **A detailed view of the revised, enlarged fin used on the NF.12 and NF.14 versions of the Meteor night fighter. The trial installation was first flown on the NF.11 WD687 shown here.** A&AEE 15938, via Tony Buttler

Below: **A close-up of the nose section of a Meteor F.4 showing the cockpit canopy and forward fuselage.** ATP 16471A, via Tony Buttler

rear bulkhead (together with the longeron extremities) was bolted on assembly to the corresponding bulkhead and longerons on the centre section.

Heavy gauge skin was used on certain parts of the outer structure and acted as deflector plates to provide, in conjunction with armour plate, some protection for the pilot. The centre section had to be very robust to house the two engines and their built-in nacelles and the main fuel tank, while also providing attachment for the main undercarriage. The extremities of the front and rear centre section spars formed attachment points for each outer mainplane while the middle portion of the centre section formed a housing for the main fuel tank and also contained within its construction the four longerons. Flaps, dive brakes and their operating jacks were collectively contained within a sub-unit assembly attached to the rear spar inboard of each engine nacelle.

As in the other two units the four longerons were carried on through the rear fuselage and, in conjunction with pressed channel frames, formed the main build-up for the attachment of the light alloy stressed skin, the latter being stiffened by 'top hat' section stiffeners. Both the skin and frames were built up in segments. Into the construction of the tail unit were embodied two upward-extending bulkheads forming at their extremities points for the high-mounted tailplane, so positioned that it would clear the jet exhaust streams.

The mainplanes were of conventional two spar design with a light alloy stressed-skin covering, the rear spar having extra depth to accommodate the jet pipes in a feature known as a 'banjo'. A special 'high speed' aerofoil section was employed and the mainplane attachment to the centre section was simple and afforded easy removal. Six main ribs were used in the wing centre section with both spars and ribs built in stainless steel. The all-metal ailerons were of simple design, they had three internal mass balance weights each and used long-chord mechanically operated servo balance-tabs. There were split flaps which were

hydraulically operated and slotted airbrakes on both upper and lower surfaces between the nacelles and fuselage. Both wingtip and trailing edge were readily detachable whilst a large number of hand or inspection panels on the undersurface provided easy access to all internal control and electrical systems for repair or maintenance. The port mainplane housed an electrically retractable landing light on its underside and there were navigation wingtip and formation lights.

The all-metal tail also employed a two-spar stressed-skin structure, the fin was integrated with the fuselage and both rudders and elevators were all-metal. Each elevator was constructed separately but joined together on assembly by a simple flange-type joint. They were balanced by an aerodynamic horn and internal mass balance weights and included in the design of each elevator was an adjustable trim tab. The Meteor's tailplane layout had required that the rudder be divided into upper and lower units and these too were joined by a

simple flange-type joint on each spar extension. The lower rudder was provided with an adjustable servo trim tab and balanced by an internal mass balance weight while the upper rudder was balanced by an aerodynamic horn and internal weights. Built integrally with the tail unit were the lower fin and emergency tail skid, the latter being provided with an easily detachable lower section or shoe.

A tricycle undercarriage was fitted, still a novel feature when the F.9/40 Meteor made its appearance, and the main legs compressed on retraction to cut down the required storage space. The undercarriage, designed by Dowty, was hydraulically operated and had knee action shock absorbers. A single 325-gallon (1,478-litre) fuel tank was housed in the centre fuselage with a 180-gallon (818-litre) external drop tank available to fit under the fuselage and two more 100-gallon (455-litre) tanks to go under the outer wings. The cabin was fully pressurised, Westland Aircraft's pressurisation experience with its wartime Welkin high-alti-

tude piston fighter having been made available to Gloster for the design of the Meteor cockpit. There were heating, ventilation, anti-icing and de-misting systems and a sliding jettisonable cockpit hood. Previously the F Mk.III had introduced to the production lines a fully transparent hood with a 'blown' centre section, the canopy sliding on runners rather than the hinged variety of the prototypes and F Mk.Is. An ejection seat for the pilot did not arrive until the Mk.8.

The four belt-fed 20mm Hispano cannon were placed in pairs either side of the cockpit (the original six-gun scheme having had two more beneath the cockpit) and a camera gun was housed in a fuselage nose fairing. On the short-span marks there were attachment points under the wings for two 1,000 lb (454kg) bombs or eight or sixteen 90 lb (41kg) rocket projectiles. The radio receiving and transmission equipment was a TR.1464.

The salient feature of the two-seat NF Mk.11 night fighter compared to previous marks was a pressurised Mk.7 type of fuselage with a longer nose to contain the radar scanner. It also had long-span wings with the four 20mm guns mounted outboard of the engine nacelles, an E.1/44 type tail unit as fitted to the F Mk.8 and external tanks which were considered to be a normal fitting (that is, a combat ventral tank plus jettisonable underwing tanks having the same capacities as on the Mk.IV). The forward portion of the nose was made of di-electric material to allow the scanner to function properly. In the cockpit the pilot occupied the front seat and the radar operator/navigator the rear cockpit, both being enclosed by a single hood which was hinged for access. In an emergency the hood could be jettisoned by either occupant and all of the structure between the nosewheel bulkhead and the front wing spar bulkhead was sealed to form a pressure cabin. Pressurisation was supplied by tapping the Derwent 8 compressor. The metal portions of the fuselage were still of semi-monocoque construction and the main fuel tank inside again held 325 gallons (1,478 litres) of fuel. The later Mk.14 night fighter introduced a two-piece clear view canopy on sliding rails plus Martin-Baker ejection seats.

Technical Data

	Span ft (m)	Length ft (m)	Height ft (m)	Gross Wing Area ft² (m²)	Gross Weight lb (kg)	Powerplant lbst (kN)	Max Speed / Height mph (km/h) / ft (m)	S/L Rate of Climb ft/min (m/min)	Ceiling ft (m)
F Mk.I	43ft 0in (13.11m)	41ft 5in (12.62m)	13ft 0in (3.96m)	374 (34.8)	11,775 (5,341)	2 x 1,600 (7.1) RR W.2B/23 Welland I	411 (661) at S/L, 446 (718) at 30,000 (9,144)	2,155 (657)	43,000 (13,106)
F Mk.II	44ft 3in (13.49m)	41ft 5in (12.62m)	13ft 0in (3.96m)	374 (34.8)	13,750 (6,237)	2 x 2,000 (8.9) de Havilland H.1	– 505 (813) at 30,000 (9,144)	–	49,000 (14,935)
F Mk.III	43ft 0in (13.11m)	41ft 5in (12.62m)	13ft 0in (3.96m)	374 (34.8)	–	2 x 2,000 (8.9) RR W.2B/23C Welland or Derwent I	– –	3,980 (1,213)	– –
					13,342 (6,052)	or 2 x 2,400 (10.7) Derwent IV	486 (782) at S/L 493 (793) at 30,000 (9,144)	–	46,000 (14,021)
F Mk.4	43ft 0in (13.11m)	41ft 0in (12.50m)	13ft 0in (3.96m)	374 (34.8)	14,460 (6,559)	2 x 3,500b (15.6) RR Derwent V	585 (941) at S/L, 550 (885) at 30,000 (9,144)	7,900 (2,408)	– –
F Mk.4 Short Span	37ft 2½in (11.34m)	41ft 0in (12.50m)	13ft 0in (3.96m)	350 (32.6)	15,175 (6,883)	2 x 3,500b (15.6) RR Derwent V	590 (949) at S/L –	7,350 (2,240)	44,500 (13,564)
T Mk.7	37ft 2½in (11.34m)	43ft 6in (13.26m)	13ft 0in (3.96m)	350 (32.6)	14,230 (6,455)	2 x 3,500 (15.6) RR Derwent 8	585 (941) at S/L 540 (869) at 30,000 (9,144)	7,600 (2,316)	45,000 (13,716)
F Mk.8	37ft 2½in (11.34m)	44ft 7in (13.59m)	13ft 0in (3.96m)	350 (32.6)	15,700 (7,122)	2 x 3,500 (15.6) RR Derwent 8	592 (926) at S/L 550 (885) at 30,000 (9,144)	7,000 (2,134)	44,000 (13,411)
FR Mk.9	37ft 2½in (11.34m)	44ft 7in (13.59m)	13ft 0in (3.96m)	350 (32.6)	15,770 (7,153)	2 x 3,500 (15.6) RR Derwent 8	592 (926) at S/L 550 (885) at 30,000 (9,144)	7,000 (2,134)	44,000 (13,411)
PR Mk.10	43ft 0in (13.11m)	44ft 3in (13.49m)	13ft 0in (3.96m)	374 (34.8)	15,400 (6,985)	2 x 3,500 (15.6) RR Derwent 8	– 575 (925) at 10,000 (3,048)	– –	47,500 (14,478)
NF Mk.11	43ft 0in (13.11m)	48ft 6in (14.78m)	13ft 11in (4.24m)	374 (34.8)	16,542 (7,503)	2 x 3,700 (16.4) RR Derwent 8	580 (933) at S/L 547 (880) at 30,000 (9,144)	4,800 (1,463)	40,000 (12,192)
NF Mk.12	43ft 0in (13.11m)	49ft 11in (15.21m)	13ft 11in (4.24m)	374 (34.8)	17,223 (7,812)	2 x 3,800 (16.9) RR Derwent 9	– –	– –	40,000 (12,192)
NF Mk.13	43ft 0in (13.11m)	48ft 6in (14.78m)	13ft 11in (4.24m)	374 (34.8)	–	2 x 3,700 (16.4) RR Derwent 8	– –	– –	– –
NF Mk.14	43ft 0in (13.11m)	49ft 11in (15.21m)	13ft 11in (4.24m)	374 (34.8)	17,287 (7,841)	2 x 3,800 (16.9) RR Derwent 9	– 585 (941) at 10,000 (3,048)	5,800 (1,768)	43,000 (13,107)

Notes:
1. Prototype DG204 with F.2 engine had a height of 13ft 8in (4.17m).
2. The thickness/chord ratio for long-span Meteors was 12% at the root, 9% at the tip; for the short-span Mks 4, 7, 8 and 9 the tip ratio rose to 10.4%.
3. Meteor's wheel track was 10ft 5in (3.18m).
4. Armament was as follows:
   All fighter marks had four 20mm cannon mounted in nose of day fighter and in wings of night fighter;
   F Mk.III, F Mk.4, F Mk.8 & FR Mk.9 had two 1,000 lb (454kg) bombs or eight or sixteen 90 lb (41kg) rocket projectiles under wings;
   T Mk.7 & PR Mk.10 did not carry armament.

Contracts and Serial Numbers

F.9/40 Prototypes

Contract SB.21179/C.23(b), placed 6.2.41.
Serial numbers DG202-DG213. This contract called for twelve prototypes, although only eight of these were completed and flown, largely because of delays in engine development. The first to fly was DG206 on 5.3.43, ironically having Halford H.1 engines (prototype of the de Havilland Goblin) rather than the intended Power Jets W.2B/23 engines that were still suffering some development problems. DG202 and DG205 flown with Rover-built W.2B/23 engines, DG203 with Power Jets W.2/500 (and later W.2/700) engines, DG204 with MetroVick F.2/1 axial-flow engines, DG206 and DG207 with Halford H.1, DG208 with Rolls-Royce-built W.2B/23 (Welland) and DG209 with Rolls-Royce W.2B/37 (Derwent). DG210 was to be the second aircraft with MetroVick F.2, but was cancelled when almost complete. DG211-DG213 were not completed.

Gloster Meteor I/II

Contracts/Aircraft/1490/CB.7(b), placed 8.41.
300 aircraft, numbered EE210-254, 269-318, 331-369, 384-429, 444-493, 517-554, 568-599. Originally intended as 200 F.I (Rolls-Royce Welland) and 100 F.II (de Havilland Goblin), F.II

cancelled when Goblin production was reserved for the DH Vampire, and order reverted to 300 F.I. Produced as 20 F.I (delivered February to September 1944), 230 F.III (delivered November 1944 to December 1946) and 40 F.4 (delivered March to December 1946).

Gloster Meteor II

Contracts/Aircraft/1490/CB.7(b), extension placed 14.8.43.
100 aircraft numbered RA365-398, 413-457, 473-493. Ordered as Mk.II, produced as F.4, delivered December 1946 to January 1947.

Gloster Meteor III

Contracts/Aircraft/5121/CB.7(b), placed 23.2.45.
300 aircraft numbered TX386-428, 531-567, 572-614, 618-645, 649-688, 693-737, 739-776, 779-804. All cancelled following the end of the Second World War in September 1945.

Gloster Meteor V/IV

6/Aircraft/658/CB.7(a), placed 7.11.46.
220 aircraft numbered VS968-987, VT102-150, 168-199, 213-247, 256-294, 303-347. Produced as 20 PR.10 (VS968-987, in lieu of the cancelled PR Mk.V, delivered May 1950 to February 1951), 199 F.4 (delivered January 1948 to March 1949) and one PR.5 (VT347, transferred

to contract 6/Aircraft/1418/CB.7(b) and crashed on its first flight, 15.6.49).

Gloster Meteor IV/V/VII

6/Aircraft/1389/CB.7(b), placed 12.8.47.
212 aircraft numbered VW255-304, 308-357, 360-371, 376-405, 410-459, 470-489. Intended as 100 F.4, 12 FR.IV, 30 PR.V and 70 T.VII. 42 F.IV (VW316-357) cancelled 17.7.49. 12 FR.IV produced as FR.9 VW360-371 (delivered July 1950 to February 1951). VW376-379 produced as PR.10 (delivered January to April 1951) with VW380-405 cancelled. VW410-459, 470-489 produced as T.7, delivered October 1948 to July 1949.

Gloster Meteor IV

6/Aircraft/1389/CB.7(b), added 20.8.47.
A single 'replacement' aircraft, serial number VW730. No record of delivery, presumed unbuilt.

Gloster Meteor IV

6/Aircraft/1490/CB.7(b), placed 3.9.47.
Twelve aircraft, numbered VW780-791. Produced as F.4, delivered January 1948.

A view of F.9/40 prototype DG204 with MetroVick F.2 engines in underwing nacelles. Eric Morgan

Gloster Meteor IV, V and VII
6/Aircraft/2430/CB.7(b), placed 17.8.48.
VZ380-385 not built. VZ386-429 and 436 and 437 produced as F.4 by Armstrong Whitworth (total 45 delivered August 1949 to April 1950), under sub-contract 6/Aircraft/2756/CB.7(b). VZ437 was produced as an F.4 by Gloster under contract 2430, delivered in January 1950. VZ438-485, 493-517 produced as F.8 by Gloster, (total 73 delivered February to June 1950). VZ518-532, 540-569 produced as F.8 by Armstrong Whitworth, (total 45 delivered June to October 1950). VZ577-611 ordered as FR.IV but completed as FR.9 by Gloster (total 35 delivered November 1950 to April 1951). VZ620 ordered as a PR.V but built as a PR.10 by Gloster, delivered May 1951. VZ629-649 built as T.7 by Gloster (total 21, delivered July to September 1949).

Armstrong Whitworth Meteor NF.11
6/Aircraft/3090/CB.7(b), placed 29.10.48.
Two prototypes numbered WA546 and WA547. WA546 f/f 31.5.50.

Gloster Meteor T.7 and F.8
6/Aircraft/2982/CB.7(b), placed 12.11.48.
137 T.7, numbered WA590-639, 649-698, 707-743, built by Gloster and delivered August 1949 to February 1951, followed by 210 F.8 (delivered October 1950 to April 1951), 35 FR.9 and 29 PR.10. The F.8 batches were WA755-794, 808-812 (45) built by Armstrong Whitworth, WA813-857, 867-909, 920-964 (133) by Gloster, and WA965-969, 981-999 and WB105-112 (32) by Armstrong Whitworth. The FR.9 (WB113-125, 133-143, delivered April 1951 to January 1952) and the PR.10 (WB153-181, delivered March to August 1951) were all built by Gloster.

Armstrong Whitworth Meteor NF.11
6/Aircraft/3090/CB.7(b).
An additional NF.11 prototype, numbered WB543, added to the contract on 24.2.49 and delivered June 1952.

Armstrong Whitworth Meteor NF.11
6/Aircraft/3437/CB.7(b), placed 31.5.49.
Two hundred aircraft, numbered WD585-634, 640-689, 696-745, 751-800. Delivered November 1950 to December 1952.

Gloster Meteor F.4
6/Aircraft/1389/CB.7(b), extended 27.7.49.
42 aircraft numbered WE625-666. These aircraft were not delivered, but the contract may relate to components delivered to Belgium for assembly as F.8 by Avions Fairey.

Gloster Meteor F.8
6/Aircraft/4040/CB.7(b), placed 2.9.49.
120 F.8, with production shared by Gloster and Armstrong Whitworth. Aircraft numbered WE852-891, 895-902 (48) built by Armstrong Whitworth, WE903-939, 942-976 (72) by Gloster, deliveries April to May 1951.

Gloster Meteor F.8
6/Aircraft/5043/CB.7(b), placed 25.4.50
89 F.8. WF639-662, 677-688 (36) built by Armstrong Whitworth, WF689-716, 736-760 (53) built by Gloster. Delivered from June to September 1951.

Gloster Meteor T.7
6/Aircraft/5044/CB.7(b), placed 25.4.50.
89 T.7. Numbered WF766-795, 813-862, 875-883, all built by Gloster and delivered between January and September 1951.

Gloster Meteor T.7, F.8, FR.9 and PR.10
6/Aircraft/5621/CB.7(b), placed 14.8.50.
This contract covered 160 T.7 built by Gloster, numbered WG935-950, 961-999, WH112-136, 164-209, 215-248, delivered August 1951 to March 1952 and 200 F.8 built by Armstrong Whitworth, numbered WH249-263, 272-320, 342-386, 395-426, 442-484, 498-513 and delivered September 1951 to March 1952. The contract also covered 25 FR.9 (WH533-557, delivered January to March 1952) and five PR.10 (WH569-573, delivered February to March 1952), all built by Gloster.

Gloster Meteor T.7, F.8, FR.9 and PR.I0
6/Aircraft/6066/CB.7(b), placed 6.12.50.
This contract originally included 373 F.8, 11 FR.9, 20 PR.10 and 126 T.7. F.8 numbered WK647-696, 783-827, 849-893, 936-955, 966-994, WL104-143, 158-191 (263 built by Gloster) and WK707-756, 906-935 (80 built by Armstrong Whitworth). Deliveries of the F.8s stretched from March 1952 to June 1954. F.8 aircraft numbered WL192-207, 221-234 were cancelled, as were PR.10 WL286-305. FR.9 WL255-265 (11) were built by Gloster (deliver-

A front three quarter view of EE387, from a set of official photographs taken at A&AEE Boscombe Down.
ATP 15556, via Tony Buttler

Meteor F.8 WK810 'E' of No 615 Squadron awaiting the scrapper at 12 MU Kirkbride on 1st April 1959, the fate of many Meteors after the disbandment of the Royal Auxiliary Air Force fighter units in 1957.
Phil Butler

ies March to May 1952), as were T.7 WL332-381, 397-436, 453-488 (126) (deliveries March to November 1952).

Armstrong Whitworth Meteor NF.11
6/Aircraft/6141/CB.7(b), placed 22.12.50.
This contract called for 192 NF.11, of which 40 were completed as NF.13 with tropical equipment for Middle East service. Numbered WM143-192, 221-270, 292-307, 368-403 (NF.11, delivered July 1952 to March 1953) and WM308-341, 362-367 (NF.13, deliveries January to March 1953).

Gloster Meteor T.7
6/Aircraft/6066/CB.7(b), extended 26.1.51.
13 aircraft numbered WN309-321 and delivered from December 1952 to August 1953.

Gloster Meteor T.7
6/Aircraft/6410/CB.7(b), placed 28.2.51.
25 aircraft numbered WS103-127 ordered for the Royal Navy, of which WS103-117 were delivered by Gloster between May and July 1952 and the final ten cancelled.

Gloster Meteor T.7 and F.8
6/Aircraft 6411/CB.7(b), placed 28.2.51.
60 T.7 and 250 F.8. All except two T.7 (WS140 and WS141 delivered in November 1953) were cancelled. The cancelled numbers were WS142-170, 183-211 (T.7) and WS230-279, 291-332, 349-394, 403-451, 476-500 and 521-558 (F.8).

Armstrong Whitworth Meteor NF.12 & NF.14
6/Aircraft/6412/CB.7(b), placed 28.2.51.
This contract, originally placed for further NF.11s, produced 100 NF.12 (WS590-639, 658-700, 715-721, delivered May to September 1953) and 100 NF.14 (WS722-760, 774-812, 827-848, delivered October 1953 to May 1954).

Gloster Meteor FR.9
6/Aircraft/7252/CB.7(b), placed 13.8.51.
82 Meteor FR.9. Twenty aircraft, WX962-981, were delivered by Gloster from May to August 1952, and the remainder cancelled. The cancelled numbers were WX982-994 and WZ103-151.

Gloster Meteor T.7
6/Aircraft/7253/CB.7(b), placed 13.8.51.
91 Meteor T.7, numbered WZ154-203, 227-267, all of which were cancelled.

Gloster Meteor T.7
6/Aircraft/6411/CB.7(b), extension of 7.8.53.

This was the final Meteor contract, for seven T.7s, numbered XF273-279 and delivered November 1953 to July 1954.

Gloster Meteor U.15
The U.15s were converted by Flight Refuelling Ltd at their Tarrant Rushton works from surplus Meteor F.4 aircraft. There were ninety conversions, under contracts 6/Aircraft/9725/CB.7(b) and 6/Aircraft/10925/CB.24(b), with the prototype being RA421. The conversions were: EE521, 524. RA367, 371, 373, 375, 387, 397, 398, 415, 417, 420, 421, 430, 432, 433, 438, 439, 441, 442, 454, 457, 473, 479. VT104, 105, 106, 107, 110, 112, 113, 118, 130, 135, 139, 142, 168, 175, 177, 179, 184, 187, 191, 192, 196, 197, 219, 220, 222, 226, 230, 243, 256, 259, 262, 268, 270, 282, 286, 289, 291, 294, 310, 316, 319, 329, 330, 332, 334, 338. VW258, 266, 273, 275, 276, 280, 285, 293, 299, 303, 308, 781, 791. VZ386, 389, 401, 403, 407, 414, 415, 417.

Gloster Meteor U.16 (later D.16) & U.21
When stocks of surplus F.4 were used up, the U.16 was developed by converting surplus F.8 airframes. Conversions were again carried out by Flight Refuelling Ltd at Tarrant Rushton. The prototype conversions were WA775 and WE934, with the complete list comprising:

VZ445, 448, 455, 485, 503, 506, 513, 514, 551, 554. WA756, 775, 842, 982, 991. WE867, 872, 915, 932, 934, 960, 962. WF659, 681, 685, 706, 707, 711, 716, 741, 743, 751, 755, 756. WH258, 284, 286, 309, 315, 320, 344, 349, 359, 365, 369, 372, 373, 376, 381, 419, 420, 453, 460, 469, 499, 500, 505, 506, 509. WK648, 675, 693, 709, 710, 716, 717, 721, 729, 731, 737, 738, 743, 744, 745, 746, 747, 783, 784, 789, 790, 793, 795, 797, 799, 807, 812, 852, 855, 859, 8767, 870, 877, 879, 883, 885, 911, 925, 926, 932, 941, 942, 949, 971, 980, 989, 993, 994. WL110, 111, 124, 134, 136, 160, 162, 163. (total 116 from F.8, plus one conversion, WK800, from RAAF U.21)

Many U.16s were used in Australia, where further (RAAF) F.8s were converted to U.21 or U.21A standard, with slightly different telemetry equipment. The first U.21 conversion was done by Flight Refuelling on WE902 at Tarrant Rushton. Flight Refuelling also converted U.16s VZ455, VZ503, WF659, WH460, WK710, WK879 and WL136 to U.21 standard before they were shipped to Australia. Fairey Aviation converted RAAF F.8s A77-157, -193, -207, -422, -510, -802, -851, -855, -863, -872, -873, -876, -882, -884 and -885 to U.21 or U.21A standard in Australia. Conversely, WL136 and A77-876 (the former RAF WK800) were shipped back to England and were then converted to U.16/D.16 for work at Llanbedr. Totals: (UK) 1 conversion from F.8, seven from U.16, (Australia) 15 conversions from F.8. Two returned to the UK and reverted to U.16.

Armstrong Whitworth Meteor TT.20
The TT.20 was a conversion of the NF.11 for target-towing duties, used by the RAF, Royal Navy, MoD experimental establishments, the Royal Danish Air Force and the Swedish target-towing contractor Svensk Flygtjänst. There were 50 conversions, the prototype being WD767: WD585, 591, 592, 606, 610, 612, 623, 629, 630, 641, 643, 645, 646, 647, 649, 652, 657, 678, 679, 702, 706, 711, 767, 780, 785. WM147, 148, 151, 159, 160, 167, 181, 223, 224, 230, 234, 242, 245, 246, 255, 260, 270, 292, 293. RDAF Nos 504, 508 (later SE-DCH), 512 (SE-DCF), 517 (SE-DCG), 518 and 519 (SE-DCI). The Danish aircraft and twenty of the British ones were converted by Armstrong Whitworth Aircraft at Bitteswell, the rest of the British aircraft being converted by the Royal Navy at Belfast/Sydenham.

FOREIGN SALES

Argentina
Fifty F.4 diverted from RAF contracts and identified as I-001 to I-050 (later C-001 to C-050), delivered to Argentina March to October 1948. (Previously RA384, 386, 388-391, 370, 385, 392, 393, 395, 396, EE570, 575, 551, 569, 554, 571, 553, 546, 544, 552, 576, 548, 532, 572, 527, 535, 537, 542, 588, 581, 582, 574, 580, 577, 583, 587, 585, 589, 586, 526, 540, 534, 547, 543, 533, 539, 536, 541.)

Fifty F.4 newly-built for Argentina, identified as I-051 to I-100 (C-050 to C-100), delivered to Argentina from December 1948 to July 1949.

Australia
(all aircraft diverted from RAF contracts)

A77-1 Mk.III delivered for evaluation in 1947, ex-EE427.

Nine T.7 delivered between 1951 and 1955. A77-2, -4, -229 (later -701), -305 (later -702), -380 (later -703), -577 (later -704), -705, -706, and -707. These were ex-RAF aircraft, respectively ex-VW410, WN321, WA731, WA732, WG974, WG977, WA680, WF843 and WH118.

Ninety-four F.8. A77-11, -15, -17, -29, -31, -46, -65, -120, -128, -134, -139, -157, -163, -189, -193, -207, -231, -251, -258, -300, -316, -343, -354, -368, -373, 385, -393, -397, -415, -422, -436, 446, 464, -510, -559, -570, -587, -616, -627, -643, -721, -726, -728, -730, -734, -735, -740, -741, -744, -793, -802, -811, -851 to -886 inclusive, -911, -920, -949, -953, -959 and -982. These aircraft were, respectively, ex-WH259, WE911, WA964, WA938, WE903, WF746, WH475, WE880, WE908, WE898, WA949, WE889, WA941, WA961, WE969, WH251, WA944, WE906, WH254, WA935, WA945, WH274, WA934, WA952, WA936, WE918, WE877, WE896, WE900, WF750, WE971, WA783, WA958, WE905, WA910, WE890, WA939, WA956, WE928, WE886, WA954, WA957, WA951, WA782, WE907, WA942, WA948, WA947, WA786, WH252, WA998, WA937, WK683, WH479, WK715, WK650, WK728, WK686, WK684, WK682, WK688, WK670, WH418, WH417, WK730, WK735, WH405, WH414, WK685, WK674, WK727, WK748, WK791, WK792, WK796, WK909, WK798, WK800, WK913, WK907, WK821, WK944, WK910, WK937, WK912, WK931, WK973, WK938, WA946, WF653, WA960, WE874, WA909 and WA950.

One NF.11, A77-3 ex-WM262

Belgium
Forty-eight new F.4 numbered EF-1 to EF-48 built by Gloster. Twenty of these later converted to T.7 standard by Avions Fairey, becoming numbered ED-13 to -32.

Three new T.7 (ED-1 to -3) built by Gloster, followed by nine aircraft diverted from RAF contracts (ED-4 to -12, ex-WF817, WF827, WF818, WL399, WL428, WL427, WL415, WH171 and

Meteor TT.20 WD629 of No 1574 Target Facilities Flight based at RAF Changi, Singapore. In the background is Hastings C.2 WJ337. via Phil Butler

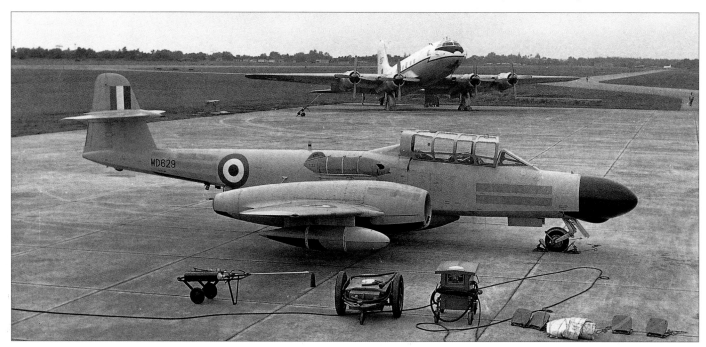

Meteor F.8 A77-207 displays the mid and rear fuselage markings of a Royal Australian Air Force Meteor. Jet Age Museum

WH174). ED-13 to -32 were conversions of Belgian Air Force F.4s by Avions Fairey. ED-33 to -37 were further diversions from RAF contracts (ex-WL486, WN320, WS140, WS141 and XF273). Finally, ED-38 to -43 were ex-RAF aircraft, delivered after RAF service (WA688, WH114, WA684, WH117, WG970 and WF814).

Belgium received large numbers of F.8s. The first Fokker-built Meteor, EG-1, made its first flight on 28th June 1950, slightly ahead of deliveries to the Netherlands. These included EG-1 to -145, all built by Fokker, and EG-146 to -150 (ex-RAF aircraft WF692, WF693, WF691, WF701 and WH448). EG-151 to -180 were F.8s assembled by Avions Fairey from components supplied by Fokker. EG-201 to -223 were further aircraft diverted from RAF contracts (VZ450, 457, 459, 499, 553, 562, 566, WA755, 870, 876, 878, 881, 883, 884, 887, 888, 889, 892, 895, 898, 900, 901, 902 in random order), while EG-224 to -260 were aircraft assembled by Avions Fairey from components supplied by Gloster.

Belgium also received 24 ex-RAF Meteor NF.11s, numbered EN-1 to -24. These were ex-WD726, 775, 777, 728, 729, 730, 727, 731, 732, 733, 735, 736, 602, 724, 622, 594, 760, 661, 590, 596, 741, 763 and WM221, 263.

Brazil

Brazil received 10 T.7 and sixty F.8 in 1953, all produced by Gloster. The T.7 were cancelled RAF aircraft with serials WS142 to WS151 and became FAB 4300 to 4309. The F.8 were numbered 4400 to 4459. The last five of these had been undelivered (embargoed) Egyptian aircraft. Deliveries completed December 1953.

Canada

F.4 VT196, which had been used for afterburner trials by Rolls-Royce, was loaned to Canada for afterburner experiments in connection with the Avro (Canada) Orenda engine. VT196 was later returned to the UK and converted to a U.15. EE282, EE311, EE361 and RA421 were also on RCAF strength for various trials.

Denmark

Denmark received twenty Gloster-built F.4, numbered 461 to 480, in 1949/50.

Denmark later received nine T.7, numbered 261 to 269.

The RDAF F.4 were replaced by twenty F.8, numbered 481 to 500.

Finally, the RDAF received twenty NF.11, numbered 501 to 520, diverted RAF aircraft originally intended as WM384 to WM403. Six of these were later converted to TT.20 standard for further service.

Ecuador

Ecuador received twelve ex-RAF FR.9 versions, via Gloster Aircraft. These were numbered 701 to 712 and were ex-VZ597, WH547, VW366, WB136, VZ610, WH540, WH543, WH549, WH550, WH553, WH554, and WH555.

Egypt

Twelve F.4, numbered 1401 to 1412, were delivered in 1950. The last seven of these aircraft were originally VZ420 to VZ426 from an RAF contract and were built by Armstrong Whitworth Aircraft.

Three T.7, numbered 1400, 1413 and 1414 were delivered in advance of the F.4 order. Three further aircraft, ex-RAF, became 1439 to 1441 (ex-VW435, WA730, WG994).

Twenty-four F.8s were ordered, only to be embargoed and cancelled. An order for twelve was then reinstated, but only four of these, numbered 1416 to 1418 and 1422, were delivered before another arms embargo was imposed. The remainder were re-allotted to Brazil and Israel. Finally, eight F.8, all ex-RAF, were delivered as 1415, 1419 to 1421, 1423 to 1426, ex-WH350, WL188, WH371, WL186, WL183, WL185, WL187, WL191, in substitution for the embargoed aircraft, after arms sales resumed in 1955.

Six ex-RAF NF.13 were delivered, numbered 1427 to 1432 (ex-WM325, 326, 328, 338, 340 and 362).

France

The French received one standard F.4, EE523, sold to them in 1948, and registered as F-WEPQ/F-BEPQ. The former Rolls-Royce Avon testbed, RA491, was also sold to France and was delivered after conversion by Air Service Training Ltd to act as a flying testbed for the SNECMA Atar axial-flow turbojet.

Two T.7, embargoed Syrian aircraft, numbered 91 and 92, were delivered in February 1951. Following the intended acquisition of NF.11 night fighters, a further eleven T.7 trainers were transferred, as F1 to F11 (F5 to F8 ex-WF832, WG997, WH136, WH168. The others were WF776, WH228, WL425, WL485, WL471, WL476 and WN312). Another ex-RAF aircraft, WA607, became F-BEAR in 1954 for the CEV. *Note: There is some confusion regarding the ex-Syrian aircraft. Conceivably they may included within the F1 to F11 batch.*

Forty-one NF.11s were supplied, nine for the Centre d'Essais en Vol, and thirty-two for Escadre de Chasse (EC) 30. These aircraft were: WD619, 628, 631, 655, 669, 674, 683, 698, 701, 756 and 783. WM153, 164, 235, 243, 265, 296 to 307, 368 to 371 and 375 to 383. The aircraft from WM368 onwards were delivered first, as new aircraft (with numbers NF11-1 to -25 in order of their RAF serials), with the remainder following after brief RAF service. The relation of RAF serials to French identities for these later aircraft is not known.

Ex-RAF NF.13 aircraft WM364 and WM365 (to '364' and '365'), used for trials work at the CEV.

Ex-RAF NF.14s WS747 and WS796 (to NF14-747 and '796') used for trials work at the CEV.

Six surplus TT.20s, after removal of their target-towing equipment, were delivered in 1974 as a source of spares for the CEV Mk.11, 13 and 14 fleet. These had previously been WD649, WD652, WD780, WM242, WM255 and WM293. All wore the marking 'F-ZABD' for their delivery flights.

Israel

The IDFAF received four new T.7 built by Gloster (numbered 2162 to 2165), and two (111 and 112) from the RAF (ex-WL434 and WL466). In December 1957/January 1958 five T.7 converted from Belgian F.4 by Avions Fairey were delivered, these being fitted with F.8 tail units.

Eleven new F.8 aircraft built by Gloster, initially numbered 2166 to 2169 and 2172 to 2178. The last three aircraft had been Egyptian ones (allotted numbers 1424 to 1426) retained at Gloster after an arms embargo was imposed on Egypt.

Belgian and Dutch Meteors being assembled in the Fokker factory at Schiphol. Via Tony Buttler

Seven ex-RAF FR.9 aircraft numbered 211 to 217 (ex-WX967, WL259, WB123, WB140, WX975, WX963 and WX980)

Six ex-RAF NF.13 aircraft as 4X-FNA to 4X-FNF (previously WM366, WM334, WM312, WM309, WM320 and WM335). The former WM312 and WM320 were embargoed and not delivered until 1958, after the Suez crisis, while WM335 was lost on its delivery flight at the same time.

Netherlands

The KLu received 34 new Gloster-built F.4, numbered I-21 to I-54. These were supplemented by 30 ex-RAF F.4s, numbered I-55 to I-80 (VZ391, 393, 395, 396, 397, 387, 400, 388, 390, 399, VW309, 286, VZ398, 402, 409, 408, VW288, 264, 291, 310, 313, VT333, VW263, VZ394, VW295, 296, 315).

The Dutch received several batches of T.7. The first twenty (I-1 to I-20) were ordered in 1948, with the first aircraft being the Gloster demonstrator G-AKPK. I-2 to I-7 were new aircraft, while I-8 to I-20 were ex-RAF (WA623, WA626, WA633, WH165, WH203, WH193, WH196, WH199, WH179, WH202, WL469, WH233 and WL482). A later batch was numbered I-301 to I-325, also ex-RAF aircraft (WH207, WH222, WL487, WH125, WG998, WL426, WN315, WH237, WL477, WH245, XF275, XF276, XF277, XF279, XF278, VW475, WH135, WH245, WL412, WA674, VW417, WA594, WA592, WF856, WH247 and WH177).

By the time the F.8 was ordered, licensed production had been arranged at NV Fokker, Schiphol, to supply both Dutch and Belgian requirements. The Royal Netherlands Air Force received Fokker-built aircraft numbered I-101 to I-255. Five ex-RAF F.8, numbered I-90 to I-94, were also supplied (ex-WF697, 698, 699, 694 and 696).

New Zealand

The RNZAF received Mk.III EE395 for evaluation. It was renumbered NZ6001.

South Africa

The SAAF received Mk.III EE429 on loan for evaluation. It was later returned to the RAF.

Sweden

Three T.7 were sold to Sweden, of which SE-CAS and SE-CAT were formerly WF833 and WH128 of the RAF. The third was SE-DCC, which was previously the Gloster T.7 demonstrator G-ANSO. All three were used for target-towing by Svensk Flygtjänst AB, a civilian contractor to the Flygvapnet (Royal Swedish Air Force).

Later four ex-Royal Danish Air Force TT.20s were purchased for the same duty (SE-DCF, SE-DCG, SE-DCH and SE-DCI).

Syria

Two new aircraft, embargoed and diverted to France. They were however used to train Syrian pilots in England as '91' and '92' in Syrian markings before being embargoed.

Reports that these two were replaced, possibly by ex-RAF aircraft, are believed to be in error. It is possible that they were ex-RAF aircraft in the first place and then became part of the 'F1' to 'F11' batch that served in France.

Twelve F.8 were supplied from Gloster production, followed by a further seven ex-RAF aircraft. The new aircraft were numbered 101 to 112, the ex-RAF examples being 413 to 419 (ex-WA785, WL174, WK868, WK984, WH503, WE965 and WH260, respectively).

Two ex-RAF FR.9 aircraft, numbered 480 and 481 (ex-WB133 and WX972).

Six ex-RAF NF.13 aircraft, numbered 471 to 476 (ex-WM332, WM336, WM330, WM337, WM341 and WM333)

TOTAL PRODUCTION

The summaries below are believed to be the most accurate breakdown of Meteor production yet published. The situation regarding overseas deliveries of Meteors has never been very clear, but as time goes on more information emerges about diversions from RAF contracts, or even 'surplus' sales of aircraft that had seen (possibly brief) RAF service. Some of these transactions have previously been assumed to be direct sales of new aircraft to overseas governments.

Gloster Aircraft Company
F.9/40: 8

F.I: 20

F.III: 208

F.4: 604
72 EE, 100 RA, 200 VT, 73 VW, 1 VZ.
50 Argentine, 48 Belgian, 34 Dutch, 20 Danish, 5 Egyptian and G-AIDC. (1 PR.5 converted from F.4)

T.7: 677
70 VW, 21 VZ, 137 WA, 89 WF, 160 WG/WH, 126 WL, 13 WN, 27 WS, 7 XF. 3 Belgian, 9 Danish, 6 Dutch, 3 Egyptian, 4 Israeli and 2 French.
(G-AKPK was F.4 G-AIDC converted, G-ANSO was F.8 G-AMCJ converted).

F.8: 702
73 VZ, 133 WA, 72 WE, 53 WF, 263 WK/WL.
60 Brazil, 20 Denmark, 11 Israel, 12 Syria, 4 Egyptian and G-AMCJ/G-7-1.

FR.9: 126
12 VW, 35 VZ, 23 WB, 25 WH, 11 WL and 20 WX.

PR.10: 59
20 VS, 4 VW, 1 VZ, 29 WB and 5 WH.

Total Gloster Production = 2404

Armstrong Whitworth Aircraft
F.4: 45

F.8: 470
45 VZ, 45 & 32 WA, 32 WE, 36 WF, 200 WH & 80 WK.

NF.11: 355
2 WA, 1 WB, 200 WD and 152 WM.

NF.12: 100 WS

NF.13: 40 WM

NF.14: 100 WS

Total Armstrong Whitworth Production = 1110

All on British contracts (F.4 and F.8 sub-contracted from Gloster). Aircraft diverted to Egypt (7 F.4), Denmark (20 NF.11), France (25 NF.11)

Fokker F.8: 300
155 to Royal Netherlands AF, 145 to Royal Belgian AF, with Fokker c/ns 6315 to 6644 (mixed batches, inc the component sets delivered to Avions Fairey).

Avions Fairey F.8: 67
From Fokker (30) or Gloster (37) components, all to Belgian Air Force.

Total from all manufacturers = 3881

RAF Meteor Squadrons and Other Units with Representative Aircraft

Meteor F Mk.1

616 Squadron	EE215, EE229
1335 CU	EE216, EE225

Meteor F Mk.3

1 Squadron	EE284, EE458
56 Squadron	EE357, EE485
63 Squadron	EE345, EE470
66 Squadron	EE349, EE399
74 Squadron	EE306, EE473
92 Squadron	EE332, EE482
124 Squadron	EE363, EE464
222 Squadron	EE247, EE450
234 Squadron	EE290, EE487
245 Squadron	EE282, EE484
257 Squadron	EE272, EE352
263 Squadron	EE353, EE404
266 Squadron	EE277, EE411
500 Squadron	EE348, EE403
504 Squadron	EE283, EE305
541 Squadron	EE409, EE410
616 Squadron	EE231, EE277
778 (FAA) Squadron	EE337
1335 CU (later 226 OCU)	EE318, EE474
CFE	EE281, EE472
CFS	EE282
CGS	EE314
ECFS/EFS	EE231
Eastern Sector Flight	EE470
Tangmere Station Flight	EE304

Meteor F Mk.4

1 Squadron	RA371, VZ436
19 Squadron	EE598, RA366
41 Squadron	VT177, VW285
43 Squadron	VT132, VT257
56 Squadron	EE591, VT304
63 Squadron	VT213, VZ417
66 Squadron	RA440, VW276
74 Squadron	RA427, VT303
92 Squadron	RA415, VW258
222 Squadron	RA443, VT233
245 Squadron	RA414, VZ410
257 Squadron	RA444, VT268
263 Squadron	RA426, VW281
266 Squadron	VT102, VT238
500 Squadron	RA474, VZ392
504 Squadron	EE584, VW272
600 Squadron	RA381, VZ411
609 Squadron	VT262, VZ436
610 Squadron	EE524, VZ436
611 Squadron	RA368, VT289
615 Squadron	VW285, VZ428
616 Squadron	RA429, VT115
226 OCU	RA372, VZ437
CFE	EE578, VT335

High Speed Flight	EE528, EE530
APS Acklington	VT135
CFE	VW787
CGS	RA365
ETPS	VW302
FCCS	EE549
Jet Conversion Flight	VT142
RAF Flying College	RA486
Yorkshire Sector Flight	VT266
203 AFS	EE590
205 AFS	EE528
207 AFS	EE517
209 AFS	RA368
215 AFS	EE529
8 FTS	RA387
12 FTS	RA368

Meteor T Mk.7

1 Squadron	VW487, WG938
2 Squadron	WH180, WL407
3 Squadron	WA656, WA662
4 Squadron	WF836, WL338
5 Squadron	WG973
6 Squadron	VW482, WA605
8 Squadron	WF855, WN313
11 Squadron	WA693, WF877
13 Squadron	WH113, WH116
14 Squadron	WF779
16 Squadron	WA657, WF789
19 Squadron	WF819, WG940
25 Squadron	WF816, WF876
26 Squadron	WF784, WL430
28 Squadron	WA675, WG976
29 Squadron	WA733, WF772
32 Squadron	WA611, WA613
33 Squadron	WA659, WF825
34 Squadron	WL422
39 Squadron	WA613, WL431
41 Squadron	WF848, WH127
43 Squadron	VW488, WA733
46 Squadron	WA742, WH209
54 Squadron	VW486, WF785
56 Squadron	WA629, WA742
60 Squadron	WH209, WH226
63 Squadron	VZ632, WA722
64 Squadron	WF793, WG979
65 Squadron	WF854, WL373
66 Squadron	VZ630, WF769
67 Squadron	WF792, WG935
68 Squadron	WH185, WH236
71 Squadron	WF786, WH117
72 Squadron	VZ629, WF783
73 Squadron	WA618, WF882
74 Squadron	VW430, WL380
79 Squadron	WH235, WL355
81 Squadron	WA681, WH119
85 Squadron	WA733, WF876
87 Squadron	WH189, WH204

89 Squadron	WA620, WL459
92 Squadron	WF813, WH223
93 Squadron	WA666, WH133
94 Squadron	WA739, WG939
96 Squadron	WF862, WN309
98 Squadron	WF813
112 Squadron	WG973, WH228
118 Squadron	WF836, WH181
141 Squadron	VZ634, WG936
145 Squadron	WH221, WH236
151 Squadron	VW471, WG949
152 Squadron	VW473, WL459
185 Squadron	VW432, WG941
208 Squadron	WA606, WL404
213 Squadron	WA622, WH113
219 Squadron	WH206, WL411
222 Squadron	VZ633, WL480
245 Squadron	VW484, WG943
247 Squadron	VZ634, WA658
249 Squadron	WA596, WA611
256 Squadron	WF862, WN310
257 Squadron	VW428, VZ631
263 Squadron	VW489, WA599
264 Squadron	WH209, WH243
421 Squadron (RCAF)	WA740, WA742
500 Squadron	VZ638, WH224
501 Squadron	WA592, WA721
502 Squadron	WF774, WF824
504 Squadron	WA610, WF845
541 Squadron	WF779, WH123
600 Squadron	WA628, WF771
601 Squadron	WA601, WF816
602 Squadron	WF773, WG993
603 Squadron	WF825, WG949
604 Squadron	VW453, WL462
605 Squadron	WA595, WH115
607 Squadron	WF833, WH225
608 Squadron	WA671, WH223
609 Squadron	WA672, WG940
610 Squadron	WF785, WH127
611 Squadron	WA743, WL470
612 Squadron	WH208, WL378
613 Squadron	WA637, WF778
614 Squadron	VZ636, WG991
615 Squadron	WA684, WA689
616 Squadron	VZ640, WH120
226 OCU	VW416, VZ629
228 OCU	VW456, WH240
229 OCU	VW450, WA729
231 OCU	VW422, VW449
237 OCU	WA697
CFE	VW478
702 (FAA) Squadron	VW436
703 (FAA) Squadron	WS103
728 (FAA) Squadron	VZ648
736 (FAA) Squadron	WS107
759 (FAA) Squadron	WL336
771 (FAA) Squadron	WA649
1 GWDS	
1 OFU	WL342

1 TWU
3 Group CF — WF772
2 TAF Communications Flight
3/4 CAACU — VW478
5 CAACU — WG984
12 Group CF — WL480
13 Group CF — WL419
23 Group CF
25 Group CF
41 Group CF
81 Group CF — WL468
83 Group CF — WL338
101 FRS — VW435
102 FRS — VW419
103 FRS — WF831
205 Group CF
1689 Flight — WF826
Abu Sueir Station Flight — WH113
Ahlhorn Station Flight — WF862
APS Acklington — WF819
APS Sylt — WL338
Bomber Command CF/CS — VW449
Benson Station Flight — WL366
CFS — WA668
CGS — VW477
Church Fenton Station Flight — WH205
Coltishall Station Flight — VW471
Coningsby Station Flight — WN318
Duxford Station Flight — VW450
EAAS — VW477
FEAFES — WA683
FCCS — VZ630
FWS — WL410
Geilenkirchen Station Flight — WN310
Gütersloh Meteor Flight — WF792
Handling Squadron — WF879
Hemswell Station Flight — WL398
ITF Nicosia — VW482
ITF Shallufa — WF853
JCU Marham — WF772
Khormaksar Station Flight — WN313
Laarbruch Station Flight — WL413
Leuchars Station Flight — WF861
Levant CF — VW482
Linton-on-Ouse Station Flight — VZ644
Malta C&TT Squadron — WF772
MEAF CF — WF795
Nicosia Station Flight — WF839
Odiham Station Flight — VW486
Oldenburg Station Flight — WL464
RAF Flying College — VW480
Scampton Station Flight — WH118
Stradishall Station Flight — VZ634
Thorney Island Station Flight — VZ644
Upwood Station Flight — WG942
Wahn Station Flight — WL407
Wattisham Station Flight — VW473
West Raynham Station Flight — WL459
Wittering Station Flight — VZ633
Wunstorf Station Flight — WF779
202 AFS — VW475
203 AFS — VW440
205 AFS — WF829
206 AFS — WL357
207 AFS — WH226
209 AFS — WA608
210 AFS — WL356
211 AFS — WA590
215 AFS — WA591
4 FTS — WL435
5 FTS — WG987
8 FTS — WH121

Meteor F Mk.8

1 Squadron	VZ454, WA842
19 Squadron	WA758, WB108
29 Squadron	WF654, WK921
34 Squadron	WF742, WL181
41 Squadron	WB110, WK888
43 Squadron	VZ440, WL114
54 Squadron	WH343, WH378
56 Squadron	VZ480, WA930
63 Squadron	VZ563, WA907
64 Squadron	WE858, WH313
65 Squadron	VZ532, WE916
66 Squadron	VZ505, WB112
72 Squadron	VZ501, WL138
74 Squadron	VZ446, WA840
92 Squadron	VZ453, WA793
111 Squadron	WK741, WL124
222 Squadron	VZ448, WA831
245 Squadron	VZ465, WA773
247 Squadron	VZ541, WK993
257 Squadron	VZ444, WF641
263 Squadron	VZ510, WA896
500 Squadron	VZ472, WF644
504 Squadron	WH255, WH318
600 Squadron	WF684, WK671
601 Squadron	WH349, WK783
604 Squadron	WH309, WK696
609 Squadron	VZ456, WK941
610 Squadron	WE891, WH302
611 Squadron	VZ484, WH365
615 Squadron	WF639, WF760
616 Squadron	WE862, WH456
226 OCU	WA808, WH256
229 OCU	WH286, WK716
233 OCU	WE946, WH354
CFE	VZ443, WE960
1 TWU	VZ467
5 CAACU	WF711
12 Group CF	WA777
13 Group CF	WE876
211 AFS	WK822
1574 Flight	WA880
APS Acklington	VZ522
APS Sylt	VZ455
Caledonian Sector Flight	WK734
ETPS	VZ451
FCCS	VZ468
FWS	WE887
Handling Squadron	VZ464
Metropolitan Sector Flight	WH380
Northern Sector Flight	WK724
RAF Flying College	VZ445
Southern Sector Flight	WA987
THUM Flight	VZ508
Western Sector Flight	WA844

Meteor FR Mk.9

2 Squadron	VW364, VZ585
8 Squadron	WH539, WX978
79 Squadron	VZ590, WB124
187 Squadron	WX967, WX975
208 Squadron	VW361, VZ606
226 OCU	WB125, WH536
CFE	VW366, WX964
Aden FR Flight	VZ601

Meteor PR Mk.10

2 Squadron	VS974, WB154
13 Squadron	WB161, WH572
81 Squadron	VW377, WB166

541 Squadron	VW376, WH573
231 OCU	WB157, WB179
237 OCU	VZ620, WB160

Meteor NF Mk.11

5 Squadron	WD740, WD776
29 Squadron	WD598, WD792
68 Squadron	WD651, WD737
85 Squadron	WD614, WD763
87 Squadron	WD658, WM183
96 Squadron	WD622, WM244
125 Squadron	WD657, WM294
141 Squadron	WD606, WM157
151 Squadron	WD590, WM270
256 Squadron	WD642, WD707
264 Squadron	WD647, WD783
228 OCU	WD702, WM230
CFE	WD585, WD799
CFE	WM191
ETPS	WD765

Meteor NF Mk.12

25 Squadron	WS612, WS680
29 Squadron	WS593, WS679
46 Squadron	WS607, WS676
64 Squadron	WS614, WS682
72 Squadron	WS591, WS700
85 Squadron	WS600, WS718
152 Squadron	WS674, WS691
153 Squadron	WS613, WS720
264 Squadron	WS596, WS675
228 OCU	WS593, WS683
238 AWOCU	WS590, WS672
CFE	WS606, WS698
CSE	WS597
FWS	WS620

Meteor NF Mk.13

39 Squadron	WM308, WM339
219 Squadron	WM312, WM335

Meteor NF Mk.14

25 Squadron	WS725, WS776
33 Squadron	WS836, WS844
46 Squadron	WS724, WS835
60 Squadron	WS754, WS800
64 Squadron	WS797, WS804
72 Squadron	WS779, WS846
85 Squadron	WS723, WS777
152 Squadron	WS735, WS805
153 Squadron	WS738, WS757
264 Squadron	WS747, WS795
228 OCU	WS731, WS844
238 AWOCU	WS829, WS847
CFE	WS751, WS848
1 ANS	WS802
2 ANS	WS788
Handling Squadron	WS731
13 Group CF	WS775
ETPS	WS845
FCCS	WS848

Meteor TT Mk.20

3/4 CAACU	WD630, WM148
5 CAACU	WM224
TTF Seletar	WD606, WM230
1574 Flight	WD591, WM246

Meteors in Colour

Gloster F.9/40. Preserved by the RAF Museum and normally on show at the Cosford Aerospace Museum, DG202, the first F.9/40 to be built, was displayed at RIAT Fairford in 2003. Phil Butler C161014

EE397, a Meteor F.3 fitted with an air-to-air refuelling probe, approaching its Flight Refuelling tanker off the south coast of England in 1949. Note the 'gate' type airbrakes slightly extended on the inboard wing sections. The camouflage is very similar to a late Second World War scheme, even to the 'sky'-coloured band around the rear fuselage. Flight Refuelling, via Tony Buttler

A fairly rare colour shot of a Meteor F.4, this one being EE531 – which was sent for scrap in 1953, only to be retrieved by the Royal Aircraft Establishment for experiments with radio aerial installations and kept at their Lasham out-station for many years. via Phil Butler

Mk.4 VT229 wears the typical silver colour scheme with yellow fuselage and wing T-bands of an aircraft from an Advanced Flying School. This shot was taken in the museum at RAF Colerne in October 1969, quite some years after this example had been retired from its time as '60' of No 209 Advanced Flying School (later No 12 Flying Training School) at RAF Weston Zoyland in Somerset. Phil Butler C21220

Meteor F.4 I-69 was flown by the Royal Netherlands Air Force, and later preserved in the RNethAF Museum at Soesterberg. Photographed at Deelen RNethAF Base on 30th June 1973. Phil Butler C61007

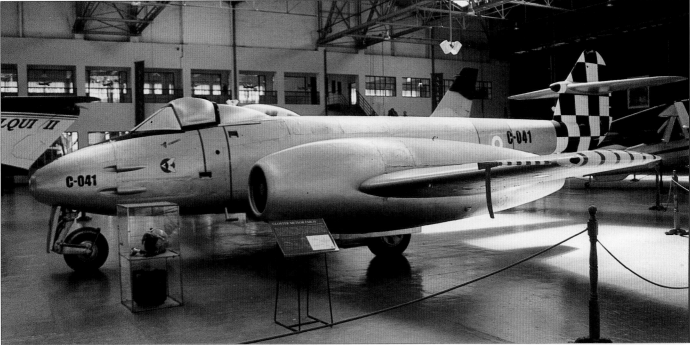

F.4 C-057 of the Fuerza Aérea Argentina in the standard camouflage scheme adopted by the FAA during the later service of the Meteors (they had originally flown uncamouflaged).
via Tony Buttler

Meteor F.4 C-041 of the Argentine Air Force in the museum at Moron, October 2003.
Gerry Manning

The red Meteor Trainer demonstrator G-AKPK, photographed at Farnborough during the SBAC Show in 1948. This was sold to the Royal Netherlands Air Force later as 'I-1'. Peter Berry

A formation of Meteor T.7s of the Central Flying School, Little Rissington, taken by Russell Adams in 1953 and showing WH241, WA615, WG962 and WA683. The letter 'O' in the two-letter combinations indicates aircraft of the CFS. Two aircraft show white bands painted around the rear fuselage, the significance of which is **not known.** Russell Adams/Jet Age Museum

T.7 WL332 of the Royal Navy, coded '571/HF' of No 728 Squadron, photographed at Hal Far, Malta in the standard 'silver with yellow T-bands' colours prevalent in the late 1950s. A E Hughes, via Ray Sturtivant

Meteor T.7 WH166, code '27' of the Central Flying School, photographed at Tern Hill, 19th September 1965 in the then-current silver and Day-Glo nose, tail and wing markings and wearing the CFS Pelican badge on its nose.
Phil Butler C10110

Enlargement of CFS badge on the nose of WH166, Ternhill 19th September 1965.
Phil Butler C10111

A T.7 in Royal Navy hands, WS103 was also flown by the FRU at Hurn. Photographed 25th July 1969. Phil Butler C13005

Meteor T.7 WA662, an aircraft of RAE Llanbedr, in the standard silver/yellow T-bands markings which had in most cases been superseded by stick-on Day-Glo patches by the date of this photograph, taken at RAF Valley on 20th August 1970. Phil Butler C31308

Meteor T.7 WA662, 'K' of the RAE, landing at Llanbedr. Gerry Manning

Meteor T.7 WA662 is shown in a late white and grey colour scheme, with the royal blue fuselage flash adopted by the Royal Aircraft Establishment, Llanbedr. Photographed at RAF Abingdon on 16th September 1978. Phil Butler C100616

Two views of Meteor T.7 WA662, photographed at RAF Finningley on 19th September 1981.
Phil Butler C103001/C110916

Meteor T.7 WA669 was for some years one of the 'Vintage Pair' flown by the Central Flying School, whose badge appears on its nose. It was written-off on 21.8.86 in a collision with its paired Vampire T.11 at Mildenhall. It is in the overall grey scheme, with the old-style yellow T-bands. Photographed at Liverpool Airport on 12th May 1973. Phil Butler C60306

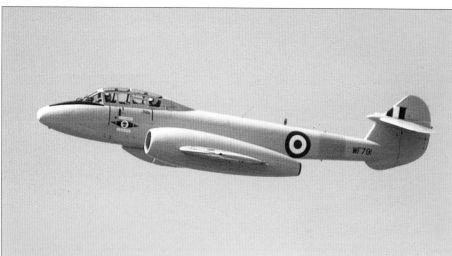

Meteor T.7 WF791 of No 5 CAACU, Woodvale, photographed in September 1971. It wears a scheme of grey polyurethane paint with 'stick-on' Day-Glo patches, then in favour as the finish on training aircraft. Phil Butler C41620

One of the CFS 'Vintage Pair', Meteor T.7 WF791, photographed at Liverpool on 21st June 1981. Phil Butler C102705

WL419 was one of the T.7 aircraft modified for trials of Martin-Baker ejection seats in the rear cockpit. It has the Mk.8-type fin in place of the usual T.7 type, thus sometimes called a 'Mark 7-and-a-half'. Photographed at RAF Abingdon 15th September 1990. Phil Butler C112405

Meteor T.7 WA638, another of the Martin-Baker testbeds, in a more recent black colour scheme. Photographed at Fairford, 20th July 2002.
Phil Butler C151818

WL419 is one of the several Meteors flown by Martin-Baker Aircraft for 'live' ejection-seat trials, with a rocket-powered seat just being launched in this shot. This Meteor is one of two still in service with M-B at the time of writing.
Martin-Baker Aircraft, via Tony Buttler

Martin-Baker's Meteor WL419 during a trial firing of a rocket-powered ejection seat on the ground. Martin-Baker Aircraft, via Tony Buttler

Opposite page:

Meteor T.7 SE-DCC of Svenska Flygtjanst AB, the contractor that provided target-towing services to the Swedish and Danish armed forces. The aircraft had formerly been a Gloster demonstrator as G-ANSO, fitted with a Mk.8-type tail unit, but reverting to the standard T.7 type before fitting out for Sweden.
Russell Adams/Jet Age Museum

Meteor F.8 WA826, aircraft 'F' of No 245 Squadron, RAF, based at RAF Horsham St Faith (now Norwich Airport). This unit flew operational trials of in-flight refuelling on the Meteor, using Flight Refuelling Ltd Lancaster and Lincoln tankers. WA826 is shown during a link-up on such a sortie. (Note: the true colours of the squadron marking are as shown on page 142, this colour image having deteriorated.)
Russell Adams/Jet Age Museum

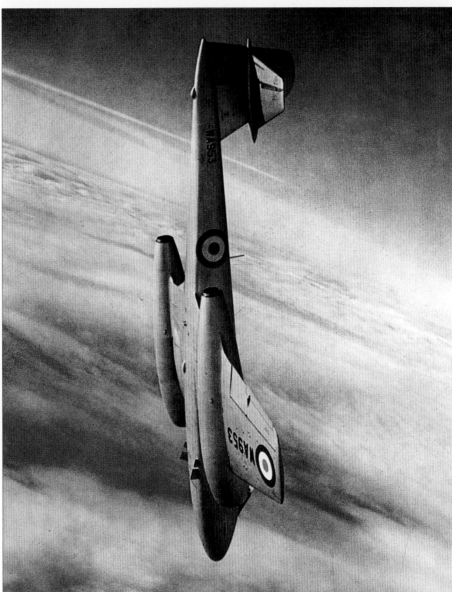

This page:

An unidentified Meteor F.8 photographed on take-off at Moreton Valence. Russell Adams/ Jet Age Museum

Meteor F.8 WA953 during an air-to-air sortie from Moreton Valence. Russell Adams/ Jet Age Museum

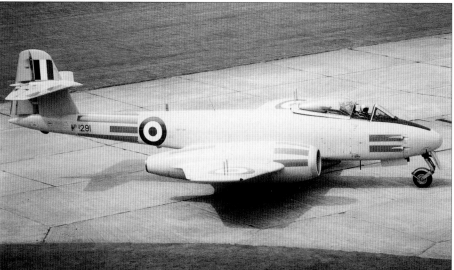

Meteor F.8 WH364, coded 'U' of No 85 Squadron, wearing the black-and-red chequerboard fuselage markings of the unit, and its octagon badge on the fin . This aircraft was photographed at RAF Abingdon on the occasion of the 50th Anniversary Review of the RAF. The Meteor was then used for towing banner targets, the squadron being a target facilities unit at that time. Phil Butler C10609

Meteor F.8 WH291 of No 229 OCU in a late colour scheme of grey polyurethane paint with 'stick-on' Day-Glo panels. via Tony Buttler

Meteor F.8 WH453, an aircraft of No 5 Civilian Anti-Aircraft Cooperation Unit, Woodvale, in a standard camouflage scheme, photographed in September 1971 before it was converted to a drone. Phil Butler C41619

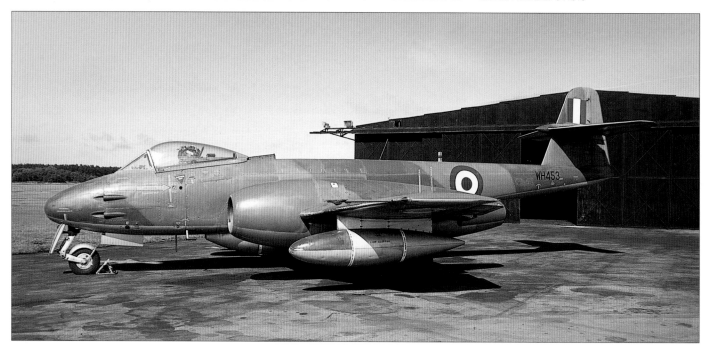

Meteor F.8 VZ467, '01' of the Tactical Weapons Unit, wore the markings of the former No 615 Squadron, Royal Auxiliary Air Force, a unit that flew Mk.8s (but not this particular one) until 1957. VZ467 was the last RAF F.8, flying as a target-tug with 1 TWU, as the unit later became, before sale as G-METE, and then going to Australia as VH-MBX. Phil Butler C93010

WL170 is a Meteor F.8 in camouflage, with an unusual pale blue fuselage band and fin tip. Photographed at Hal Far, Malta, in 1961, probably in use by No 64 Squadron. A E Hughes, via Ray Sturtivant

This page:

The Sapphire Meteor, WA820, photographed in a vertical climb by Russell Adams in 1950, presumably the Meteor T.7 camera-ship would have difficulty keeping up! WA820 was later flown in RAF exercises, simulating the climb of a rocket-powered fighter.
Russell Adams/Jet Age Museum

A77-510, an RAAF aircraft, was photographed at Kimpo in South Korea during the Korean War. The RAAF Meteors retained their overall silver colour scheme during the war; note the rocket projectiles on rails under the wing.
via Tony Buttler

Opposite page:

Meteor F.8 VH-MBX at the Avalon air display in Australia in February 2003. Gerry Manning

A preserved aircraft of the Belgian Air Force (Force Aérienne Belge, F.Aé.B), Meteor F.8 EG-224 was photographed at Coxyde on 10th August 1968. Phil Butler C10907

A Meteor F.8 of the Royal Netherlands Air Force, coded 3W-3 of No 322 Squadron, seen in 1957. Courtesy Aart van Wijk, via Coen van den Heuvel

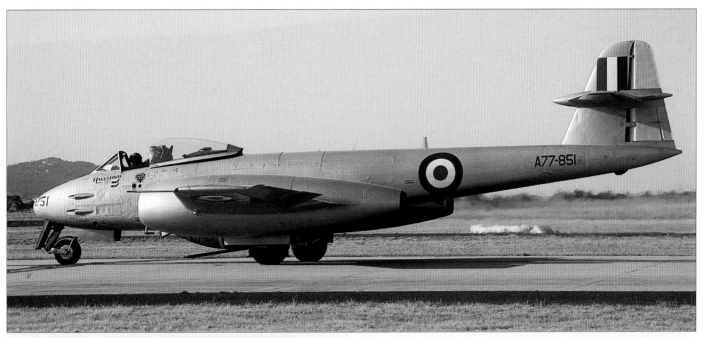

A pair of No 322 Squadron Meteor F.8 of the Royal Netherlands Air Force, taxying for take-off in 1957, the lead aircraft being '3W-31'. Aart van Wijk

A formation of two Syrian F.8s during a training flight in England. Russell Adams/Jet Age Museum

This shot of WB118, in the markings of No 2 Squadron, was taken at a Battle of Britain open day in the mid-1950s, showing an example of an RAF fighter reconnaissance (FR.9) version.
Peter Berry

Meteor FR.9 712 of the Fuerza Aérea Ecuatoriana, photographed by Russell Adams, Gloster's Chief Photographer, shortly before delivery. This was an ex-RAF FR.9, returned to the Gloster Aircraft Company for refurbishing before delivery to Ecuador. Russell Adams/Jet Age Museum

Meteor FR.9 FF-123 of the Ecuadorean Air Force at the Quito museum in September 1997.
Gerry Manning

This page:

Meteor FR.9 VW360 is believed to have been photographed by Russell Adams in 1950. Russell Adams/Jet Age Museum

A shot of NF.11 WD597 taken in April 1951, probably while in Armstrong Whitworth's hands for trials, and showing the grey/green camouflage applied at the factory. A E Hughes, via Ray Sturtivant

Opposite page:

WD790, a rather non-standard NF.11 Meteor in a non-standard colour scheme, the so-called 'raspberry ripple' colours favoured for Royal Aircraft Establishment aircraft in the 1990s. The modified nose radome was installed for trials of radar for the BAC TSR.2 at the RRE. A E Hughes, via Ray Sturtivant

One of the few Meteors still flying on the display circuit is NF.11 G-LOSM (previously WM167). Photographed at Kemble 15th June 2003. Phil Butler C152409

Meteor NF.11 NF11-1 was used by the French Air Force (Armée de l'Air). At first a front-line night-fighter, it was later used for the flight development of experimental equipment at the Centre d'Essais en Vol (CEV) at Bretigny. Note the camera ports in the aircraft's nose. Photographed at Le Bourget, 7th June 1979. Phil Butler C101213

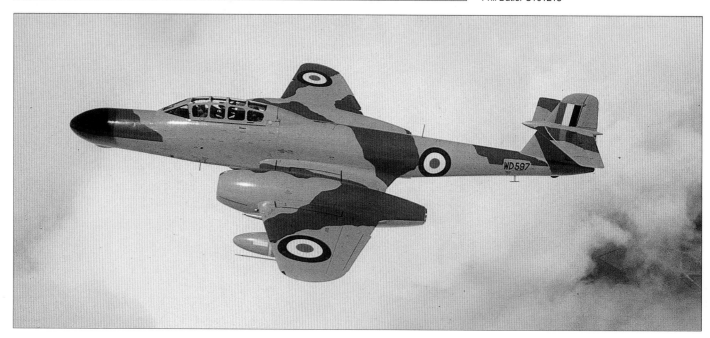

This page:

Meteor NF.12 '7065M', still marked as 'C' of No 72 Squadron. In fact the Ground Instructional 'M' number should read 7605M, 7065M having actually been allotted to a Vampire. Photographed at Henlow. via Tony Buttler

Meteor NF.13 WM367 is a rare version of the Meteor night fighter, being a tropicalised variant of the NF.11 which served with two squadrons of the Middle East Air Force. This example was employed as a trials aircraft at the A&AEE, having earlier also flown at RAE Farnborough. Photographed at Abingdon on 20th June 1968. Phil Butler C10611

WS804, a Meteor NF.14 in use as a night fighter trainer, in silver with liberally-applied Day-Glo stick-on panels, and showing the much neater sliding canopy of the Mk.14. via Tony Buttler

Opposite page:

A photograph of NF.14 WS723 in the colours of No 85 Squadron. Ministry of Defence T:0028, via Tony Buttler

Another view of an NF.14, this time WS744, showing the long-span wings of the night fighters, and the underwing fuel tanks normally fitted (the radar operator's seat occupied the space used for a fuel tank on the day fighters). Ministry of Defence T:2094, via Tony Buttler

Meteor NF.14 WS838 was photographed on 28th June 1972, at the Colerne Museum where it had arrived from Farnborough in February of that year. It had previously also served with the Royal Radar Establishment at Pershore, the A&AEE at Boscombe Down and the RAE at Bedford, the unusual overall yellow colour scheme dating from its days at Bedford. Phil Butler C51312

Meteor NF.11 WS843 is preserved at the Cosford Aerospace Museum in the markings of No 64 Squadron. Photo at Cosford 14th July 2003. Phil Butler C160213

Meteor NF.14 WS843 was photographed at RAF St Athan on 18th September 1971, in a non-typical grey/Day-Glo scheme. It wears a Malaysian national marking on its fin, probably a 'zap' from Malaysian students passing through the resident No 4 School of Technical Training. The shot shows the clear-view canopy and extended fin (around the 'bullet') of the NF.14. This aircraft had been relegated to ground instructional use at St Athan in 1967, but its allotted number, 7937M, was not worn at the time this photo was taken. Phil Butler C41706

Meteor NF.14 WS774 of the All-Weather Operational Conversion Unit (formerly No 228 OCU) with liberal application of Day-Glo paint over its camouflage. via Phil Butler

WF716, a Meteor U.16 of No 728B Squadron of the Fleet Air Arm, photographed at the unit's Hal Far base in late 1961. The aircraft is coded '658' and has the standard red and yellow scheme used on UK and Malta-based drones. A E Hughes, via Ray Sturtivant

Meteor U.16/D.16 WK800 'Z' of RAE Llanbedr photographed at RAF Valley on 18th August 1979. Shown in its red/yellow drone colour scheme, it had been delivered to the RAAF as A77-876 and flown in Australia, before being converted as a U Mk.21 drone by Fairey Aviation in Australia. After service at the Weapons Research Establishment, Woomera, it was returned to the UK and took up its original RAF number, changing to a U.16 version after the revision of its drone telemetry equipment. It was the last RAE drone, being retired in November 2004. Phil Butler C101804

WK800 is a very historic Meteor, having flown with the RAAF during the Korean War as A77-876. It was then converted to U.21 drone configuration in Australia and served at the Woomera research establishment, before being shipped home to England. At this point it reverted to its RAF serial number WK800 and became a D.16. The photo was taken during trials of a 'missed target' system by Marshalls of Cambridge. Marshalls, via Tony Buttler

Meteor U.16 WK747 'D' photographed taxying at Llanbedr. The words in yellow on the nose say 'RAE Llanbedr'. Gerry Manning

Meteor U.16 WH320 'N' after take-off at Llanbedr. Gerry Manning

The flight line at Llanbedr in July 1969, showing Meteor T.7 WA662, Meteor U.16s WH320 and WK747 and a Hawker Hunter. Gerry Manning

Meteor U.16 (later D.16) WH420 was one of the 'drone' unpiloted targets normally based at RAE Llanbedr, and converted from a standard F.8 version by Flight Refuelling Ltd at Tarrant Rushton. The drone versions were flown as pilotless targets for experimental missile firing, although they could be piloted for ferrying purposes or when required for observing experiments. This example is in the standard red-and-yellow colour scheme of the drone versions, and wears the individual code letter 'S'. Photographed at RAF Valley on 20th August 1970. Phil Butler C31306

Meteor TT.20 WD630 'Q' of No 3/4 Civilian Anti-Aircraft Cooperation Unit at Exeter, in silver with extensive stick-on Day-Glo patches and the diagonal yellow/black stripes worn by target-towing aircraft. via Tony Buttler

A Royal Navy TT.20 of the FRU, WD780, shows the Rushton winch mounted above the starboard wing, which distinguished this version from the night fighters. Phil Butler C13004

Meteor TT20 WM159 '040' of the Airwork-operated Fleet Requirements Unit at Hurn in the usual colours of black/yellow diagonal-striped undersides, with silver topsides and yellow fuselage band. via Phil Butler

WM147, a Meteor TT.20 of No 728 Squadron, Hal Far, showing the black/yellow undersides painted on target-towing aircraft, and the yellow winch above the starboard wing. Also discernible are the guard cables from the tailplane tips. A E Hughes, via Ray Sturtivant

An example of the target-towing conversion, photographed at Hurn on 25th July 1969, where WM159 was flown by the Airwork-operated Fleet Requirements Unit, with individual code '840'. Wears one of the normal TT.20 colour schemes of silver with alternate black/lime-green Day-Glo bands on its undersides. Phil Butler C13003

This shot of all-silver Meteor F.8 WA953 was taken in 1951, and shows the original type of canopy with the metal rear section. WA953 went on to serve briefly with No.56 Squadron before being written-off in an accident at RAF Waterbeach.
Russell Adams/Jet Age Museum

1 Squadron

29 Squadron

2 Squadron

33 Squadron

5 Squadron

39 Squadron

8 Squadron

41 Squadron

11 Squadron

43 Squadron

19 Squadron

46 Squadron

25 Squadron

54 Squadron

56 Squadron

72 Squadron

60 Squadron

74 Squadron

63 Squadron

79 Squadron

64 Squadron

80 Squadron

65 Squadron

85 Squadron

66 Squadron

87 Squadron

68 Squadron

92 Squadron

96 Squadron

219 Squadron

111 Squadron

222 Squadron

141 Squadron

245 Squadron

151 Squadron

247 Squadron

152 Squadron

256 Squadron

153 Squadron

257 Squadron

208 Squadron

263 Squadron

264 Squadron

609 Squadron

500 Squadron

610 Squadron

504 Squadron

611 Squadron

600 Squadron

615 Squadron

601 Squadron

616 Squadron

604 Squadron

Armament Practice Station

Note: The squadron markings illustrated here were originally drawn by Chris Butler from colour drawings made by Phil Butler at the time when the markings were in current use. The Armament Practice Station marking used at RAF Acklington (and similar ones used elsewhere) were based on the pattern used on the 'banner' targets used in air firing practice.

BRITISH SECRET PROJECTS
Jet Fighters Since 1950

Tony Buttler

A huge number of fighter projects have been drawn by British companies over the last 50 years, in particular prior to the 1957 White Paper, but with few turned into hardware, little has been published about these fascinating 'might-have-beens'. Emphasis is placed on some of the events which led to certain aircraft either being cancelled or produced. Some of the varied types included are the Hawker P.1103/P.1136/P.1121 series, and the Fairey 'Delta III'

Hbk, 282 x 213 mm, 176 pages
130 b/w photos; 140 three-views, and an 8-page colour section
1 85780 095 8 **£24.95**

BRITISH SECRET PROJECTS
Jet Bombers Since 1949

Tony Buttler

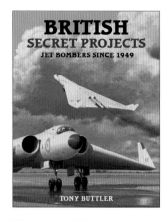

This long-awaited title forms a natural successor to the author's successful volume on fighters. The design and development of the British bomber since World War II is covered in similar depth and again the emphasis is placed on the tender design competitions between projects from different companies. The design backgrounds to the V-Bomber programme, Canberra, Buccaneer, Avro 730, TSR.2, Harrier, Jaguar and Tornado are revealed.

Hbk, 282 x 213 mm, 224 pages
160 b/w photos; 3-view drawings
9-page colour section
1 85780 130 X **£24.99**

BRITISH SECRET PROJECTS
Fighters & Bombers 1935-1950

Tony Buttler

This volume again places the emphasis on unbuilt designs that competed with those that flew, and covers aircraft influenced by World War Two – projects that were prepared from the mid-1930s in the knowledge that war was coming through to some which appeared after the war was over. The latter includes early jets such as the Attacker, Sea Hawk and Venom which all flew post-war but to wartime or just post-war requirements.

Hbk, 282 x 213 mm, 240 pages
228 b/w, 6 pages of colour photos, plus c192 line drawings
1 85780 179 2 **£29.99**

Aerofax
VICKERS VALIANT
The First V-Bomber

Eric B Morgan

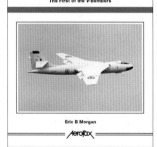

The Valiant was the shortest-lived of the post-war V-bombers, first flying in 1951 and with production of 104 aircraft ending in 1957, and official withdrawal in January 1965 after investigation had shown that the main wing spars were suffering from metal fatigue. Valiants participated in British atomic bomb tests and made noteworthy long-distance flights, principally operating from Marham and Gaydon. Includes a full listing of each aircraft's history.

Sbk, 280 x 215 mm, 128 pages,
155 b/w and colour photographs,
plus line drawings
1 85780 134 2 **£14.99**

Aerofax
MIKOYAN-GUREVICH MiG-15

Yefim Gordon

In this Aerofax, compiled from a wealth of first-hand Russian sources, there is a comprehensive history of every evolution of the Soviet Union's swept-wing fighter and its service. Notably in this volume, there are tables listing intricate details of many individual aircraft, a concept which would have been unthinkable in any publications only a few years ago.

There is extensive and detailed photo coverage, again from Russian sources, almost all of which is previously unseen.

Sbk, 280 x 215 mm, 160 pages
214 b/w and 21 colour photographs,
7pp col sideviews, 18pp b/w drawings
1 85780 105 9 **£17.95**

SEA HARRIER
The Last All-British Fighter

Jamie Hunter

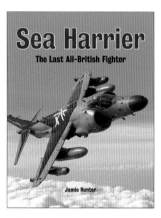

The Sea Harrier had proven its worth in combat over the Falklands within three years of entering frontline service. A Cold War warrior, and a veteran of recent actions in the Balkans, the Persian Gulf and Sierra Leone, the 'Shar' now finds itself at the end of its career. As well as extensive archive material and images from Sea Harrier pilots, the volume is illustrated with recent air-to-air and ground material taken by the author during the last two years of Sea Harrier operations.

Sbk, 280 x 215 mm, 160 pages
241 colour, 50 b/w photos, plus
drawings/cutaway
1 85780 207 1 **£17.99**

Red Star Volume 4
EARLY SOVIET JET FIGHTERS

Yefim Gordon

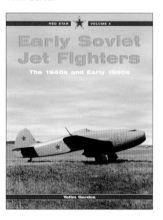

This charts the development and service history of the first-generation Soviet jet fighters designed by such renowned 'fighter makers' as Mikoyan, Yakovlev and Sukhoi, as well as design bureaux no longer in existence – the Lavochkin and Alekseyev OKBs, during the 1940s and early 1950s. Each type is detailed and compared to other contemporary jet fighters. As ever the extensive photo coverage includes much which is previously unseen.

Sbk, 280 x 215 mm, 144 pages
240 b/w and 9 colour photos,
8 pages of colour artworks
1 85780 139 3 **£19.99**

Top: **A shot of Martin-Baker's black-painted Meteor WA638.** Martin-Baker, via Tony Buttler

Above: **Meteor F.8 WH364, coded 'U' with 85 Squadron, was used for towing banner targets.** Phil Butler

Front cover illustration:
Meteor NF.14 WS838, in its striking yellow colour scheme, while in use as a 'shepherd' at RAE Bedford. RAE Bedford, via Tony Buttler

An imprint of
Ian Allan Publishing

www.ianallanpublishing.com

ISBN 1-85780-230-6

9 781857 802306

USA $36.95 UK £19.99

Printed in England

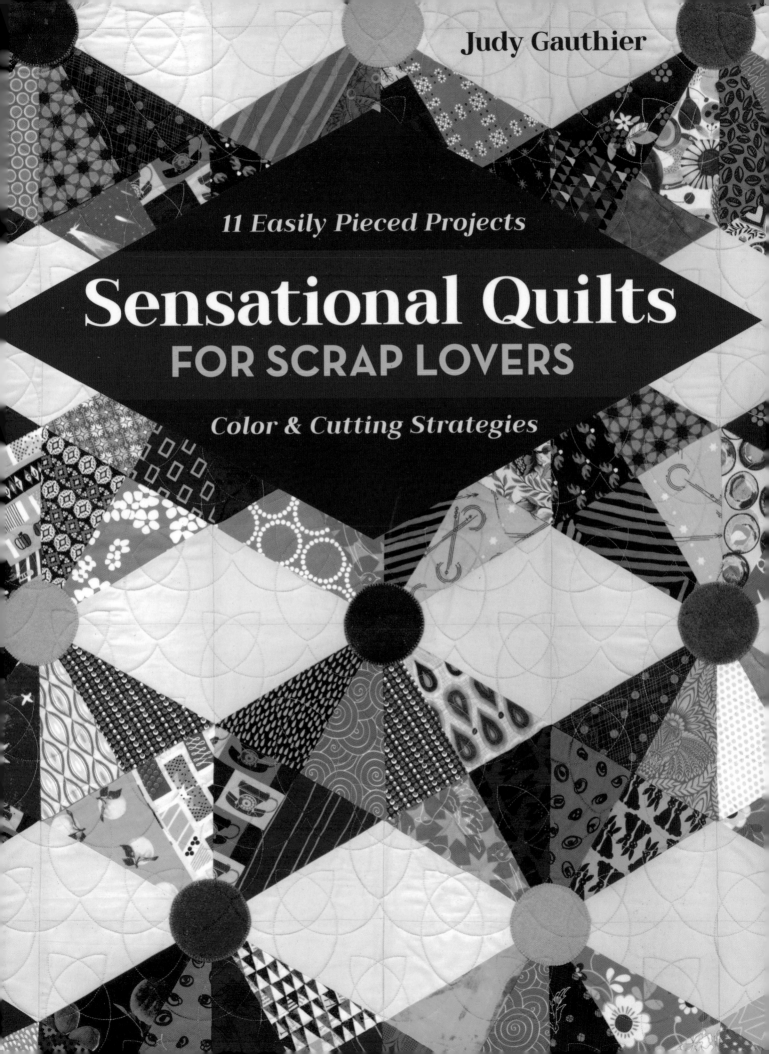

Judy Gauthier

11 Easily Pieced Projects

Sensational Quilts
FOR SCRAP LOVERS

Color & Cutting Strategies